76. 19ª

CRIME AND THE SOCIAL STRUCTURE

SOCIETY TODAY AND TOMORROW

General Editor: A. H. Halsey

*Fellow of Nuffield College and Head of the Department
of Social and Administrative Studies, Oxford*

*

THE SECONDARY MODERN SCHOOL
   by William Taylor, *Principal Lecturer in Education, Bede
   College, Durham*

THE CUTTESLOWE WALLS: A Study in Social Class
   by Peter Collison, *Department of Social and Administrative
   Studies, Oxford*

CRIME AND THE SOCIAL STRUCTURE
   by John Barron Mays, *Senior Lecturer, Department of Social
   Science, University of Liverpool*

Crime
and the Social Structure

JOHN BARRON MAYS, M.A., Ph.D.

Senior Lecturer
Department of Social Science
University of Liverpool

FABER AND FABER LTD
24 Russell Square
London

First published in mcmlxiii
by Faber and Faber Limited
24 Russell Square, London, W.C.1
Printed in Great Britain by
Western Printing Services Limited, Bristol

CONTENTS

PREFACE

This is not intended to be a comprehensive textbook on criminology, although many different aspects of crime are touched on from time to time. My intention is not to be exhaustive or to produce a completely detailed and rounded analysis of the nature and extent of criminal activity in modern society. What, however, I have tried to do is to underline the social components in the etiology of crime and delinquency which nowadays are often overlooked. I have done this because I believe that factors operating in the general social framework contribute greatly to the origins of crime and have a direct bearing on methods of treatment and, above all, of prevention.

Amid the contemporary concern about the alleged increase in criminal behaviour it seems to me immensely important that we should get our facts in perspective, and that, before rushing into more drastic penological methods, we should take a hard, long look at the nature of our society to see whether or not there are social and environmental forces which foster delinquent attitudes against which our efforts could more profitably be exerted. To say this is not to deny individual autonomy but to underline our corporate responsibility for weaknesses and stresses within the structure of our society which we could, if we so willed, go a long way towards eliminating. I am concerned that the present concentration on the treatment of individual offenders may serve to obscure much of the truth about the nature of crime and so absolve us of blame for those social conditions and practices which are equally culpable. The delinquent can so easily become the social scapegoat and so salve our consciences but fail to solve our problems. I have endeavoured, therefore, in this book to concentrate less on the individual offender and more on the nature of social organization

PREFACE

because this is so often neglected in public debates and discussions about crime.

Before presenting this book to the public I have consulted various friends and colleagues whom I would now like to thank. I am especially indebted to Professor T. S. Simey for criticizing the work as a whole and for making invaluable criticisms which have served to restrain my theoretical exuberance. Dr. Philip Pinkerton, the well-known child psychiatrist, very kindly read through my brief chapter on *The Psychology of Crime*, and made useful comments. Neither Professor Simey nòr Dr. Pinkerton, however, should be associated with the general expressions of opinion in which the book abounds. These and all other tendentious material are entirely my own responsibility and their shortcomings must be laid at my door not at theirs.

I must also pay a warm tribute to my colleague in the Department of Social Science, Liverpool University, Miss Elizabeth Gittus, M.A., who prepared the statistics on crime which she very kindly permitted me to include as a valuable appendix to this book. I should also thank Professor David Marsh of the University of Nottingham for generous permission to reprint a statistical table from his book, *The Changing Social Structure of England and Wales, 1871–1951*, and Dr. Hermann Mannheim, lately Reader in Criminology at the London School of Economics, and Mr. Leslie Wilkins of the Home Office Research Department, for a table from their book, *Prediction Methods in Relation to Borstal Training*, which is reproduced by permission of the Controller of H.M. Stationery Office.

Liverpool, 1962.   J.B.M.

CHAPTER I

INTRODUCTION

I

A crime is an offence against society. It consists in the commission of acts which have been legally proscribed. It may, at the same time, be regarded as a symptom of psychological disorder, or it may, more frequently, be interpreted as an index of social stress and strain. But basically it is a simple concept, with no absolute moral connotation whatsoever. A criminal is merely a man who has transgressed the legal norms of the society in which he lives. If he is apprehended and found guilty by a court of law he becomes an official offender. But this need not make him a bad man in the moral sense. It may do so, of course, but only in a society where for the most part the legal and moral codes are identical. We can all name societies however in which good men were punished under immoral laws and where patently evil men occupied the seats of power.

Strictly speaking we ought not to talk about individuals as criminals unless an offence has been proved against them. This is, in fact, the only operational definition of a criminal or a delinquent that we can employ as strict criminologists. In the course of this study, however, we will go beyond this definition to include, for some purposes, those delinquent impulses which we all harbour and occasionally express in legally permitted ways together with such immoral acts as ought, in our opinion, to be brought within the province of legal sanctions.

But the official crime statistics are based on the number of offences reported to the police and the number of persons who are prosecuted in any one year. They tell us nothing about the 'larval' criminal tendencies we all nourish or the near-delinquents who under a different dispensation would be brought to justice.

Much more will be said on this topic of criminal statistics later and about the problem of assessing how delinquent we really are. Here I only want to point out that, even when we define crime narrowly as actual law-breaking, it is salutary to bear in mind that any one of us might at any moment break the law and thus become a criminal. In modern society we are hedged about by so many laws that the chances of our breaking one or another of them are getting greater each decade. However trivial the offence may appear to us, however mitigating circumstances may allay our sense of guilt and however public opinion or the judgement of our friends may condone our act, once we have broken the law and been found out we pass from a state of innocence into that of being 'a man with a record'. It is a sobering thought that we would do well to ponder. The law is indeed something of a social leveller; it cuts us all down to size. As Professor Sprott wrote recently, 'it brands as "criminal" an enormous number of people who would not ordinarily be called "criminals", and so much the better' in that 'it puts the so-called "criminal classes" into perspective'.[1]

II

For some of us, indeed, the beginning of our interest in criminology springs from the realization that we ourselves are very far from being perfect and from the kindred discovery that many of our cherished friends and associates have appeared in court at some stage of their lives. My own particular research into delinquency developed from my work as a boys' club leader on Merseyside. I found out after a while that an astounding proportion of my club members had broken the law at some time or another or had actually been found guilty of some offence. I say I was astounded because in the main a boys' club is thought to cater for ordinary sorts of boys and not for the delinquent or maladjusted as such. There is indeed more than a suspicion that the ones who are retained by the youth organizations are usually a cut above their contemporaries. Yet many

[1] *Howard Journal*, Vol. X No. 4. 1961, p. 257.

of these good, solid, reliable types were in fact delinquents. Privately they told me of their illegal exploits and exposed a part of their lives which had hitherto been quite unknown to me; that part which corresponded to the private, unsupervised leisure which they shared only with their contemporaries. This is what our transatlantic colleagues like to refer to as 'the peer group' culture, and, which, in less sophisticated days, we knew as gang life.[1]

Now what amazed me was not so much that many of my club members had broken the law. I had sufficient contact with the local probation service to know that several offenders were numbered among my flock. It was that almost every boy, even those I thought of as my 'best', had taken part in illegal exploits at some time in childhood and early adolescence. Moreover, in their chats with me they gave chapter and verse for many more illegal acts than those for which they had been prosecuted, and these were of both a petty and more serious nature, for which thus far they had got off scot free.

One boy said, telling me about shop-lifting parties which used to operate on Saturday mornings during his schooldays, that they always knew on the night before exactly where they were going. He also told me how he and his mates broke into a grocer's shop. They watched it very carefully for several days to discover the best way of entering and to see whether or not anyone lived above. Then they took advantage of a moonless night to force a back window, having taken the precaution to leave 'dowses' (sentries) both front and back to give warning of any approaching danger. While the actual raid was on, he said, it was very thrilling, but best of all was 'when you knew you'd got clean away and were walking back up the street'.

Another boy spoke of a 'tenement gang' to which he had once belonged. Many of their exploits were planned in advance and, in his own words, 'we put our heads together in the Dwellings'. He described to me how one more daring youth would incite the others to take greater risks. He once saw a boy coolly remove a whole chemistry set from a shop counter, tuck it under his coat and walk off with it. Such escapades were talked about with relish and admiration.

During most of the discussions I had with these lads it was

[1] See Appendix I for typical case histories of these boys.

remarkable how little sense of guilt was expressed and how they talked about delinquency as something which everyone they knew took part in during his youth. 'You used to enjoy yourself,' one boy said, although like many others he admitted that 'at the time it made you sweat'. One young man recalled how he and his pals deliberately broke into one shop merely in order to be able to brag in the neighbourhood that they were the first to do it. Once committed to this dare-devil, delinquent life, it was extremely difficult to withdraw without being branded as a coward. They just kept on doing dangerous and criminal things because they did not know how to stop. Everybody did them. It was part and parcel of the life they knew.[1]

III

The discussions I had with these club and ex-club members quickly led to a thorough reorganization of my ideas both about crime in general and the neighbourhood in which I was living in particular. The question was, how to account for this enormous amount and extent of illegal behaviour? Clearly the pattern of life which the juvenile males traditionally led thereabouts was simply saturated with delinquency. Petty theft, shoplifting, raiding from open markets and lorry-skipping were all activities in their own rights in which the great majority of boys at some time indulged. In particular, the period from 8 to 15, that is to say from the time of transfer from the infant to the junior school and right on up to the end of school life, was especially dangerous. After leaving school and assuming the status of worker and young adult, the risk seemed to be considerably reduced. In other words, delinquency was part of the pattern of life of boys growing up in a special kind of locality —a locality rich in temptations and weak in discipline and controls. It was phasic in character and it was far from being abnormal.

Of these aspects of 'the delinquent community', I will say much more later. At the moment I am concerned with my own reaction to this investigation. I was both intrigued and chastened. Once I accepted the fact that many, if not all, of

[1] For a fuller description of this research material see pp. 64–6 below, and the author's book, *Growing up in the City*, Liverpool University Press, 1954.

my best club members had 'a record' or might have had a record of offences against their names if things had gone differently, I had to face the question, not only of how this came to be, but, further, whether or not a radical reappraisal of their characters and personalities was not necessary? Had these lads previously succeeded in pulling the wool over my eyes? Had I been carried away by mere surface impressions? Or were they really the sound, lovable boys I thought I knew so well?

As far as I am concerned the answers to these questions were never long in doubt. All my experience told me that I was not mistaken in my judgement. That being so, only one alternative explanation remained. There was something seriously wrong with the environment in which they lived. If they were not basically anti-social characters, then clearly the causes for their delinquency must be social in origin.

The truth is that delinquency was part and parcel of most of these boys' early life history. It was indulged in, not so much for its own sake, but because it was only by taking part in delinquent escapades that they proved themselves both to their own and to their pals' satisfaction. It was something they did in order to be 'one of the lads'. It admitted them to the happy band of brothers who dominated the street or the tenement block. The penalty for abstention was, in all but exceptional cases, social isolation and the contempt of their peers. The path of virtue was a lonely road in that neighbourhood along which few could hope to travel unsupported by unusually interested persons or other adult guides. All too often the reward of deviation from the pattern of juvenile life would be social ostracism and hostility. It was a price which few could pay.

IV

The idea that there are particular neighbourhoods or parts of big cities whose residents are specially prone to commit certain kinds of offences is now fairly well established. Since they have been shown to be more or less co-extensive with the poorer and slummier localities the idea of the delinquent community is acceptable not only to sociologists but to the majority of respectable citizens. Moreover, the point made at the beginning of this chapter—namely that any one of us might at any time become an offender—would probably also be conceded by most thoughtful people, who would, however, almost certainly add very quickly that the kind of offences they have in mind are somewhat petty in character and are more akin to infringements of regulations than to positive criminal activity.

In this essay I want to take the argument one significant stage further. I maintain that, in addition to us all being potential offenders and over and above the heavy concentration of convicted delinquents in specific localities, there is reason to believe that society as a whole, the way in which our total social and economic life is organized, has strong criminogenic components. I have no wish to exaggerate this position to the point at which one is obliged to claim that every social institution is evil or that every apparently harmless activity is merely a mask for some racket or anti-social practice. All I wish to suggest is that criminal behaviour arises naturally enough out of the ordinary daily affairs in which all of us are engaged. The routine methods of doing business, of plying one's trade, of making a living and of obtaining other human objectives, such as status and friendship, contain within themselves the seeds of criminality. Pushed one degree further, or scrutinized in the more exacting light of absolute morality, many of the things we take for granted in both personal and corporate life are undeniably unethical and are frequently illegal. It is at this point that many of those people who have gone along with my argument so far will want to part company. I shall hope to show in the course of succeeding chapters, however, that I am right and they are wrong. Or rather, to put it more modestly, that there is evidence in support of my thesis substantial enough for them to reconsider their own position.

The point is, I believe, of profound importance. It drastically affects both our personal attitude to those who break the law and our group treatment of convicted offenders. Moreover, as I shall hope to show, it is upon where we stand as a community on this basic topic that our ultimate chances of ever being in a position to bring and keep delinquency under control really depend.

In theoretical language, the debate is about how far crime and delinquency can be thought of as essentially normal conduct to be dealt with, in consequence, at the rational and ethical level as a form of acquired behaviour. Before modern times this question would hardly have been posed. Until comparatively recently it was generally accepted that criminals were merely bad people and that their anti-legal behaviour was immoral. It was thought that they indulged in delinquent acts to promote their own ends and that the appropriate social reaction, therefore, involved punishment of the miscreant and a system of deterrence for potential law-breakers. If you punish them severely enough, so the argument ran, they would therefore amend their ways and conform to ordinary decent standards of behaviour. This belief in a simple pleasure-pain psychology underlying most human conduct, although manifestly inadequate to account for all the facts, survived for thousands of years and is still far from dead. As a basis for penological theory and practice it is not so much false as extremely limited in its applicability. Punishment as a deterrent is in fact only effective with psychologically normal people and only in certain circumstances with them. It is true that the majority of ordinary and, in the main, law-abiding citizens can be restrained from committing minor offences by fear of the consequences. But there is a substantial minority who will not submit to be disciplined in this simple schoolboy way. They can be divided into two types.

First, there is the essentially normal group who, rightly or wrongly, for the moment see the results of punishment as less serious than the rewards of delinquency. Such offenders, on the whole, have little to lose by prosecution, public exposure and the shame of conviction. Secondly, there is a much smaller minority of confirmed criminals and recidivists who are also unimpressed by traditional sanctions for rather different reasons. Punishment either serves to confirm their belief that society is hostile towards them or satisfies some deep craving for masochistic self-pity, or is simply irrelevant, since they have positively dissociated themselves from society and view themselves as being above blame or censure. There is also a small maladjusted group for whom the forbidden act is either a drug or a distress signal sent up to draw attention to themselves and to their plight.

We may perhaps illustrate this distinction between normal and abnormal reactions to punishment by considering two types of motoring offenders. Both suffer from a temptation to excessive speeding. One, *l'homme moyen sensuel*, is caught exceeding the speed limit and fined five pounds with the result that, next time he finds his right foot pressing too heavily on the accelerator in a built-up area, he remembers what is the possible result and, because a fiver is quite a lot of money to chuck away, overcomes the temptation and keeps his speedometer wisely flickering around about the thirty mark. On the other hand, there is a type of driver to whom sheer speed is an addiction, a drug or a stimulus as the case may be, who finds ordinary caution and the possibility of retribution an insufficient deterrent. Speed he needs and speed he must have. So, like the late T. E. Shaw on his motor bike, he goes crashing around the countryside indulging his pathological craving as one possessed of a demon. He may end up like Shaw by killing himself, or as many do, somebody else.

The problem presented by the persistent offender, which will be dealt with elsewhere, is thus radically different from the problem of the ordinary individual who happens to fall foul of the law. Whether the way in which we deal with him is termed punishment or treatment is largely irrelevant. What we ought to be concerned about is the right way to help or prevent him from committing similar acts again. And this task cannot satisfactorily be undertaken with *a priori* assumptions about the effectiveness of punishment or the eternal rightness of the *lex talionis*.

V

It should now be clear that the distinction between normal and abnormal conduct which I have been trying to make is of crucial importance for the understanding and treatment of offenders. The question is one which probably could not have been raised in these terms as a serious intellectual issue before the twentieth century. Now, however, the growth of psychological study, and more especially, the rapid expansion of the influence of psychoanalytic theory has wrought a profound change. The old idea that if you could make it unpleasant enough for the thief the problem of theft would automatically disappear has been seen to be fallacious. Many have swung to the opposite extreme of invariably regarding crime as an illness of some sort and of thinking of delinquency as abnormal behaviour arising from personality stress and emotional upset in a majority of cases. Explanations based on the concept of unconscious motivation have not only modified the assumptions of unsophisticated pleasure-pain notions of how the human mind works, they have further led to a crucial lack of interest in normality. Rational, moral, common-sense considerations are undramatic and hence of little interest today in an age which has feasted on perversions and outlandish speculation.

In the field of penology one serious consequence has been our somewhat pathetic belief that if only we could get more specialist advice and psychiatric treatment all would be well. The increase in the provision of child guidance centres and the availability of psychiatric services in prisons and borstals is seen by many *avant garde* criminologists as the dawn of enlightenment and the earnest of ultimate triumph. While limited successes may be achieved in this way, I cannot help believing that this will prove to be yet another side-track leading us into deeper disillusionment. The great weakness, as I see it, of most current theories of the origin of crime lies in their inability to grasp the significance of the social setting in which the condemned behaviour develops and occurs. They often lack sociological content altogether. In the great majority of cases the offenders are not sick. They do not need psychological treatment so much as social re-education. Many in fact break the law simply because they *are* normal. Their behaviour is rational, and until we seize hold of this simple truth all our more elaborate attempts to reduce the incidence of crime will in the main be of little avail.

CHAPTER 2

CRIME—SOME FACTS AND FIGURES

I

Before going on to examine the various explanations for criminal behaviour that sociologists and psychologists have advanced, it is necessary to look at what we may call 'the hard facts about crime'. How do the present figures compare with those for previous years and earlier generations? For the answers to these and similar questions we have to turn to the official statistics on crime which are made available every year by the Home Office in a blue book called *Criminal Statistics: England and Wales*. But the uninitiated layman will find these hard going indeed and must turn to the criminologist and the statistician to interpret them for him. Unfortunately, as so often happens, the experts are by no means agreed about the way in which the official figures are to be interpreted. There are indeed some specialists who seem to suggest that it is well nigh impossible to make any reliable deduction from them whatsoever: even worse from our point of view, a few experts regard them as positively misleading.

Why should this be so? What is the matter with the way in which these statistics are compiled and recorded that not only their usefulness but also their fundamental reliability is called in question?

The main reasons why we cannot put very much reliability upon criminal statistics for either comparative and historical purposes or for gauging the actual amount of crime being committed at any one time are threefold: they arise from changes in the law itself, from changes in the attitude of the public and from changes in police procedure. We will take a brief look at each of these factors in turn.

It is quite obvious that changes in the law will have an important bearing on the amount of criminal activity. If there is a multiplication of possible offences, that is to say if more things are forbidden by statute, there will almost certainly be an increase in the number of offences and offenders. Perhaps the most striking illustration of this is to be found in war-time conditions when a whole new series of defence regulations is brought abruptly into operation. Infringements of blackout, black-marketeering, refusal to submit for medical examination or to register for national service and other temporary peccadilloes help to swell the volume of recorded crime. Moreover, the tremendous increase in motoring has brought with it a corresponding increase of laws and controls, all of which produce a spate of prosecutions which threaten to overwhelm the courts of summary jurisdiction which have to deal with them. Parking in urban areas is a case in point of a social discomfort which has ultimately led to legal prohibitions which many people are prepared to infringe as the lesser of two inconveniences. The use of parking meters and the appointment of traffic wardens empowered to deal on an *ad hoc* basis with offenders are indications that the courts cannot possibly cope with the deluge of petty offenders thus created. It is worth pointing out at this stage that some 60 per cent of all crimes are in fact traffic offences, some of a very minor but a few of a much more serious nature.

Changes in the attitude of the public towards particular offences have also been responsible for fluctuations over the years. They can exert both a local and a national effect. Perhaps the best illustration of this kind of bias is to be seen in prosecutions for some kinds of sex offences which could, at one time, be generally tolerated but at a later date might become such a focus of public concern that police officials would decide to step up the number of arrests for these particular cases. Homosexual practices conducted in specific public places are especially subject to this kind of variation. There are rendezvous, such as certain down-town urinals, which are known to be meeting places for individuals who wish to participate with like-minded fellows in the enjoyment of many perverted practices. Police officers on patrol usually move such offenders on with contemptuous reprimands, but, if the local justices or M.P.'s have been directing awkward questions at the higher ranking police officials then they are much more likely to prosecute. It is therefore theoretically possible for the actual amount of crime of a specific character to be less in a certain year *even though the number of cases for that offence dealt with by the police shows a sharp increase.*

Another closely associated phenomenon is connected with public confidence in the courts. Whenever people have greater confidence that the courts are able to deal adequately with offenders there is likely to be an increased willingness on the part of the ordinary law-abiding citizens to prosecute delinquents. The classic instance of this is the increase in the numbers of juveniles brought before the juvenile courts following the passing of the *Children and Young Persons Act* in 1933. By the mid-1930's police and public alike realized that it was often in the child's best interest that a prosecution should take place. This was because the welfare rather than the punitive aspect of the juvenile courts' work was coming to be more widely appreciated.

Changes in police procedure cover a number of variations between one police district and another and also more general changes of method over a number of years. Some police forces make a considerable use of the power of caution while others use it comparatively sparingly. In Liverpool, for instance, the development of a special department to deal with early and minor offenders, known as the Juvenile Liaison Officer scheme, has caused many youngsters, who would otherwise have been prosecuted, to be dealt with by what we may term social work methods.[1]

It is almost certain that new attitudes and changes in the organization of police work greatly affect the number of less serious offences, such as drunkenness and casual larcenies, which ultimately get into the official statistics. Moreover, the method of keeping records is still far from uniform. Before 1938, when a more standardized method of recording was universally introduced, the position was very confused. Indeed it is not possible to make use of the pre-1938 figures for comparative purposes at all. That is why most of the tables of criminal

[1] We shall have something further to say about this particular type of police service in a later chapter as it has aroused considerable controversy since its inauguration a dozen years ago. See pp. 216–19.

statistics referred to in this chapter and those printed in the appendix commence in that year.

The classic example of an apparent crime wave, which was produced as a result of an alteration in methods of recording offences, occurred when Lord Trenchard became Commissioner of Police for the Metropolis. He discovered that the practice in vogue at local stations was to keep reported offences in two separate books. One was *Crimes Reported*, the other was called *Suspected Stolen*. Only the entries in the first book were used in compiling official returns. Lord Trenchard ordered that in future the two should be combined and the result of this administrative decision can be seen in the number of larceny offences which were reported in the Metropolitan Police District for the consecutive years, 1931 and 1932. In 1931 the total stood at 9,534, but twelve months later it had risen to the amazing figure of 34,783. Anyone unfamiliar with what had taken place behind the scenes might well have concluded that the criminal population of London had trebled its number and that every one of them was working a double shift!

This cautionary tale should be kept in mind whenever we open the Blue Book or peruse local Chief Constables' reports. Every police district likes to be considered efficient at its dual task of maintaining law and order and apprehending felons. This is a laudable ambition and accounts for the desire on the part of chief officers to eliminate offences which are very dubious or trivial or wellnigh impossible to clear up. Imagine a neurotic housewife turning up at the local bridewell declaring that her engagement ring has been stolen. Much apparently factual evidence can be paraded to substantiate the claim that a felony has taken place, so the alleged theft must be recorded. The woman's ring may eventually turn up when months later, while spring cleaning, she finds it under a carpet. She may very well breathe a sigh of relief, replace the cherished jewellery on her finger and not trouble to let the police know what has happened. Money is a particularly tricky commodity to keep an accurate check on. A shopper may find her purse open, imagine that five pound notes have been stolen when in fact she carelessly dropped them in the street. A spate of pocket-picking in the local region may be sufficient to convince her that she had indeed been robbed. Hence the reason, or at least part of the reason, for the local police keeping a book labelled *Suspected Stolen*. Some crimes are indeed imaginary but how is a poor bridewell sergeant to know when to distinguish between hysteria and genuine theft? It is almost certain that a proportion of fictitious offences are now collected in the official statistics, but it is generally agreed that this is an error on the right side as many other offences which are actually committed are never in fact reported.

C. H. Rolph, the well-known criminologist, in discussing the inexactness of our criminal statistics in a review printed in the press some years ago, said:

'But among those who have actually watched the machinery of compilation at what might be called the feeding end, it must be difficult to keep a straight face when the figures come out every year.[1]

The reasons for confusion and the opportunities for error in the compilation are so numerous, he argued, that they are 'enough to reduce the whole system to a solemn farce'.[2]

Rolph, we must remember, is not only a criminologist, he is also an ex-police officer and is therefore less likely to be gullible than either a member of the public or even the academic student of crime might be.

II

But there is a much more serious source of error in our national statistics than any we have so far discussed. This concerns not what goes into the pot but all those ingredients which are omitted. And here we are not merely concerned with differential cautioning procedures on the part of the police, omissions and errors of recording, but with that unknown volume of crime committed in any one year which never comes to the attention of the authorities at all. This is sometimes referred to as 'the dark figure' and it corresponds to that section of the iceberg, to use a familiar metaphor, which is below the level of visibility. In the case of the iceberg we can of course investigate below the water line and, when this is done, it is discovered that the bulk of the object is in fact generally out of sight. It would be merely speculative to suggest that a similar picture would hold good for crime; to claim, in fact, that our official figures correspond

[1] *New Statesman*, London, 10th December, 1955.   [2] Ibid.

only to a minor fraction of the total amount of illegal behaviour actually committed. Nevertheless, the proportion of unknown offences must be very substantial.

Quite clearly there are some offences which it is particularly difficult to conceal. The most obvious of these is homicide. Getting rid of a corpse is a tricky technical procedure. Similarly, arson, manslaughter, suicide, mailbag robbery, have dramatically demonstrable features that are hard to disguise. But, as Rolph says, burglars tend to be more reticent. And thefts are by no means always known about, nor are they invariably reported. One very obvious reason for this failure to report a larceny is that it is often an uneconomic proposition to do so. A business man has to weigh the chances of regaining his property (these are often very remote indeed) against the inconvenience and actual monetary loss resulting from the palaver of police enquiries, a morning spent in court waiting for the case to come up, possible delay resulting from remands, further enquiries or an appeal. In many cases, unless fairly substantial sums are involved, he will probably decide that it is not in his interest to pursue the matter any further, although from the public viewpoint this is most deplorable. Take the case, again, of a large shop, a member of whose staff detects a shop-lifter in the act. Prosecution would mean the worker having a long session off duty. This in turn might involve a reduction in sales or even risk of further larcenies taking place in his absence. Providing the goods are regained it is not worth the firm's time calling for the police and pressing a prosecution. This is particularly the case with children; and many juvenile shop-lifters, even when caught in the act, are sent away with a warning instead of being brought before the court.

There must also be a considerable number of crimes which are 'hushed-up' in other ways. One thinks of the thefts that take place inside every large institution that are dealt with internally in order to avoid undesirable publicity. If a member of the staff of a bank peculates, it is often wiser to dismiss him or transfer him to a post where there is no immediate temptation than to bring him before the court and risk the whole thing being blazoned in the local press. Naturally banks want clients to believe that their deposits are safe with them, that the bank officials are above suspicion, and they can hardly retain this public image if they have recourse to prosecuting any of their supposedly impeccable employees. Again, a great many thefts take place in schools, colleges and universities which never become official offences. I remember, for example, during my own schooldays there was a long hoo-ha over bicycle stealing. Something like twenty were mysteriously stolen from the shed until the culprit was finally discovered, seen by someone who recognized him abandoning one of the stolen machines on a piece of waste land. He was not prosecuted. He was sent to a psychiatrist and subsequently flogged. The chances were that had the boy lived in a poorer part of the town and attended a less bourgeois school he would have been taken in the first instance, before the court. In which case he would perhaps have had his diagnostic session with a psychiatrist by order of the magistrates and almost certainly been put on probation, thus avoiding the flogging!

There is simply no way of discovering how much unreported theft takes place in any one year, but when we think of the number of institutions who deal internally with their own delinquencies—in the case of firms by dismissals or change of job and status, in schools by means of expulsion, corporal punishment or warning, in colleges and universities by systems of internal fine or by sending down or cautioning—it must comprise a considerable addition to the 'dark' figure of crimes not known to the police. And if it be objected that such offences are always of a petty character, we might well point out that so are a number of those which get into the official statistics.

It is quite impossible to discover by perusing the official figures how many of the offences classified under the same heading are in this sense petty. I say 'in this sense' because such an interpretation makes the *a priori* assumption that an offence which involves only a small amount of money is therefore petty in its significance for the offender and gives an accurate indication of his future development. In fact the prognosis for a child who steals the odd coppers may prove, upon examination, to be much worse than that for a child who actually commits a breaking-in offence. As social scientists we have to look at an offence in two different perspectives: one based on the extent of the injury to society and the person offended against, the other concerned with the meaning of the offence in terms of the individual offender's psychological condition. The gravity imputed to the offence therefore can substantially alter depending on which way we are looking at it and for what purposes.

III

It is the practice in this country to divide all crimes into two main categories, those called indictable and those called non-indictable offences. The distinction is of mainly juridical interest and arises from the peculiar way in which British law has evolved, and need not concern us here. For practical purposes indictable offences are those which are triable by the higher courts, that is to say Assizes or Quarter Sessions, while non-indictable offences are those which are dealt with summarily by magistrates in the lower courts. In practice many indictable offences, minor thefts and larcenies for example, are dealt with summarily by agreement between the bench and the offender. This is a common-sense way of reducing the volume of more serious offences coming before the higher courts and of avoiding the delays this would involve. More important for our purposes is the widely held view that indictable offences are more serious in nature than non-indictable offences and for this reason, when considering the general state of crime in the country as a whole, it is customary to deal with the indictable class alone. This division between the serious and the trivial can be misleading. While indictable offences include larceny, breaking and entering, receiving stolen property, frauds, false pretences, sexual offences, violence committed against the person and homicide, the non-indictable category includes, amongst a whole host of peccadilloes, such things as malicious damage, cruelty to children, assaults, offences by prostitutes and many motoring and traffic offences. Attempting suicide is an indictable offence but living on a prostitute's earnings is not. Cruelty and neglect of children is non-indictable but stealing a postcard is. Such arbitrary distinctions seem anomalous. Therefore, the custom of using only indictable offences as an index of criminality is to some degree misleading. Baroness Wootton has recently drawn attention to the fact that motoring offences which continue to lead the statistics—something like half those convicted in all criminal courts—are still not thought of as crimes.[1] She asks why not and the question inevitably poses itself whether there is some deep-rooted bias on the part of the motoring public (which includes the better-off sections of the community) against taking such potentially dangerous offences more seriously.

Lady Wootton has also made some pungent comments on the indictable and non-indictable distinction. 'A category which includes the most trivial offences of stealing by children eight or nine years old, but omits the great majority of dangerous and drunken drivers, brothel-keepers and those who live on the earnings of prostitutes, along with cases of cruelty to animals, and often children as well—such a category is not a reliable index of serious criminality.'[2]

IV

My colleague in the University, Mr. Harold Silcock, made a valuable study of *The Increase in Crimes of Theft 1938–1947*, which blew gaping holes into the official statistics.[3] The 'Black Market' which flourished during those years of shortage was, he argued, supplied by the proceeds of theft. Between 1938 and 1947 crimes of theft, which in all their forms accounted for about 90 per cent of all indictable offences known to the police, showed an increase of 78 per cent. Mr Silcock estimated that the loss as a result of stolen property rose from being £2·5 millions in 1938 to the phenomenal sum of £13 millions in 1947. Much of this theft was never in fact reported to the police. It was merely lost in transit. Many articles of both imports and exports simply vanished on the journey from one place to another. Textiles seemed to be especially vulnerable to this sort of theft. Packed at Point A they set out on their journey by road or rail and failed to reach their destination at Point B. In some cases their loss was reported, in other cases it was merely written off as the result of unavoidable quasi-natural hazards.

A further fact that we must bear in mind is the detection rate

[1] *Social Science and Social Pathology*, Allen and Unwin, 1959.
[2] *Contemporary Trends in Crime and its Treatment*, The Nineteenth Clarke Hall Lecture, 1959.
[3] Liverpool University Press, 1949.

on which the police forces usually work. This is somewhat lower than it was pre-war and, although there are regional variations, it is on average somewhere between 40 and 50 per cent. There has been an increase of about 8 per cent in the population since 1938, which has some bearing on this reduced detection rate, but a more likely explanation is to be found in the fact that most police forces are operating below their desired capacity. Anyone, therefore, who commits an offence can reckon on having at least a fifty-fifty chance of getting away with it, and the old parrot cry of 'Crime Doesn't Pay' is patently at variance with the facts.

We have perhaps already spent too much time considering the limitations and shortcomings of the criminal statistics. But this is necessary in view of the generalizations that are often based on such insubstantial foundations. It is important to know exactly what we are talking about when we start advocating administrative or legal policies which we think will reduce the incidence of crime. It is also necessary, before going on to look at the figures, to know how they are obtained and what they represent. Forewarned is forearmed, and this information may assist us to make more cautious deductions than we otherwise would and prevent us jumping too quickly to gloomy conclusions.

It is generally agreed by experts that the criminal statistics collected before the year 1938, when steps were taken to introduce some degree of order and uniformity into chief constables' returns, are of little value for comparative or deductive purposes. In this chapter we will merely pick out what we consider are the more significant figures during the past twenty years or so. In particular we will be concerned with trends and regularities over a fair period of time, rather than with temporary fluctuations or fringe phenomena.

V

The first fact that stands out with startling clarity is that the total amount of allegedly more serious crime has apparently increased by substantial proportions. In 1938 the number of indictable offences known to the police in thousands was 283·2. In 1959 the figure had rocketed to 675·6. That is to say the amount of reported crime had more than doubled over twenty-one years, while the population had increased by rather less than 10 per cent. In the year there were 626,500 indictable offences committed, and although many were of a seemingly trivial nature, there were also indications that some of the nastier type of offences had gone up disproportionately, as between the years 1938 and 1959. Crimes of violence against the person had gone up by over five times, sexual offences were nearly four times as frequent, breaking and entering was well over two and a half times as common, larcenies had more than doubled, as had receiving, frauds and false pretences.

Over the same period the numbers of people who were found guilty of indictable offences correspondingly increased. In 1938 those found guilty per thousand of the population numbered 78·5. In 1959 the figure had risen to 153·2. What we do not and would very much like to know is how many individuals have between them been successfully prosecuted for these offences, Unfortunately, as the statistics are presented to us, there is no means of finding out how many times one individual was found guilty of offences in the same year. This is a serious limitation in our knowledge, for, as Lady Wootton pointed out in her Clarke Hall lecture in 1959, there is certainly more crime, but are there very many more criminals? 'What we do not know,' she said, 'is how far this means that more people are breaking the law and how far it reflects more persistent or more extensive criminality on the part of those once convicted. Certainly it is of interest that year by year the total number of findings of guilt per 100 different persons convicted seems to be going up. In 1950 every 100 individual males convicted of an indictable offence were responsible between them for 136 findings of guilt; the corresponding figure for females being 129. In 1957 the figures were 149 for males and 141 for females. Is there a hint here that the contemporary problem is not so much a matter of the general decay of law-abiding habits as of failure to deal effectively with a determinedly anti-social minority?' This is a vital question which could only be answered by more thorough-going research into the statistics than has yet been attempted.

So far we have established that there is more *known* crime nowadays than there was pre-war, and furthermore there seems to have been an increase in the nastier offences involving violence against the person and sexual offences. There has also been a shift from simple larceny towards more breaking and entering. We may now look at the figures to see whether or not any particular age group is more apt to commit certain kinds of offences than in pre-war days, and here the evidence is remarkable. It suggests that the older teenagers are unusually delinquent and that their offences are rather more aggressive in nature than they used to be. As between 1938 and 1959 the number of crimes with violence against the person for the 17 to 21 age group has gone up by about ten times while their breaking and entering offences had nearly quadrupled. Moreover, if we take all kinds of indictable offences the 17 to 21 age group has more than doubled the amount of its criminal activities. The 21 and over group has almost doubled its criminality while the 8 to 16 group is only a little way in arrears of this achievement.

This phenomenon of an increased teenage delinquency has recently been examined by Mr. Leslie Wilkins of the Home Office research unit in a paper entitled *Delinquent Generations*.[1] In this study Mr. Wilkins has shown from an examination of the official statistics for the years 1946–57 inclusively that a particular generation of boys born between 1935 and 1942 have been exceptionally criminal. These young people who grew up during the most unsettled war years, who were between the ages of four and five during some of the most socially disturbed phases, subsequently produced the highest delinquency rates. These findings were not only true for boys and girls in England and Wales but also for the same age groups in Scotland. There is therefore a strong *prima facie* case for connecting the general upset in family and social life during the war years with the anti-social behaviour of young people who, at a particularly susceptible and sensitive stage of their psychological development, had to endure exceptionally adverse conditions. If this is true, and the evidence points strongly in favour of this theory, then these subsequently abnormally delinquent youngsters are to be thought of more as the victims of circumstances than as being exceptionally depraved or vicious. This, in turn, suggests that those members of older generations who had the good fortune to grow up in more favourable conditions and who occasionally in their irritation give vent to demands for more

[1] H.M.S.O. 1961.

drastic punitive measures to be adopted to deal with the so-called 'post-war crime wave' might usefully assume a more sympathetic and constructive approach.

A second important finding in Wilkins's study is that these youths who were between the ages of 17 and 21 from 1955 onwards proved, not only to be more delinquent than any previous generation had been, but even more criminal in adolescence than they were in the prepubertal period. This seems to imply that growing up in wartime or in similar times of unusual stress is not only particularly damaging for the four- to five-year-olds deprived of adequate home life and social discipline, but further that there is a delayed reaction which manifests itself most acutely immediately prior to adult maturity and evidences itself in a sort of last-minute fling against authority. The generation of children who were toddlers in wartime proved extremely antisocial in their youth. We may therefore hope that this particular epidemic of adolescent unruliness will abate as the individual members of the disturbed generation settle down and marry and, we trust, outgrow their problems. Such optimism seems justified by the further fact that those children who were actually born during the war years have not as yet shown any tendency towards excessive criminality—perhaps because life had become more stable by the time they were old enough to take notice of the wider environment. We may perhaps, on the strength of these findings, look forward to a period of increasing stability in which juvenile misbehaviour will at least be contained within reasonable bounds.

Year after year the official statistics have shown that crime is closely associated with childhood and youth, that, while in adult life it is far from inconsiderable, it remains a substantially juvenile and adolescent activity. At the present moment the peak age for all kinds of offences is fourteen, whereas in the past juvenile delinquency reached its zenith rather later in adolescence, round about the age of sixteen. But in recent years the trend has been in the direction of a lower peak and has curiously been associated with the statutory school leaving age. The authors of the Crowther Report, in an interesting section, have drawn attention to this phenomenon and made some pertinent comments which are well worth quoting.

'There is one aspect of juvenile delinquency with which the

schools must be very closely concerned—it is the fact that the last year of compulsory education is also the heaviest year for juvenile delinquency, and that the steadily increasing rate in the secondary school years is reversed when a boy goes to work . . . moreover, when the school-leaving age was raised from 14 to 15 in 1947 there was an immediate change over in the delinquency record of the 13-year-olds (who until then had been the most troublesome age-group) and the 14-year-olds took their place in 1948 and have held it consistently ever since.[1]

As the report goes on to suggest, once a boy gets to work he has far less time for illegal acts, and, in so far as juvenile delinquency is a childish phase, its diminished incidence in working life is only to be expected. This explanation does not account for the fact, however, that, while in the years immediately prior to 1947 the peak age was round about thirteen, a generation or so earlier it was located in later adolescence, well after boys presumably started their working lives. In 1936 in England and Wales it was somewhere between fourteen and sixteen, while in 1933 it was between sixteen and twenty-one. A curious fluctuation has therefore occurred which is difficult to account for. Changes in administrative practice, following the 1933 Children and Young Persons Act and the growing confidence of the public in the work of the juvenile courts may have helped to lower the peak age for known offences, but it is also conceivable that other more general social and physiological changes may have been at work. In the 1930's, for instance, the incidence of unemployment for all age groups was particularly high and there was accordingly much more poverty in families. This may have induced some of the older and possibly unemployed youths to commit thefts as a form of retaliation and protest and been an index of their social unrest. Moreover, in post-war years there has been some medical evidence produced to indicate an earlier age of physiological maturity in British youth.[2] If this is so, it could presumably have a bearing on earlier psychological stability and so lead to an earlier outgrowing of the juvenile delinquent phase.

[1] *15 to 18*, Report of the Central Advisory Council for Education—England, H.M.S.O., 1959, p. 42.

[2] See in this connection Dr. J. M. Tanner, *Growth at Adolescence*, Blackwell, 1955.

CRIME—SOME FACTS AND FIGURES

Whatever the reasons for these fluctuations, it is clear that crime and immaturity are associated phenomena, and that the older we get the less likely we are to commit illegal acts. This is a most important general fact which by implication tells us a great deal about the nature of crime and the nature of modern society. In some ways, too, it is a most heartening feature since it gives support to the idea that delinquency is very often a phase through which most boys and fewer girls have to pass before ultimately attaining social sagacity and ethical maturity. If we do indeed tend to grow out of crime, then the sooner we do so the better, and the lower the peak age falls the healthier the younger generation may be presumed to be.

VI

The second fact which emerges with startling clarity from the official criminal statistics is that the vast majority of all offences are committed against property. Figures given by Professor David Marsh for the period 1900–1951 inclusive, for offences known to the police, show that what we may call the pattern of crime has remained constant over half a century. It is clear from his figures that crimes against the person, such as homicide, manslaughter, rape, indecency, incest and infanticide, had remained at roughly no more than 4 per cent of all offences; that offences against property with violence, such as burglary and housebreaking, also remained fairly steady round about 17 per cent of the total; that offences against property without violence, such as embezzlement, false pretences and various kinds of theft, accounted for between 75 and 80 per cent of the total; that malicious injuries to property, such as arson and other acts of deliberate damage, were never more than 1 per cent; and finally, that a miscellaneous group of rare offences, such as treason, attempted suicide, occurred with similar infrequency; and that forgery and currency offences were never more than 1 per cent.[1]

In other words, no less than 90 per cent of all reported crimes in this country in the first half of the twentieth century have comprised offences against property, with or without violence.

[1] David C. Marsh, *The Changing Social Structure of England and Wales, 1871–1951*, Routledge and Kegan Paul, 1958, p. 245.

34

INDICTABLE OFFENCES KNOWN TO THE POLICE IN ENGLAND AND WALES. 1900–51

Offences	Annual average number						No. for year	
	1900–04	% of total	1925–29	% of total	1935–39	% of total	1951	% of total
1. Offences against the Person	3,522	4	5,181	4	7,238	3	21,149	4
2. Offences against property with violence	9,277	11	20,505	16	44,569	17	96,820	18
3. Offences against property without violence	67,732	80	97,823	77	209,328	78	392,538	75
4. Malicious injuries to property	485	1	306	·2	549	·2	4,993	1
5. Forgery and Offences against the currency	536	1	904	·7	1,680	·6	3,378	1
6. Other offences	2,695	3	2,921	2·0	3,922	1·0	5,628	1
TOTAL	84,247	100	127,640	100	267,286	100	524,506	100

35

This picture remains substantially unaltered today. The crime problem, then, is fundamentally a problem of honesty and respect for other people's possessions. To an overwhelming degree the law is concerned with safeguarding private property and preventing its damage and theft at the hands of other members of the community. This single fact tells us a very great deal about the structure of British society and about the way in which the nature of social organizations influences the behaviour and character of individuals.

VII

The third striking fact which criminal statistics reveals is that crime is predominantly a masculine activity. Men are much more criminal than women and boys are more delinquent than girls. This remarkable differentiation between the crime rates of the sexes is constant over the years and quite unaffected by any changes in the social structure.

Persons Found Guilty of Indictable Offences per 100,000 Population
England and Wales

	Males	Females
1938	393	51
1948	612	87
1951	645	79
1957	612	73
1958	680	84
1959	710	84

This phenomenon is world-wide. As Sutherland said: 'The male sex has a great excess of crimes in all nations, all communities within a nation, all age groups, all periods of history for which organized statistics are available, and all types of crimes except those which are somewhat intimately related to the female sex such as abortion and infanticide.'[1]

The reasons for this state of affairs are fairly obvious. Apart from physiological and constitutional differences, which tend to

[1] *Principles of Criminology*, Edwin Sutherland and Donald Cressey, 5th edition, Lippincott, 1955, p. 111.

make women less energy expending and physically aggressive than men, there are important cultural distinctions in nearly all known societies which define the male and female roles in markedly different terms. While men are the breadwinners and the protectors of the family they must always be encouraged to adopt a more aggressive attitude to the world. The feminine role is more confined to the care of children and safeguarding the emotional solidarity of the family and is consequently more pacific, tender and home-centred than the man's. Moreover, women have traditionally less access to occupations which offer opportunities for embezzlement, fraud and large-scale theft. Their roles tend to confine them to petty pilfering and illegal sex practices. And their education and social training reinforces the limitations of their roles and underlines the expressive rather than the instrumental aspects of their social functions. Thus little boys are encouraged to be rough, to play with guns and to stage mock battles. When they are older they are expected to enjoy vigorous games, to climb trees, to box and play football. Little girls are given dolls and prams and expected to imitate mother, to keep themselves clean and take an interest in clothes and personal toilet. Identification with the maternal role comes early and easily to girls and may be one explanation of the generally recognized fact that they 'mature' earlier than their brothers. Maturity is often defined in terms of whether or not expectations of role behaviour are realized by the individual and is therefore a somewhat 'circular' definition.

We may summarize what we have said in this section by saying that, although we can never know in an absolute way what the extent of crime is at any one moment in society, there are good grounds for believing that there has been a substantial increase in this country over the past twenty odd years. Moreover, certain regularities in the statistics occur year after year with such persistence and apparent universality that we are in a position to make some broad generalizations. These are (a) that the vast majority of all offences are committed against property and involve various forms of theft, (b) that crime is particularly associated with childhood and youth and attains its climax at the age of fourteen or thereabouts, and (c) that crime is predominantly a masculine activity. What we may term, then, the lay image of the criminal in contemporary

British Society is not a Bill Sykes or a Fagin, not a professional offender dedicated to the antisocial life, but a schoolboy in the act of shoplifting or breaking and entering in his unregulated leisure hours. Criminality is primarily an aspect of immaturity, social and psychological. It is mainly but not solely a juvenile phenomenon. Older offenders are by no means negligible, however, and, as we shall see, present more intractable problems to the penologist.

Author's Note. Since this chapter was written the law relating to attempted suicide has been altered. The latter is no longer an offence and, therefore, the comment on p. 27 is no longer valid.

Chapter 3

WHITE COLLAR CRIME AND BUSINESS OFFENCES

I

At this point I want to say a little about crime and morality and then pass quickly on to a consideration of the extent to which dubious and illegal conduct permeates the whole of our society.

The question of crime and morality need not delay us long, as it more properly appertains to the sphere of the philosopher and theologian than the sociologist. But one thing we must get clear is that crime and immorality are not necessarily one and the same thing. There is undoubtedly a certain amount of overlap between them but they are not identical. Inevitably acts forbidden by moral codes tended to become proscribed by legal systems. But our ancestors were perversely eclectic in their selection of certain spiritual offences rather than others for incorporation in their list of prohibited acts. There is a very real danger that we can become so bemused by notions of legality and illegality of behaviour that we may fail to make distinctions in the moral quality of varying acts. This is, of course, the hoary sin of phariseeism so severely castigated in the New Testament and which seems to be man's inseparable shadow-companion, his *doppelgänger*, in whatever culture or milieu he happens to dwell. It is all too human and simple to bracket law-breaking with immorality, to assume that a man who offends against the law is *ipso facto* less moral than one whose activities remain within the legally permitted. Yet a few moments' honest reflection will convince us that the mere fact of transgressing the legal code or not tells us very little about our spiritual condition.

Many a man who lies in gaol may be less sinful than others who occupy important posts outside who yet have perpetrated acts which are spiritually abominable. There is not likely ever to be a public record of the various forms of hypocrisy, of confidential slander, personal muckraking and malicious denigration, of despicable toadyism, sycophantic time-serving, lying, deliberate withholding of credit, cheating, subtle blackmailing and calculated emotional torture which are everyday occurrences in so-called normal social relationships. Who dare cast the first stone? And may these spiritual sins not contain more downright wickedness than many a physical assault on the person or theft of property? As the late Sir Norwood East, the eminent forensic psychiatrist wrote: '. . . as the criminologist looks out upon the world, and sees men and women in important positions making false and often unscrupulous assertions in order to secure personal advantage, he can hardly fail to conquer their moral turpitude with that of those who break the law.'[1]

Perhaps this argument might best be summed up by saying that the legal and moral codes overlap but are not identical. Crime is a socio-legal and not necessarily a moral concept. The standards of morality presumably are unchanging. Legal codes change from time to time in the same society: what is forbidden at one stage is permitted at another. What the Nazi government treated as an offence is not necessarily regarded in a criminal light by the West German state today. The law prohibits and punishes certain forms of immoral conduct but not others. It condemns murder but permits hypocrisy, forbids theft of goods but is powerless to prevent filching of ideas and undermining of reputation. It deals with physical neglect but finds emotional cruelty beyond its power to chasten. Concerning the supreme New Testament sin of uncharity it is, even in ostensibly Christian societies, remarkably silent. Historically, the law came into being to safeguard certain elementary human rights and to secure private property. It favoured the haves against the have-nots and to a certain extent it still does. There is little doubt that police action also often reflects this class bias.

A magistrate's son took his parent's car and drove it without a licence recklessly to the public danger. The police informed his father but took no further action on that occasion. Had the

[1] *Society and the Criminal*, H.M.S.O. 1949, p. 210.

youth been dressed in certain attire, spoken with an uncouth accent and not been the son of a distinguished father, prosecution would almost certainly have followed. Such instances could be multiplied and documented and would make a penetrating sociological thesis. As Barbara Wootton pointed out in her famous book *Social Science and Social Pathology*, hierarchical assumptions infect the law and its practice in this country: 'the prevalence of criminality among the lower classes is, for instance, easily demonstrated by the use of definitions which automatically exclude those crimes to which the upper classes are most likely to be addicted.'

During the last war even such institutions as the tribunals set up to deal with conscientious objectors to military service were deeply and patently influenced by social class factors in the appellates. If a man had a good education, was literate and articulate in his own defence and had some intellectual subtlety to match against the insidious questions that the members of the tribunal used to try to undermine the applicant's confidence, he usually got more sympathetic treatment. But the half-educated man from a poor social background received, on the whole, much harsher treatment and was more likely to have his appeal turned down and thus be faced with the prospect of imprisonment.

To a sociologist, of course, it is not surprising that those sections of the community who possess the power should use it to their own advantage and for the protection of their special class interests. Nor is it unlikely that those who make the law and those whose job it is to maintain its integrity should share a common interest reflecting this bias. In a good middle-class residential suburb it is assumed that police officers are there to safeguard the interests of the residents. When officers speak to local residents they assume a quasi-deferential manner and usually address them as 'sir'. But down on the dock road where hostility between police and local inhabitants is traditional, a different attitude is observable. In slum neighbourhoods, police tend to take a more aggressive line and are much less likely to use the titular courtesy in addressing people.

Throughout society class differences exist and are tacitly recognized. As Lady Wootton suggests, the law is more rigorously exercised against the kinds of offences which lower class people are more tempted to commit. At the same time it often fails to classify as serious crimes the kinds of delinquencies which better-off people are more likely to commit. To some extent our easy-going tolerance of many kinds of motoring offences can be attributed to this class-bias. The attitude may, of course, be unconsciously influenced by such prejudices, but conscious or not, discrimination is apparent and those who are concerned about notions of justice and morality would be wise to take cognizance of its existence, to take out, in this way, what may be termed an insurance policy against hypocrisy and humbug.

A much more serious group of actual or near offences are those to which criminologists have given the generic title of 'white collar crime'.

The late Edwin Sutherland, who was a pioneer in this field, defined white-collar crimes as 'crimes committed by persons of respectability and high social status in the course of their occupations'.[1] As he pointed out, although there are grounds for believing that they are fairly widespread, 'an index of their frequency is not found in police reports'.[2] Not only is there a reluctance to prosecute such offences, but they are notoriously difficult to detect or pin down. The fact that these offenders occupy top positions in industry, commerce or public office, and the fact that they commit their offences only in this limited and specialized field and do not make the mistake of straying over into common or garden theft or fraud, makes them more or less impregnable. Some of the so-called 'perks' which business men enjoy are institutionalized forms of theft. I knew, for example, a manager of a large firm employing its own maintenance men to look after its vehicles, who used to take his own car regularly into the firm's garages, have it serviced and repaired at their expense and thus save himself over the years a considerable sum of money. Such instances could be multiplied easily and would reach astronomical proportions. Every large industry or commercial undertaking is wide open to this sort of plucking by the higher administrative staff—and others with rather less authority too. Expense accounts are notoriously tricky propositions. Inland revenue officials permit this form of camouflaged salary increase, judging it a legitimate business expense similar to a reasonable outlay on advertising. While most fair-

[1] Op. cit., p. 40.   [2] Ibid.

minded people would agree that some expenses must be allowed and that an employee, however exalted, ought not to be financially out of pocket as a result of promoting the firm's interests, it is extremely difficult to know where the line ought to be drawn. If an executive has to entertain an important buyer it will necessitate an outlay on food, tobacco and alcohol. But how much? £10? £20? £30? And how often do these occasions occur? Is it feasible to keep accurate records and present receipts for every item over a twelve month period? Or do we settle for a nice round sum, say £500 or £1,000 a year?

There is also the hoary institution of the *quid pro quo* and of the thank-offering for favours received.

A man has a large contract to dispose of, and there are two almost equally efficient firms competing for it. He decides on balance to give the job to firm B rather than firm A and a month later firm B dispatch a crate of whisky to his home or send a diamond ring for his wife. One cannot say this is bribery in the ordinary sense of the word. In the world of private business it is certainly not a delinquency, although in public life such things are not supposed to happen. A government or corporation official who is found out receiving such presents gets into trouble, largely because of the wind of scandal that blows up. But it is extraordinarily difficult to distinguish *morally* between bribery and corruption and the operation of the *quid pro quo* network. 'In some cities and states,' says Sutherland, 'any purchase of commodities which is strictly honest is an oversight.'[1] We may console ourselves by saying that Sutherland is writing about North America, but there is no reason to believe that similar rackets do not take place in this country. In 1950–1 the U.S.A. citizens were shocked by the mass of evidence collected by the Kefauver Committee 'into realization of the hugeness of the problem of racketeering, its ramifications into the field of legitimate business, and its dominant influence over government in many cities'.[2] It found 'the gambling interests in some cities so powerful they could dictate to government and could corrupt police and other law-enforcement agencies'.[3]

One of the best illustrations of how racketeering operates as

[1] Op. cit., p. 45.
[2] Donald Taft, *Criminology*, New York, Macmillan, 1956, p. 231.
[3] Ibid., p. 247.

a form of quasi-legitimate business in a big North American city is contained in William Foote Whyte's classic study *Street Corner Society*.[1] In Boston, according to Whyte's account which has, to my knowledge, never been refuted, the racket most widely practised involved mass illegal gambling by highly organized syndicates operating on what one can only call sound business lines. Gone are the days of internecine gang warfare which characterized American urban crime during the hey-day of bootlegging. Violence is now subdued so competition, as in other commercial concerns, has given way to rational co-operation. The philosophy is: let us unite our illegal practices and divide the spoils, with agreed shares for all racketeers and nobody gets hurt. The police occupy an important role in this organized crime since they possess the power, if not to stamp out unlawful betting then at least to interfere seriously in its extent. Too frequent prosecutions would be bad for business, therefore the police have to be incorporated into the whole concern. Says Whyte: 'The cops are paid off. They call it the "union wage". The patrolman gets five dollars a month for every store on his beat that sells numbers. . . . They divide up the territory between themselves.'[2] From time to time, in order to allay public anxiety, they make a pretence at enforcing the law. Some of the lesser people who take and transmit the bets allow themselves (for a financial reward of course) to be prosecuted and sent to jail, having pleaded guilty in order to avoid fuss. Whyte suggests that in Cornerville 'the primary function of the police department is not the enforcement of law but the regulation of illegal activities'.[3] Organized gambling hence operates as a system. All its parts are closely inter-related and individuals, who may come or go, occupy specialized positions in the system. The purpose of the organization is to provide a service to certain members of the public who desire it, i.e. gambling. At the same time it gives the little men involved in the business a reasonable living, offers the police a useful emolument and furnishes the top level racketeers with substantial profits. And seldom does anybody get hurt! What could be more rational?

The question which this illustration poses most acutely is whether such rackets ought not to be made lawful. Is this not a

[1] Fourth impression, University of Chicago Press, 1947.
[2] Op. cit., p. 123. [3] Ibid., p. 138.

vivid example of the way in which modern societies create their own crime? As the law stands such activities are illegal, but are they really immoral? It is not much use arguing that betting is an essentially evil practice. It may or may not in individual cases become a damaging vice. But because one man ruins himself by backing horses, is that any justification for forbidding the rest of the community? Many a man has ruined himself on the stock exchange, but we don't therefore call for a banning of the sale of stocks and shares. Prohibition in America led to bootlegging which in turn led to criminal wars and rival gangs. But what an idiotic law it was! It is a sound legal proposition that if a law is held in contempt by a substantial body of citizens, then that must be a bad law. A good law, on the other hand, while it must sometimes be broken to show that it is necessary, should receive the approval of the majority of the people. In this way it is apparent that the possession of a body of laws serves to bind members of a society together. When a serious crime is committed—when, that is to say, a law we are all agreed about is broken—we unite together to seek out the criminal and bring him to justice. A homicide seldom receives asylum but is hounded by every good citizen. Thus law is socially cohesive and confirms feelings of community. But a bad law acts divisively. If it is invoked, it divides public opinion sharply and makes for disunity. An example of a bad law, almost everywhere held in contempt, is that on the British statute book obliging everyone to attend divine service on Sunday. The Sunday Observance and kindred acts have never been revoked but they are not respected. Imagine what a kurfuffle would ensue if anyone attempted a prosecution under the Sunday Observance Act!

To return to William Foote Whyte's *Cornerville* study, we must note two significant things. First, that the existence of anti-gaming laws results in police officers being placed in a position of acute temptation. The patrolman who is 'honest' and who will not co-operate with the racketeers and accept his bribe is a source of considerable embarrassment to the whole system. He has to be removed before he creates a scandal and the most effective way is for his superiors to transfer him to another branch of police work where he is not brought into contact with the numbers' racket. So they put him on traffic control duty, an arduous and unpopular task, *pour encourager les autres*. The second point one has to make, and this is a grave consideration, is that once the racket is in being many people, and the police in particular, have thereafter a vested interest in its continuation. If gambling on numbers were to be made legal, it would no longer be necessary to pay off the cops and they would all be out of pocket. Thus we can see that, in some cases, not only does the society create its own offences but it also tends to develop attitudes of mind favourable to their perpetuation. Once crime becomes a social system it has all the characteristics of other social systems, viz. stability, tradition, individual interests, capital investment and so on.

That this is so is convincingly demonstrated by Marshall B. Clinard's scathing exposure of the machinations of black marketeers in the United States during the war against Hitler Germany and in the later Korean campaign. As a result of his investigations he concluded:

'Although the foregoing accounts of the black market show considerable variation, there can be no question that it extended throughout the entire nation, among all classes of society, from the thief and counterfeiter to the businessman, at all levels of our economic structure, from consumer to large manufacturer, and in numerous commodities.'[1]

The traffic in scarce goods was not confined to rationed articles only but invaded the production, distribution and retailing of commodities at all levels, which seems to indicate that a widespread attitude of mind developed during the war years. There was, naturally enough, a big black market in gasoline and meat, accompanied by counterfeiting of coupons and wholesale issuing of false statements and claims. Landlords, too, cashed in while the going was good, and such illegal practices as key money (in Britain) and charges for hidden rents (in both countries), whereby owners extorted extra payments for almost fictitious additional facilities, flourished. The black market was a nationwide phenomenon, not exclusively associated with one racial group or with a few geographical regions or cultural groups and its manifestations ranged from the more traditional kinds of sharp practice to outright conspiracy to defraud. Basically,

---

[1] Marshal B. Clinard, *The Black Market, A Study of White Collar Crime*, Rinehart and Co., New York, 1952, pp. 48–9.

Clinard claims, it was closely related to many ordinary peace-time commercial activities and transactions, and hence was marked by a general lack of guilt feelings on the part of those who operated the network.[1]

While no author to my knowledge has so witheringly exposed the underlying unscrupulousness of British business practice and uncovered the working of the black market in this country, there can be little doubt that similar things, though possibly on a smaller scale, happened here and for identical reasons.

Somewhat alarmingly, Sutherland discovered that public no less than private corporations were far from being above-board in their business deals. He found that many of the largest operated corruptly in placing contracts for public works, more-over even in Britain a close tie-up between certain business concerns and local government is far from being unknown. In other words, ordinary so-called above-board business infiltrates into political life in order to secure economic advantages, and individuals all along the line facilitate the process to their own profit. Clearly the dividing line between the legitimate and illegitimate wears transparently thin in many important aspects of our public life, and the perplexed individual conscience is put to intense strain to maintain any sort of ethical standards.

Not all white collar offenders, however, get away with their illegal practices. Sometimes, if their timing of activities goes wrong, their nefarious machinations are uncovered and a public scandal ensues. This happened not long ago in the notorious case of the misuse of funds belonging to the State Building Society when Friedrich Grunwald and Herbert Hugh Murray, former officials of the society, were gaoled for fraudulently converting to their own use money received for investment by buying shares in their own names. How often money entrusted to officials gets temporarily utilized in this way to promote private gain and, if all goes well, subsequently gets returned to its proper uses, is an open and disturbing question that many small investors must now be asking themselves.

[1] Interestingly enough, Clinard shows that while black marketeering was on the increase, the statistics of 'ordinary' crime showed an opposite trend, as though the sources of delinquent energy had been channelled into an alternative track rather than that the number of law-violators had substanti-ally increased.

It is probably true to say, however, that in this country organized peacetime rackets, such as Whyte had described in Boston, U.S.A., are of a somewhat different nature and much less widespread. British society contains many built-in safeguards which prevent criminal systems developing to any great extent. The proud boast that we possess both an independent judiciary and an incorruptible police force is not a mere patriotic piece of self-deception. In most, if not all, the American states judges and police captains are political appointments. So are public prosecutors. This gives the party political machine and its bosses almost unlimited power in social affairs. Sutherland said that, in the United States, 'All large cities and most of the smaller cities have persons who make a business of "fixing" cases for professional thieves'.[1] He goes on to claim that 'The police, bailiffs, clerks, prosecutors, and judges frequently cooperate with these "fixers", either for direct money payments or under orders from political leaders who control appointments and elections.'[2]

In Britain it can be said, without any shadow of doubt, that the judiciary, although by no means infallible, is entirely uncorruptible. And the police, since they are not directly subject to political control, can, if they wish, act without fear or favour. While it could not be maintained that they never exercise discretion to the point of discrimination and differential treatment, in the main they carry out their arduous and demanding task with honesty and a sense of public responsibility. This does not mean that individual police officers do not themselves sometimes break the law or accept bribes. In recent years we have had the notorious example of the Brighton Police Trial to remind us that every system is no stronger than its individual parts. It is always possible for a man to sell immunity to lawbreakers in return for gifts. But whether or not police officers in this country accept bribes from, for example, owners of shebeens or illicit drinking clubs, it would certainly be very difficult to assemble evidence to that effect. In the nature of things, those who accuse law enforcement officers of running protection rackets at their expense are themselves such dubious characters and of such a reputation that, without independent corroboration, no jury would be likely to pay much attention

[1] Op. cit., p. 46.　　　　　[2] Ibid.

to their evidence. Nevertheless, it would be idle utopianism to maintain that individual officers never err. But the system—and this is the important point which distinguishes the British police from that in many other countries—is not *as a system* subject to external pressures emanating either from political or other socially powerful groups, and is therefore less exposed to possible corrupting influences. Moreover, the police force itself exercises a constant and searching scrutiny into its own activities and any breach of the code leads to dismissal or demotion of tainted members. For these reasons, therefore, we may say that, the failings of individuals apart, we have in this country a police system of high integrity. And when we add this to the admitted fact that our judiciary is practically incorruptible we have the explanation for the absence of organized systems of crime and political corruption which is so shameful a part of public life in the United States.[1]

But while the big rackets are few and far between, we undoubtedly have our share of smaller racketeering. Something more will be said about organized and professional crime in a later section. It certainly exists in Britain but the vast majority of the people convicted in our courts of law are not professional criminals. They are small-scale crooks, occasionals or ordinary enough men, women and children who succumb to immediate temptations. Small-scale crooks who are probably inadequate personalities incapable of competing in the ordinary affairs of society, eke out a precarious living, frequently interrupted by spells in gaol, imitating the rackets of the real professionals. In a Liverpool court not very long ago a man was charged with and found guilty of extracting protection money from street-traders. His *modus operandi*, as the police like to call the petty criminal's technique, was to criticize a stall-holder's or barrow-boy's wares and then say that if he wanted to remain in business he must hand over regular protection money. Any refusal on the part of the street-trader resulted in his barrow being overturned and personal assault. The police inspector giving evidence against the accused man stated that there were other cases of traders who had had their barrows overturned but who were too frightened of further trouble to complain to the police.

[1] For a full documentation of this see *Crime in America*, by Estes Kefauver, Gollancz, 1952.

He said that 'one new vendor had been put entirely out of business because he could not afford to pay what was demanded of him'.[1] So, too, perhaps we may categorize the stable boy who is tempted by twenty pound notes to administer drugs to the horse in his care on the night before the big race as a small-scale crook, at least in embryo. Clearly the line between the casual offender, who steals on the impulse, and the 'wide-boy' mentality that is always ready to make a bit on the side, even if this involves breaking the law, is hard to draw. One merges into the other. But the one thing they have in common, which differentiates them from the genuine professional criminal, is their pettiness. Many of the petty offenders are found guilty of fraud and false pretences—which crimes are on the increase, incidentally. Sometimes this involves hire purchase fraud and selling articles obtained on account, or is associated with various larcencies, often of a casual, unpremeditated nature. People who fall into this kind of life-style often become chronic offenders and end up, as the protection racketeer in the Liverpool case cited above did, with ten years' Preventive Detention.

So far we have in the main been discussing crime as a business. But it is possible to look at things the other way on, to consider business as crime. Such an apparent reversal of normal values is often shocking to many people who have been brought up to consider that business is next to godliness and who regard the social order and the economic structure of our society as something sacrosanct. In considering business as crime we do not mean cases of business people who misuse their powers illegally, as for instance the directors who fraudulently converted over £3 million of the funds of the State Building Society to their own use in the recent notorious public prosecution. This scandal which was often referred to in the press as 'The Takeover Deals Trial' pointed to the existence of crime in high places and, like the Brighton Police Case or the Proceedings of the Bank Rate Tribunal in 1959, created a good deal of public alarm. This has in recent years however tended to concentrate more and more on what, in the past, many people would have described as legitimate business practice. In other words some of us are asking whether or not some of the currently acceptable and legal methods of conducting commercial enterprises ought

[1] *Liverpool Daily Post*, 18th November 1960.

not to to be made illegal because they appear to us to be immoral and undesirable. Many would like to see the laws of the land reformed to prohibit and punish various forms of sharp practice and wilful deception which are obviously fraudulent in purpose and in any case socially demoralizing. The Roman Catholic Archbishop of Liverpool, Dr. John Heenan, criticized the way in which some business take-overs come about. While agreeing that no moralist should condemn mergers which lead to economic expansion and higher wages, he added, 'It is not unknown for firms to be taken over simply to be destroyed. Directors who accept profitable offers without guaranteeing the future welfare of those they employ are plainly immoral.'[1] The comparatively recent institution of the 'golden handshake' to retiring directors of firms which have submitted to being taken over by a larger concern suggests, but does not prove, some kind of self-interested unde standing between the leaders of the undertakings concerned. Golden handshakes can consist of phenomenally high sums, many thousands of pounds which, being of the nature of a gift and not earned income, are presumably free of tax.

Books and articles have recently drawn attention to the hitherto somewhat mysterious activities of what is known for short as 'The City'. The City is an international centre of trade and finance, and 'city men', as they are called, financiers, bankers and stockbrokers, are both influential and wealthy. They often make large fortunes, occasionally they lose them. At times of boom, such as followed the Conservative Party victory at the Polls in 1959, anyone trafficking in stocks and shares stood to make a handsome and immediate profit.

The Stock Exchange is an extraordinarily fascinating social institution. Essentially its successful function depends on the honesty of its members, whose motto, *Dictum meum Pactum*, is no trivial Latin tag, but the very formula of business. In the hectic bustle and occasional bedlam of the exchange at the zenith of its activity, it is not possible to rely on anything more than a man's spoken word, which presumably could later be retracted, but which in fact is seldom dishonoured. If it were, the entire edifice would prove unreliable and ultimately unworkable. Your regular city man conducts his business with

[1] *The Catholic Herald*, 5th March 1961.

impeccable integrity, within certain agreed limits. He is merciless in pursuing profits or in making business agreements and is out to make the most he can when he has the advantage. At the same time he obeys the rules implicitly and his customers and professional colleagues know exactly where he stands. His word is his bond.

All this, of course, is to the good. The point at which concern arises over the trafficking in stocks and shares is when business becomes mere speculation and, in its turn, speculation looks uncommonly like gambling. Gambling, that is, with other people's money to a large extent. 'The speculator hopes', says Paul Ferris in his lucid and entertaining account of city life, 'for rising prices, and buys shares he has no intention of paying for; or he hopes for a fall and sells shares he doesn't possess. In the first place he is a "bull", in the second he is a "bear"—the phrases "bull market" and "bear market" are extended to cover a rising and falling market. Various technical devices help him perform this pocket-lining function of free markets everywhere, so natural to its practitioners, so strange and sometimes reprehensible to outsiders.'[1]

The great increase in the number of investors over recent years has greatly influenced the operation of the stock market. Many ordinary citizens who, during these affluent years, have been able to save up a few hundred pounds are keen to invest in stocks and shares, hoping not only for good dividends but also led on by the prospect of being able to sell out during a bear market and make a substantial profit. By doing no real work and without making any genuine contribution to the common welfare, individuals who successfully manipulate the buying and selling of stocks (either on their own or under the guidance of an experienced broker) can make in a day what a skilled craftsman would earn in a year. Such a situation causes moral unease in the minds of some citizens, particularly, a cynic might suggest, in the consciences of those who would like to but dare not risk their own money or who have no free capital to invest.

The issuing of new stock in companies is a matter about which those who are jealous of the good name of the city are much concerned. Says Ferris: 'Flotation of a public company is the point where mugs can be most easily relieved of their

[1] *The City*, Gollancz, 1960, p. 27.

money, and British regulations are devised to protect the applicant for shares in a new company. But are the regulations sufficiently strong? Opinion is sharply divided.'[1]

The 'con' men have a self-justificatory philosophy which says that the mug whose money you obtain by a swindle deserves all he gets since he was, for his part, anxious to get rich at someone else's expense. This is a decidedly criminal outlook and is beyond the pale of legitimate business. But it must be admitted that in motivation it is only distinguishable in degree from that of many business men. Is it morally right for one man to profit from another's cupidity, ignorance, error or misjudgement? With certain safeguards, the city business man and most people who engage in commerce of any sort would answer 'yes'.

The profit motive, however legitimate it might be as a rule for conducting business in a free society, may become a source of criminal temptation in individual cases. Carried beyond a certain point, it degenerates into fraud. But the important thing to note is that the profit motive is institutionalized in our kind of society. In the City, as it functions at its best, we can see this institutionalized profit-seeking in its legitimate guise. But there is a shadowy borderline between fair trading and fleecing which is not always clearly defined. And the take-over bids are examples of ways in which the interests of investors and of the staffs employed by companies concerned in such transactions are jeopardized to a degree which, although not illegal, seems to many people to call for some sort of state control. One of the things that directors who receive a juicy bid ought to do is to make sure that the offer is backed by adequate resources before taking any further action. As John Kenneth Galbraith has pointed out in regard to the financial transactions of Ivar Kreuger, 'we may lay it down as an absolute rule that, given an excess of confidence, there will be confidence men to take advantage of it.'[2] Kreuger, the match king, was, of course, no ordinary financier or speculator. He was an international crook and larcenist on a prodigious scale. Galbraith epitomizes him as 'the Leonardo' of the craft of those manipulators 'whose genius and imagination are unconstrained by integrity'.[3] His first theft, according to Shaplen, was of an envelope of pressed wild flowers belonging to a school-mate.

[1] Ibid, p. 43.   [2] *The Sunday Times*, 30th April 1961.   [3] Ibid.

Somewhere, then, legitimate business merges into crime. Monopolies and restrictive practices in business are close to that borderline. Restrictive Practice Courts set up by act of Parliament in recent years are empowered to intervene in cases where mergers making for monopoly are clearly seen to be inimical to the public interest. They can annul such mergers and agreements. Price maintenance agreements, for example, in the cotton trade were condemned by the R.P. Court as being contrary to public interest. In the United States the Sherman Anti-Trust Act of 1890 made it an offence to monopolize any kind of trade. The view in that country has always been that private enterprise should remain free. But in Britain the spate of mergers and take-over bids had led many critics to wonder whether the anti-monopoly legislation is adequate. It is, of course, a highly complicated and technical matter and the sole purpose in raising the issue in this chapter is to highlight the way in which unbridled profit-seeking in business can, if left unchecked, reach such an anti-social pitch as to make it virtually criminal.

This seems to be the appropriate place to consider the ethics of modern advertising. Here again we have an example of a perfectly legitimate and necessary business practice which at one extreme borders on downright dishonesty. Of course manufacturers and salesmen must inform the public what commodities are available. The trouble arises when the advertisement either suppresses relevant information or makes claims for the article which are purely fictitious. In modern society we are literally bombarded with adverts. Posters shriek at us from hoardings; loud-speaker vans advise and beseech us like the voice of coming doom; newspapers and magazines grow fat on expensive sales insertions; and at night, closeted in the dim-lit privacy of parlour or lounge, we are at the mercy of the wheedling, authoritative, succulent, bombastic, insidious, confidential, persuasive, imperative, glossily sleek and so-modern voices and faces that flicker across our T.V. screens from the independent and commercial studios. It has been shown that for the cost of a few minutes' television time you can sell almost anything. You can even get customers to besiege the shops asking for non-existent goods, so powerful is the persuasion generated by this modern medium of communication. Advertising through television brings certain sales. Conversely, failure to make use of this vehicle is likely to result in public apathy and reduced sales. Once inveigled into advertising on a big scale, the manufacturers cannot risk withdrawing. They are committed to an ever increasing advertisement rat-race.

In recent years various devices have been introduced to counter the more insidious and blatantly spurious claims of advertisers and sales-promoters. They may be thought of as techniques to safeguard the interest of the buyers against sheer exploitation. The Consumer Association now publishes a magazine called *Which* that is concerned with the relative values of various similar commodities and which, indirectly, is helping to make shoppers more sophisticated and discriminating. The old principle of *laissez-faire* economy, *caveat emptor*, let the buyer beware (of dishonesty), is clearly an inadequate protection against the subtle, calculated deception that modern salesmanship entails. The appeal to be more modern, up-to-date or chic, is, perhaps, permissible. But appeals to customers' sexuality or snobbery are more dubious. Why should it be necessary to sell a grand piano by means of a poster showing a girl in a tightly-fitting bathing dress? Indeed, everything from a razor blade to a motor cycle seems to require some sexual titillation of the customer's appetite to recommend it. Or so the people responsible for floating the commodity seem to think. The appeal to snobbery is somewhat more nauseating. 'This is the car for the go-ahead young business man' or, 'The up-and-coming man wears such and such a shirt', are much of a muchness with 'The X hair-perm brings the men to your feet'. The urge to get on and get up, to make good i.e. acquire a lot of money and possessions, no doubt reflects the values of a materialist, commercial society. The sex-appeal stuff probably gains its power from the general sex-neurosis. But there are other widely publicized phrases which have more humour than genuine one-upmanship. 'Top people read *The Times*' is really very funny. It could easily be the caption of a Punch cartoon.

Mass advertising does two things which make contemporary society very different from anything that has gone before: (a) it encourages salesmen to deceive, and (b) it whips up the general appetite for consumer goods. Both these phenomena have a direct bearing on the crime-rate. They mutually reinforce one another, tending towards the creation of a general state of mind which is hedonistic, materialistic, unethical and greedily egocentric. Just as the nature of the culture bed determines what sort of seedlings will prosper there, so in societies the common philosophy, general attitudes and widely-repeated clichés influence personality and condition behaviour. And crime, we have constantly to remind ourselves, is a form of socially conditioned human behaviour. It is, moreover, in the main concerned with the acquisition of money and goods—other people's! The criminal and law-abiding, then, are activated by similar motives; their goals, objectives and values are similar in almost every respect except one, that is the precise means they employ to attain their ends.

CHAPTER 4

ARE WE ALL DELINQUENTS?

I

From the viewpoint of the social scientist, criminal behaviour like any other form of action is essentially 'learned behaviour'. That is to say it is, in the main, the result of social processes and experiences. The criminal or the delinquent is the product of his social background and training. Thus, in this view, criminals are made and not born. Either circumstances prove too much for them and they inherit a delinquent sub-culture pattern or suffer from too frequent or too early association with other law-breakers. This position has been staunchly maintained by the famous American criminologist, Edwin Sutherland, and embodied in his so-called law of 'Differential Association' which some psychologists and criminologists have assailed.[1] Briefly, this law says that if the preponderance of influences in the social environment is anti-social or criminal, then the chances of an individual becoming an offender are greatly increased, and vice-versa.

The significance of this approach is that it narrows the gap between the criminal and the non-criminal, between the ordinary man-in-the-street and the habitué of the cell and familiar of the bridewell. It leads us to the alarming conclusion that any one of us might have been branded as a criminal and that, in all probability, we *were* juvenile delinquents. It is not so much a case of 'There, but for the grace of God, go I', which rather immorally presupposes some sort of special guardianship and divine protection denied to others, as 'There, but for greatly altered circumstances, I would myself very likely be'. This

[1] For a fuller exposition of Sutherland's Theories, see Chapter 6, pp. 85–7.

chastening thought must cross the mind of any honest social scientist who visits the assizes and casts his eye on the accused in the dock, and of every cultural theorist who chances to drop in on the juvenile court.

Is there then no distinction between the man-in-the-street and the man-in-the-dock, between you and me and the known offender? Is it due to nothing more than luck that our lives have followed along different lines? Or is it that we were never found out? Or merely that the sort of offences we committed were deemed too trivial, the kind of delinquencies and petty fiddles that everyone indulges in and that are endemic in most if not all strata of society? Or was it that, in their early stages, our apparently trivial offences were treated quietly, wisely, humanely?

We were not stigmatized as law-breakers. But that ought not to put us in an entirely different category from those who were. It is a popular misconception that there exist what used to be called 'criminal classes' or 'criminal types'. It was a convenient conventional notion which made for smug self-satisfaction on the part of the unconvicted and permitted the 'good' citizens to make it as hot as possible for the delinquents, without any qualms of conscience. But that ideology is no longer viable.

The idea that there is a law-respecting, peaceable, moral majority and a desperate, lawless, tough, unfeeling, unscrupulous subhuman minority on the other hand, is nonsense. Most offenders are pathetic creatures, failures and misfits down on their luck, and even in their truculent moods they are obviously inadequate personalities. When you visit an approved school, for instance, it is not the boys' toughness that strikes you but their immaturity. Scratch the skin and find the baby! In prison this sense of inadequacy on the part of many persistent criminals is even more apparent. There go but ghosts of men that might have been. And our ghosts, too, if we had the knowledge and imagination to realize it, if the dangerous corners in our lives had not been miraculously avoided, if a wise parent or a shrewd teacher had not intervened at a critical stage in our development, if love had been denied too long or not freely given when we needed it most.

ARE WE ALL DELINQUENTS?

II

We have been working round to the idea that delinquency is so widespread a social phenomenon that, in most of its varieties, it can be regarded as normal. In certain situations breaking the law is almost a convention. When one asks ex-servicemen to look back on their military life this point of view finds ready acceptance. They all remember how articles used to be 'won'. They all recall the term 'scrounging' for behaviour which, in another social context, would be called downright stealing. They all laugh, some a little guiltily to be sure, when such topics are touched upon. But the fact that 'everyone did it',[1] and that the military system itself actively encouraged this kind of behaviour makes such delinquencies seem excusable. Closely related to this military misdemeanour is our attitude towards communally owned property. If things belong to the War Office—a vague, remote and somewhat hostile body of brasshats and boffins— their theft or damage is not regarded as a serious matter. It is not personally felt by anyone. Not only can public property be openly abused in most circles, but individuals do not feel much shame in so doing. An officer who fills his tank with petrol intended only for the use of army lorries, so that he can go off on a joy ride with his pals, does not consider such conduct a crime. We all do it in a sense. Every job has its perks. Clerks in offices take home stationery for their own use. They would probably not take postage stamps and would be even less likely to filch the petty cash. They might ring up their girl friend on the office phone but they would hesitate (the majority would even be genuinely appalled by the idea!) to steal fourpence from the till. We make a distinction between one act and another yet *both* are predatory. But in one case the delinquency has some support and approval from the group. Others do it. They would not condemn you for it. There is a tradition for it even. Theft of cash is generally regarded as reprehensible. But very, very few people would regard the misuse of time for which they were being paid as stealing. If a man steals the boss's car he is adjudged a criminal, but if he only steals an odd afternoon off work or half an hour at the end of every day he is still

[1] This is, of course, a pardonable exaggeration. Quite a number were strongminded enough to refrain.

59

reckoned to be honest. He might even be applauded as a good union man! And what happens about income tax offences? And frauds against insurance companies? The state is impersonal, so is a large business corporation. Again we may note that the offence is not personally felt by any individual, hence public outcry against these sorts of offences is weak, whereas offences against the person or thefts from individuals are received with indignation. We learn a great deal—perhaps more—about a society by noting what is accepted than by noting what is forbidden. Public opinion, as has been indicated earlier in this book, is vital arbiter of the general conscience. In the United States the bribing of ball players was so rife in the years 1950–1 that the outraged public could only be placated by severe punishment. The penalty for giving bribes in athletic contests became thereafter more severe than for robbery with a gun![1]

III

It is often claimed that, as a community, we are much less moral than we used to be. There is some evidence to support this view, apart from the official crime statistics. The little delinquencies committed by ordinary people are probably more common than in the past, and, if this is so, there are grounds for believing that there has been a shift in the social norms which regulate our conduct. Rowntree and Lavers showed that thefts from railways and hotels and public institutions had increased enormously in the post-war years.[2] And Geoffrey Gorer found that two-thirds of his respondents regarded evasion of rationing and other regulations as practically universal.[3] One may reasonably argue, as Collier has done from these admissions, that the majority in this instance were indirectly admitting that they did it themselves.[4] 'Fiddling', as it has come to be known, extends from top to bottom of our society. The now notorious Bank-Rate leakage, which became the subject of a government

[1] Edwin Sutherland, op. cit., p. 93.

[2] Seebohm Rowntree and G. R. Lavers, *English Life and Leisure*, Longmans 1951.

[3] *Exploring English Character*, Cresset Press, 1955, pp. 228–34.

[4] K. G. Collier, *The Social Purposes of Education*, Routledge and Kegan Paul, 1959, p. 44.

enquiry, high-lighted the moral and social quicksands on which many influential public men walk in order to conduct their daily affairs. The Radcliffe Report, which was issued after the tribunal had looked into the alleged irregularity, eventually came to the conclusion that although 'no general leakage of advance information as to a rise in the Bank Rate' had occurred, added, 'it does not, of course, follow that there may not have been individual cases in which dealings were promoted by the improper disclosure or use of confidential information'.[1] It is a delicately-poised statement which both reassures and alarms. As Paul Ferris remarked of it, 'It was like a tiny flaw in a large block of crystal'.[2]

What matters as far as the general public is concerned is that the flaw exists. It could presumably widen. Ordinary men and women wonder whether, in upholding the standards of honesty and integrity that conventional morality urges upon them, they are not being mere 'mugs'. They listen to the statements of their national leaders and they wonder even more. It is almost true to say that no comment on foreign policy made by a representative of any government is ever based on consideration of truth but on dubious considerations of political expediency. When the news of the American U.2. flights leaked out, officials of the United States government immediately denied they had taken place. This barefaced lie was later corrected when the evidence became available. But it cannot be ignored that the lie sprang easily to official lips. More recent evidence about the activities of the late Senator McCarthy in disseminating lies about men in positions of public trust and in whipping up hate against innocent men by publicizing deliberate untruths cannot tend to calm suspicions about the leaders of modern states.[3] People in the public eye are under constant observation. Their actions are noted and may be made models for other people to follow. We read of the Quiz scandal in America, of how certain contestants were told the answers before the questions were put to them, and that about a hundred witnesses lied to the New York Grand Jury which initially investigated these television scandals.

Turning to Britain again, the man who reads his daily paper

---

[1] Ferris, op. cit., p. 157. [2] Ibid.
[3] See Richard Rovere, *Senator Joe McCarthy*, Methuen, 1960.

finds frequent reports of events which suggest that 'fiddles', both great and small, are rife in contemporary society. He reads for example Mr. Patrick Gordon Walker's account of the 'cheque-book election' of 1959, of how organizations, financed out of the profits of big business concerns, campaigned in the Conservative cause and vigorously opposed nationalization. The amount of money a party can expend on an election is regulated by statute. In a democracy this must be so, otherwise the financially poorer parties would never be able to state their case to the public, but would be overwhelmed by the propaganda of the richer party. Said Mr. Walker in the House: 'This deserves to go down in history as the "chequebook election" in which the tie-up between the Conservative Party and big business was more naked than ever before.'[1] He claimed that before the election the Aims of Industry organization made anti-nationalization leaflets available to firms to put into the pay packets of their employees. 'This strikes me as the meanest, most underhand and dirtiest form of political propaganda. . . . There are some very grave implications from all this which must arouse great anxiety. Should these expenses be allowed against income tax? It is really monstrous and pernicious that the whole body of taxpayers should be made to bear expenditure which is incurred in favour of a particular party.'[2] The implications, of course, of this attack are that elections are no longer free, in the full sense of the word. Money gives power to a disproportionate share of the means of swaying the electorate; it gives a wealthy party an unfair advantage for promoting its point of view by every means of propaganda available. As the popular phrase has it, 'Money talks'.

IV

Equally serious, and, from many points of view, considerably more dishonest, are the recent disclosures that have been made about election rigging by some trade union officials. Allegations that the general secretary of the Electrical Trades Union was in 1960 elected by dishonest trickery was substantiated in a civil hearing over which Mr. Justice Winn presided in June 1961. It was clear from the enquiry that the responsible officials

[1] Press report in *Liverpool Daily Post*, 22nd July 1960.   [2] Ibid.

had deliberately overprinted the number of ballot papers to be used by branches which were known to support the Communist Party. The accused officials, Foulkes, Hazell, McLennan, Frazer and Humphrey were found to have conspired together in breach of their union rules to prevent Byrne, the lawfully elected candidate, from acceding to the office of General Secretary by the use of fraudulent and unlawful devices. So great was the shock to the prestige and integrity of the trade union movement in general that T.U.C. council members subsequently pressed successfully for the expulsion of E.T.U. from their Congress.

My contention is that the revelations of what goes on in business life and financial affairs, of how public officials use calculated lies to promote their ends, of how powerful interests can line up to support an individual party in political elections, of how white collar crimes often go unpunished (in the legal sense), and the way in which privilege can often buy immunity from the law, combine to create a climate of opinion, an attitude of mind which is ethically disillusioned and cynical. Such a climate of opinion is, I believe, conducive to crime. It takes the strength out of social discipline and weakens personal restraint. It leads to the view that 'Everything's a fiddle and every man has his price'. It removes the buttresses of social morality and invites every man to take part, by whatever means is available to him, in the scramble for easy money and the acquisition of more and more goods and commodities.

In the light of examples of corruption and dishonesty which have been presented in this and preceding chapters, is not the assumption of such fervent moral indignation over the shoplifting of a slum child out of all proportion and seen for what it is as a sham covering to the dubious practices everywhere carried on in our social life? For some reason, when we discuss crime, we put on blinkers. We consider only certain types of crimes and certain types of offenders. We point to the increased number of child offenders, wax eloquent about the decline of moral values, indicting the individual yet blandly deluded about the nature of our society itself which is the matrix in which developing minds are moulded. We indeed strain at gnats and swallow camels.

V

The comparative universality of delinquency has been made the topic of an interesting essay by Joseph Trenaman and B. P. Emmett.[1] On the basis of their calculations (which, however, I imagine few academic statisticians would support very far!) they suggest that one in every nine males becomes delinquent *over the lifetime of a whole generation*, that is to say over a period of considerable length approximating to seventy years or so as criminal risks. They reckoned that in those sections of the population where crime is known to be highly concentrated (i.e. in delinquency areas, as Shaw would call them), as many as one in every three males would have an offence recorded against his name in the lifetime of his generation. While it must be admitted that Trenaman's and Emmett's formula is speculative, it is, as they point out, no less misleading than the commonly accepted method for showing the number of delinquents at any one time. The latter is normally based on the ratio of those in any one year who are found guilty to the total number of people in a population at risk, that is to say old enough to be prosecuted by present law. The weakness of this method, they argue, is that it conceals the actual number of convicted offenders at large in the community at any one time by merely showing those prosecuted within the twelve month period. Moreover, delinquency may have already occurred but gone undetected. It may, as they argue, be latent and waiting some propitious circumstances to trigger it off. For these reasons they conclude that 'in order to estimate the incidence of delinquency, one needs to know more than just the annual ratio of offenders to population. One needs to consider the outcropping of crime throughout the lifetime of a whole generation. One needs to know the probability of any child born at any given time becoming a delinquent some time during his life.'[2]

If one accepts the force of their argument, without necessarily committing oneself to their actual mathematical calculations, one is led inevitably to the conclusion that there are more criminals and offenders in the community than is commonly supposed. Some support is given to this contention by a small piece of research I carried out myself, amongst members of a

[1] *Out of Step*, Methuen, 1952, Appendix A, pp. 204–9.   [2] *Ibid.*

dockland boys' club at the beginning of the 1950's.[1] Briefly, I found that no less than 30 out of 80 boys whom I questioned had been convicted of an indictable offence on one or more occasions. That is to say 37·5 per cent were official delinquents. Two further boys were convicted after our interview and 2 others had appeared in court for non-indictable offences, making in all 34 or 42·5 per cent who actually appeared before a juvenile court at some time in their boyhood. Further investigation of the 46 who had clean sheets showed that 22 of them, an additional 27·5 per cent of the sample, admitted having committed offences on a variety of occasions *without being found out*. These undetected offences were by no means always of a petty character, and involved shoplifting and breaking and entering. One lad had as many as twelve individual offences which he had got away with. All these boys committed their delinquencies in gangs and all their offences were against property. The group of undetected offenders resembled the official offenders in every way bar one. They had not been apprehended. They came from the same social background, had similar interests and identical education. A still further group regularly lorry-skipped and stole from parked lorries but said they had not committed the more serious types of offence. They too had not appeared before the court. If we add together all these offenders, the petty and the more serious, the detected and undetected, we obtain a grand total of 62 out of 80, no less than 78 per cent, either officially delinquent or straying across the dangerous threshold of delinquency. This seemed to me a truly phenomenal proportion and I was so impressed by these findings that in depicting the area in which they lived I described it as a 'Delinquent Community'. One point we have to bear in mind when considering the implications of this piece of research is that all the boys in the sample were members of a boys' club which operated a fairly strict programme in which all were obliged to participate and which had comparatively strict rules. For example, no smoking was permitted during club activities— a severe regulation in a working-class neighbourhood. Any boy found smoking was either fined or suspended from membership.

This enquiry, like Trenaman and Emmett's mathematical speculations, covered more than one year. The age range of my

[1] J. B. Mays, *Growing up in the City*, Liverpool University Press, 1954.

boys was, as far as their offences were concerned, from seven to seventeen.

My research was carried out with only a small section of the population, with the boys attending a good youth club. One could only guess what the extent of delinquent activity might be amongst those lads who were not club members. In all probability it would be even higher. Nor was any consideration given to adults in the locality. But, partial as my enquiry was, it served to underline the extent of illegal behaviour to be found amongst the juvenile population of a poor, working-class area in a large modern city. One can only conclude, with Trenaman and Emmett, that in contemporary urban society crime must be accepted as a mass phenomenon. It concerns the majority, not a psychologically disturbed or sick minority. It is normal rather than abnormal. If we are ever to understand its nature and meaning, we must ask ourselves two searching questions. They are, first, why do so many members of the community break the law, and second, why is it that some individuals do not succumb to the temptation? Not until we have answered both queries satisfactorily can we hope to control or prevent the growth of delinquency in modern society. It is not so much the problem of the occasional so-called crime-wave, times, that is, when the official statistics soar, that must engage our scrutiny. We must diligently and objectively turn our attention to a study of those attitudes and values institutionalized and widely accepted in the community which appear to foster and promote anti-social and criminal conduct. It is to the structure and quality of society itself, rather than to the aberrations of individual psychology, that we must look if we are to find the solution. This means that we must face the fact that crime is endemic and not epidemic in character, that we are all either actual or potential delinquents.

CHAPTER 5

THE SOCIOLOGY OF CRIME

I

In preceding sections it has been argued that criminality is almost certainly more widespread in the community than the rising annual crime rate suggests. Not only are there a considerable number of people with criminal records in the population at any one time, but one of us might at any moment become an offender of some sort. Breaking the law, therefore, is to be thought of as illicit behaviour in which normal as well as abnormal people might and, in fact, do indulge. Probably the most significant contribution that sociologists have made in the criminological field is to stress the essential normality of crime as far as the vast majority of offenders go. This important theoretical advance, which seems to have begun with the work of Emile Durkheim in the early years of the century, has been responsible for the development of less punitive and more re-educational penological methods being widely adopted.

Unfortunately, theoretical speculation can go too far and outstrip common-sense experience. Durkheim himself argued that since crime was normal it was part and parcel of the social process. To Durkheim and his fellow thinkers crime is functional in society. That is to say, it has a job to do and a part to play in keeping the society intact and in promoting its objectives. 'To classify crime amongst the phenomena of normal sociology,' Durkheim wrote, 'is not to say merely that it is an inevitable, though regrettable phenomenon, due to the incorrigible wickedness of men; it is to affirm that it is a factor in public health, an integral part of all healthy societies.'[1] Such a view is, we at once

[1] *The Rules of Sociological Method*, 8th edition. Free Press, Illinois, 1939, p. 67.

feel, in direct conflict with common sense. It is an outrage to decency. If it were to be taken as it stands would it not mean that we should become completely tolerant of crime and would not this undermine the basis of social morality?

There can be no doubt about the answer of these expostulatory questions. If criminal behaviour is to be accepted as an essential part of the nature of society it is an outrage to decency, and public morality can no longer be upheld. Durkheim was himself acutely aware of the paradox of his theoretical position. He maintained that 'what is normal, simply, is the existence of criminality, provided that it attains and does not exceed a certain level, which is perhaps not impossible to fix in conformity with the preceding rules'.[1]

Nevertheless, he does not offer us any help in determining the level of criminal activity which can be tolerated by society and beyond which it becomes a menace. For it is clear that if predatory tendencies should extend too far the community would undoubtedly degenerate into a free-for-all jungle existence. That is to say, it would cease to be a society at all!

The argument that crime is not necessarily evil is analogous to the view that pain, although generally experienced as malign, can be shown physiologically to have a limited functional value. Pain notifies the seat of a disorder, it draws attention to disease and insofar as it does this can be said to have a benign aspect *within limits*. But widespread pain is always regarded as the epitome of evil. The common-sense view is that, while pain usefully draws our attention to the onset of a disease, once it has made its signals we should do what we can to dispel it. One can argue that if men did not feel pain, they would probably die earlier, if not from the diseases then from accidents. Hence pain has a useful, if limited, function. But can one say the same of crime?

To some extent I think we can. Crime undoubtedly draws attention to disorders within the body of society. It registers some kind of stress or strain between individuals and between groups. It indicates a point of conflict and potential threat to which the guardians of the community should direct their attention. But one would surely not go on to argue from this that crime and pain are good things in themselves. Maybe they

[1] Ibid., p. 66.

have their uses and we can accept the warning they give us. At the same time one cannot say that cases of assault or robbery are in themselves functional for the promotion of socially desirable ends, any more than ulcers are prerequisites for the 'good life'.

Durkheim argued that collective sentiments are reinforced whenever a crime occurs, therefore the occasions, i.e., the crimes, which produce this desirable end are necessary. Thus, in his view, the criminal will no longer be thought of as 'a totally unsociable being, a sort of parasitic element, a strange unassimilable body introduced into the midst of society. On the contrary he plays a definite role in social life.'[1] His predatory activities serve to underline the basis of group morality. The consequence of his act is to bind people closer together as a result of the indignation they share over his unlawful behaviour. He performs a socially integrative function for the majority. We may hate him but at the same time regard him as necessary to social wellbeing. Hence, we must stop thinking of crime as an unqualified evil to be uprooted and destroyed. A reduction in the crime rate then should not be made the occasion for self-congratulation 'for we may be certain that this apparent progress is associated with some social disorder'.[2] The number of cases of assault, he noted, is especially low during times of economic want. The reason for this is, we may suppose, that large sections of the population are too lacking in spirit, too insecure and depressed, or even too under-nourished physically, to register their protest in deeds of violence.

While there may well be important ideas in this analysis which we ought to consider seriously, we must also state categorically that, as a whole, the argument is unfounded. Certainly sentiments of corporate responsibility are socially desirable. It is good that the members of the group should be aware of all the things they have in common and should realize that their individual welfare is intimately linked up with that of other people. Unity of purpose, solidarity and feelings of comradeship are known to be desirable and beneficent. But collective sentiment can be promoted in a whole variety of other ways than by uniting against criminals, and there is no reason whatsoever to think that crime is functionally more useful for this

---

[1] Ibid., p. 72.   [2] Ibid.

purpose than many other things. A sense of common purpose can as easily be focused around the cure of cancer or the rebuilding of slums. Moreover, these latter examples do not mean that the majority unite against the minority. Crime divides a society, even when it unites most of its members. Some, the offenders, are excluded, and put into special institutions which take them out of social circulation for a while. It is only when we endeavour to meet a common enemy outside society that we can say that the attack on a common problem serves to unite us all and is, therefore, socially integrative.

Durkheim's main position is hence untenable and illustrates the way in which speculation sometimes runs away with reason. And the various philosophical notions that he invokes do not make his case any stronger. The evolution of morality and law, he argues, depend upon freedom of individual choice. In order that the idealist and innovator may be enabled to work for social changes, it is inevitable that what he terms 'the originality of the criminal' should also exist. Without freedom to deviate from the norms there can be no change, and hence no progress. Here one thinks of the alleged crimes of Socrates, whose fearless pursuit of truth tended to disrupt the assumptions of Athenian society. Some forms of sex offences today might conceivably fall within this type of criminality. In *The Division of Labour in Society* Durkheim maintained that punishment is not primarily aimed at reforming the offender but rather at reinforcing the collective values of the community. 'We must not say that an action shocks the common conscience because it is criminal, but rather that it is criminal because it shocks the common conscience.'[1]

This sort of argument has something to commend it, although in the study of crime it can be very misleading. If societies are to develop and change, individuals and groups must have sufficient freedom of action to pursue their ends in their own ways. While we might generally agree regarding those ends, it is clear that different people set about achieving those ends by differing means. But there is, in democratic societies at least, a consensus of opinion about what is proper and legitimate and what is not. Non-conformists are tolerated within degrees and freedom of conscience is widely upheld as an ideal. Those who

[1] *The Division of Labour in Society*, The Free Press, 1947, p. 81.

wish to make innovations in behaviour must begin by subjecting themselves to ridicule and misunderstanding, even to legal sanctions, but they live and work in the hope that in the end they will persuade the rest of their fellow citizens to see, if not the correctness of their point the view, at least that it should be tolerated. So Socrates went to his death virtually as a martyr, not as a felon. But most criminals do not wish to urge a new way of life on their fellows. Indeed the thief would find his trade menaced by a general acceptance of the legality of thievery! The thief relies upon most people being honest for most of the time. He is himself honest in many ways and theft plays a small part in his total life.

It does not seem to follow, therefore, that to have good we must also have evil, although the potentiality of evil may be necessary. But potentialities need not become actualities. At heart, the criminal is not a man bent upon the reconstruction of his society, although in our folly we may temporarily be misled into branding prophets and visionaries as criminals.

Crime is in many ways normal in any society but this does not mean that it is good. Crime seems to result from the imperfection both of human personality and social organization. We are not perfect individually nor have we collectively as yet discovered a social system which operates with complete justice in the Platonic sense. The existence of crime and delinquency indicates our group and personal failure, and when the crime rates go up *without alterations in the law or changes of police procedure* we can reasonably argue that we are in some respects failing more grievously than before. But it is wise to remember that crime is only one index of strain or failure within the social structure. Poverty and disease (both physical and mental) are other indices which we should keep a wary eye on. One might, indeed, argue that, of the three indices referred to, crime is the least obnoxious. But one would also want to go on to qualify that statement by indicating what kinds of crime one is talking about. As far as offences against property go—and even conceivably some crimes of violence—this view could be upheld. But homicide, infanticide and crimes of violence against the person involving savage physical attack would surely be regarded very differently.

THE SOCIOLOGY OF CRIME

II

To believe that crime is undesirable and socially divisive and that in its grosser manifestations is utterly abominable, need not blind us to the residuum of truth that survives from our examination of the Durkheimean analysis. It is still very apparent that crime is not merely evil-doing but that it is closely connected with many of the ordinary everyday activities and motivations of social living. Insofar as this is so it may, sociologically speaking, be regarded as normal.

We have already indicated the ways in which business can be conducted on the borderline of graft and sharp practice yet remain narrowly within the law. This tendency together with the phenomenon of white collar crime to which it is spiritually allied reveal the latent criminality in many aspects of our commercial life. Moreover, we can with justification extend the argument a stage further by pointing out that the 'get-rich-quick' mentality is itself a product of powerful influences which are constantly in operation in the social milieu and which are conducive to the development of an amoral and sometimes even immoral attitude of mind. Success in business and the ruthless search for markets at home and abroad fosters a general attitude that is restively hedonistic and materialistic and which regards the possession of goods and money as the most important individual and social objective. Donald Taft, speaking specifically of American conditions, said some years ago: 'Crime is correlated with social change. Our dynamic culture is criminogenic.'[1] When sociologists speak in these terms they are not moralizing but striving to describe objective facts in the structure of the societies they are studying. Their job is to look at societies as wholes, to isolate important structural regularities which operate more or less independently of the individuals who temporarily make up that society. A society is not merely an agglomeration of individuals but a collectivity made up of individuals who are related in social structures. Human personality, therefore, and human behaviour are profoundly, though not entirely, influenced by the nature of the society into which as individuals men are born. Social institutions and the ways in which the society is formally organized modify inherited pre-

[1] *Criminology*, Macmillan, New York, 3rd edition, 1956, p. 39.

dispositions and decide to some extent how constitutional endowments are likely to develop. If a child, for example, is born with exceptionally high intelligence, but has to grow up in a society in which upward social mobility is impossible, either his innate intellectual gifts will be stultified, or, if they do develop, they will probably lead him into anti-social activity as the only way open to him to satisfy his reasonable demands for significance, status and possessions.

A sociological analysis of crime, therefore, must examine society as a whole and explain those features in the social structure which make for criminality. It must pinpoint tendencies to lawlessness and indicate how these tendencies come into existence in individuals and in larger groups. It must at the same time make a clear distinction between social and other factors predisposing to delinquency. This involves isolating and describing those things which are largely external to the individual and which operate more or less independently of him and which are in a genuine sense the properties of social wholes or societies rather than of persons. Sociological factors must be distinguished from both hereditary and constitutional factors, and, as far as possible, from mainly psychological ones. To some people such an analysis may seem unreal. How can we decide what is a social and what is a psychological factor, and how do we distinguish between the hereditary and the psychological? Are not they all aspects of one and the same thing?

The short answer to such queries is that these things are not identical and that we can go a long way towards separating them. Although it is quite true that they overlap to a considerable degree and are always in real life encountered in varying shades of inter-relatedness, they are, nevertheless, generically distinct. Constitutional, hereditary and psychological factors are primarily associated with specific individuals. They are essentially personal and in some measure the qualities of unique beings. They will be dealt with in a later chapter. In this section we are concentrating on criminogenic forces which are external to the individual, which are to be found in his environment and which are located within social systems to which the individual is exposed as a member of a particular community. These are forces and influences to which most, if indeed not all, members of the social group are susceptible. For example, the existence of social class and of a hierarchical status system are things which exist outside the individual, although, of course, as a responsible citizen he can strive to modify and even to eliminate them. Nevertheless, when he encounters them in his experience he sees that they were in operation before he was born and are artefacts of society. Individuals may have brought them into existence but he meets them as hard facts in the social system itself. On the other hand, an individual's sexual perversions or his hatred of his wife are facts of a different order and we do not usually need to delve deeply into the social structure in order to understand their genesis. Not that social factors are entirely irrelevant, but they are obviously merely secondary influences in these particular cases.

III

All I want to do is illustrate the distinction between the mainly social and the mainly personal causal factors in the etiology of crime, because I believe that such a distinction is valuable, not only in the development of criminological theory, but more importantly perhaps in the preparation of preventive services and in the devising of appropriate penological methods.

Modern industrial societies are all characterized by high crime rates which seem to be getting higher and higher every generation. The sociologist sees a connection between these two things, which he expresses by saying that many of the values which are explicit or implicit in social institutions are conducive to crime. It may be that the desire to accumulate personal wealth is ethically neutral in the abstract, but in specific social settings it tends to make some people break the law.

The hunger for more goods and commodities in a society which is so arranged that they must inevitably be disproportionately distributed leads certain groups and individuals to seek to obtain them by illegal means. I think we might go further and claim that the increasing productivity of more goods and commodities to which our economy is dedicated imposes a severe strain on some people who would, in a less competitive milieu, find little difficulty in keeping the law.[1]

Another way of stating these propositions, and one which

[1] A fuller examination of this hypothesis will be found in chapter 14.

may be more acceptable to many people, is to concentrate on the characteristics of societies which have low crime rates. We can then surmise what are the features of modern industrial urban culture most closely related to the prevalence of crime and delinquency.

According to Walter C. Reckless, such a comparison can be made and produces important clues to which most criminologists would give their assent.

'Societies of infrequent crime appear to be societies of relative isolation, with little mobility of population, little change, homogeneity of population in race and culture, little institutional disorganization, minimum differentiation in classes and social groupings, a single system of customary rules or a single code of customs, and a high degree of control over their members.'[1]

In other words, what we term primitive and rural communities tend to have less criminality involved in their affairs than do the restless, profit-seeking, highly mobile, mixed populations of modern industrial societies. Moreover cities even in modern countries are more criminal than country districts. The characteristically peasant community changes little and hence is relatively crimeless.

Another feature of our modern industrial society is the extent to which internal conflict is encountered. There are all sorts of differences of race, religious belief, social class and enthnic cultures which make for lack of homogeneity and what Durkheim first called 'anomie' or the absence of group norms. The lack of agreed ways of behaving and differing standards of conduct, especially in the older and poorer quarters of large cities, undoubtedly makes for conflict and hence unauthorized conduct. The folkways of West Africa are not identical with those accepted by the majority of British citizens and hence immigrants may behave in some matters in ways which bring them into sharp conflict with the host society. There are, also, within existing society groups of native born people, who have developed codes which are equally unacceptable to the majority of their fellow citizens. Such people seem to have developed over the generations a way of living which in some important instances brings them into conflict with the values of the wider

[1] *Criminal Behaviour*, McGraw Hill, 6th impression, 1940, pp. 26–7.

society. Inhabitants of the rooming-house districts of big cities, slum-dwellers and other socially unconnected groups seem to possess their own subcultures which often encourage lawbreaking. For example, in the dockland community of Merseyside which I knew myself over a number of years it was clear that a substantial number of residents regarded petty theft and particularly theft from impersonal entities such as chain stores and big businesses in a very casual light. One could indeed go so far as to say that in subcultural areas the climate of public opinion favours certain kinds of law violation and is thus to be categorized as criminogenic as far as the children are concerned.

But it would be misleading to argue that such conflicts as these which undoubtedly operate within the main body of society always serve a functionally useful purpose. Lewis Coser has urged, 'Groups require disharmony as well as harmony, dissociation as well as association; and conflicts within them are not altogether disruptive factors'.[1] Nevertheless, some kinds of conflict are socially disfunctional and disintegrative. And many kinds of crime seem to be of this nature. Bank robberies and forgeries, murders and woundings can have no conceivably useful purpose in themselves and do not serve to knit up the community but to make people and groups suspicious and wary of one another.

At the same time, some conflict situations contain within themselves the possibility of progress and amelioration. It is probably true, in a general way, to say that in the clash of competing ideologies lie the seeds of social change. It is also arguable that some illegal activities may be of this kind. The disorders caused by the suffragettes or more recently by anti-nuclear-armament factions are ultimately creative in purpose. Some offences against the existing sexual code could also be viewed in this light, together with offences against property which are the expression of a socially depressed and underprivileged section of the community of the type that will be dealt with in the succeeding chapter.

If this is so, clearly our objective should not be an entirely equable and law-abiding society but one in which stability, limited conflict and change can co-exist. It may, therefore, be inadvisable for social workers to strive in every instance to help

[1] *The Functions of Social Conflict*, Routledge and Kegan Paul, 1956, p. 31.

an offender adjust to the existing social conditions if by so doing they serve to bolster up an unfair and unjust order. If social work and measures designed to prevent crime merely aim to make malcontents and misfits more socially adjusted they would appear to have a very limited purpose and, to some extent, to be working against the best interests of both individuals and the wider society.

Not only social workers, but even some social theorists have been led into mistaking social adjustment for wise and beneficial social policy. There has been a tendency for some contemporary sociologists, such as Talcott Parsons[1] and George Homans,[2] to treat disharmonies in the social structure as necessarily disfunctional for the society. Their attitude is probably deeply influenced by psychoanalytical ideas and the definition of mental health which has been given wide currency in recent years as a form of social adjustment. This view implies that absence of stress is socially desirable and that the ideal for the individual is to nestle snugly into the social system. The man who does not make this kind of adjustment to his environment is the social misfit. He is classed as a deviant, categorized as maladjusted, and is generally considered to need some kind of treatment to bring him into line with his neighbours. Much of the stock-in-trade of what is often called 'group dynamics' is concerned with this business of adjusting the individual to his group, of reducing strains and tensions and to improving the mechanisms of social control. William H. Whyte[3] has dealt a trenchant blow at this philosophy in his mordant indictment of the conformist tendencies in modern American middle-class business and social life which have produced what he describes as 'organization men', happy mixers who make it a virtue to get along easily with other people. For such men, conformity and the absence of conflict has become an ethical imperative to the detriment of personal moral initiative. Multiple group affiliations and resultant conflicts of ideas and interests which these entail are, however, in Coser's view often socially healthy signs. They help to sew up the social fabric into a tough yet

[1] Passim.
[2] Homans, *The Human Group*, Routledge and Kegan Paul, 1951.
[3] *The Organization Man*, Jonathan Cape, 1957; Penguin Books edition, 1960.

flexible whole. Thus we can see that it is easy to misunderstand the meaning of certain conflict situations in modern society and to mistake them for pathological symptoms. The fact that strikes occur, that interests openly clash, that group factions wrestle it out together does not necessarily deny an underlying unity. Nor does the absence of strikes mean industrial health. It may indeed spring from the opposite—low morale all round.

IV

We may, therefore, conclude this rather difficult and tricky argument by saying that crime in bulk does not serve a socially useful function and that Durkheim and others who have subsequently espoused this view have allowed themselves to be seriously misled. At the same time, certain kinds of offences do seem to serve a socially useful purpose. Hence all conflict situations occurring within the social structure are not to be treated as necessarily bad or disfunctional for the society, but may in the end prove beneficial.

The important point is surely that criminal behaviour and the nature of social conditions are always intimately related. Certain kinds of societies produce certain kinds of crime which appear to be characteristic. As Durkheim suggested, but ultimately did not succeed in proving entirely satisfactorily, suicide rates may be closely connected with what we may call the degree of social integration.[1] Where the individual feels that he belongs to a closely knit social unit he may be less inclined to commit suicide or other kinds of offences than if he is a member of a much more loosely connected collectivity. This view has received some support from the observation that in times of war and serious crisis the behaviour of children seems to deteriorate.

Juvenile delinquency figures, at any rate, can be shown to rise during these times of national dislocation. This is probably due not so much to the threat of invasion or the apprehension of acute physical danger as to the removal of parental discipline and the breakdown of family and social life. Meanwhile the adult crime rate appears to remain fairly constant, at its pre-war level. This is possibly because the claims of military service remove many potential civilian offenders and also because the

[1] *Suicide*, ed. George Simpson, Routledge and Kegan Paul, 1952.

sense of common danger engenders in adults feelings of corporate loyalty and responsibility to a greater degree than children can possibly experience.

Our information on this and related topics is woefully inadequate and there are many gaps which at the moment can be filled only by tentative speculation. Nevertheless, it seems apparent that crime and the social structure are closely related and that changes in the latter can deeply affect the former. Nowadays, many critics blame the fact that mothers go out to work for an alleged increase in juvenile crime. Whether this is so or not does not matter for the moment. But it is clear that the reasons why many more women go out to work than in the past and why the modern family tends to contain more than one earner are intimately related to social changes and to the pressures of an expanding economy. We could not, indeed, maintain our present standards of living if women did not go out to work in the numbers they do, and for this reason they are positively encouraged by the authorities to take up either full or part-time employment. It is no good, therefore, attacking mothers for being irresponsible and neglecting the welfare of their children when powerful forces operate in the general structure of society to encourage them in this supposedly harmful behaviour.

We may conclude by saying once again that crime, in the majority of cases, is best thought of as normal behaviour arising from the operation of ordinary social processes. Some of these processes are strongly criminogenic. But even when they are not, stresses and strains generated within the social structure can produce delinquency either directly or as a by-product. Crime is, therefore, if not inevitable, always a potentiality in social life which very frequently becomes an actuality.

CHAPTER 6

PARTICULAR SOCIOLOGICAL THEORIES WITH A BEARING ON CRIME

I

It is impossible to do justice to the sociological explanations of criminal behaviour without saying something about specific theories which have each in their turn proved influential. The earliest of these were in the main what is termed ecological, that is to say they endeavoured to show the relationship between the actual physical environment and the way people behave: between what is often called the social milieu and the kind of lives associated with it. Common observation indicated that certain neighbourhoods contained many more offenders than others. Or, to put it in another way, there were very many more ascertained criminals living in the slums than in the more prosperous residential areas. Clifford Shaw and his colleagues in Chicago went one stage further by demonstrating statistically that common observation was correct. They showed that, in Chicago, and later in fifteen other major American cities, the rates of juvenile delinquency varied remarkably between different parts of the city; that while in some areas not a single juvenile was convicted in a twelve-month period, in other less salubrious localities the delinquency rate could be anything up to 20 per cent of the youthful population.[1] High delinquency areas were invariably located in the poorer neighbourhoods where the lowest rents were found and especially close to the

[1] Clifford Shaw and Henry McKay, *Juvenile Delinquency and Urban Areas*, University of Chicago Press, 1942.

city centre and the commercial and industrial zone. Delinquency rates decreased more or less progressively from the urban centre so that the lowest rates were found on the periphery.

Shaw and McKay also showed that high delinquency rates were associated with the existence of other socially pathological factors, such as truancy, the presence in the locality of substantial numbers of adult offenders and foreigners, bad housing, rapid population changes and the prevalence of mental illness. They proved, moreover, that despite the change of population over a period of time, the delinquency rates remained more or less constant. Areas with high rates in 1900 had equally high rates in 1930, although the population of the localities had almost completely changed. Crime was thus seen to be a function of the locality rather than the product of individual psychology. Theoretically one might suppose that if all the families living in the black areas of Chicago in 1900 had removed elsewhere, thirty years later, the people who replaced them, being different in almost every possible way, would behave either more or less criminally. That the delinquency rate stayed more or less stable implies that we must look to extra-personal and social causes for the explanation of the phenomenon. This common element they described as 'social disorganization or the lack of organized community effort to deal with this condition'.[1]

Crime and delinquency seemed to become part and parcel of the social traditions of these areas and were handed down through successive generations of inhabitants very much in the same ways that language and other customs are transmitted. The social norms, the common attitudes and accepted values of these 'delinquency areas' incorporated a proportion of illegal and destructive behaviour to which the younger residents, as they grew up there, were exposed and which, in the course of time, they came to accept as normal conduct. Juveniles in such neighbourhoods, therefore, were not necessarily maladjusted or anti-social. In terms of the norms obtaining within his own social group the delinquent often appeared to be normal and well-adjusted—a good member, that is to say in this case, of a delinquency-prone community.

This latter explanation is in many ways a contradiction of the

---

[1] Professor E. Burgess, Preface to *Juvenile Delinquency and Urban Areas*, p. (XI).

thesis which Shaw, and others associated with such researches, had earlier propounded. It conflicts with the idea of 'social disorganization' in so far as it points to the existence of community sentiments and activities as causal factors connected with the creation and transmission of a delinquent pattern of life. The disorganization therefore is more apparent than real. It is apparent to someone who comes to study such a community with his mind already prejudiced by living in other social climates. To the middle-class observer, the district round the Loop in Chicago no doubt seems disorganized. It is confused and disturbingly dissimilar from the neat law-abiding society which he takes as his reference group. But it is also a society, the difference being that in some respects it has highly individual characteristics. Later investigations revealed that the disorganization theory was largely the result of misunderstanding the relationship between the smaller and the wider social group. Shaw and McKay never seemed to face the implications of their research work adequately. They apparently wanted to have social disorganization at the same time as the delinquent's 'own social world' to whose norms he could be said to be well-adjusted. It was left to later theorists to sort out the tangle and show how these seemingly contradictory concepts could be woven into one embracing theory.

Shaw and McKay also fenced rather than grappled with the problem of how and why such delinquency areas came to exist *in the first place*. In their classic work, *Juvenile Delinquency and Urban Areas*, in which their life's work came to fruition, they wrote suggestively:

'This explanation, it is assumed, must be sought, in the first place, in the field of more subtle human relationships and social values which comprise the social world of the child in the family and community. These more distinctively human situations, which seem to be directly related to delinquent conduct, are, in turn, products of larger economic and social processes characterizing the history and growth of the city and of the local communities which comprise it.'[1]

The very fact that people lived in such areas indicated social inferiority and low status. They comprised underprivileged communities, where 'fewer opportunities are provided for

[1] Op. cit., p. 14.

securing the training, education and contacts which facilitate advancement in the fields of business, industry and the professions'.[1] For such people, denied the legitimate means to acquire high status and financial rewards, 'the economic and social values generally idealized in our culture', crime represented an illegal but necessary step to achieve what luckier people achieved in conventional ways. What Shaw did not do, and this is absolutely essential if we are ever to understand the full meaning of crime in modern societies, was to indicate why, in a richly endowed and prosperous country like the United States such underprivileged groups were allowed to exist at all. This would necessitate examining the nature of capitalist society, more pertinently the American variety, and its concomitant philosophy of unfettered individualism. It is surely obvious that if any man may make a fortune, and if a section of successful manipulators of the business machine are permitted to acquire for themselves comparatively excessive shares of capital and goods and other rewards from increased productivity, there must also be others who fail and are correspondingly deprived. The question whether it is necessary to have a poor minority, i.e. an unemployed or depressed section of the population, in order to make the economic system work is one we need not be concerned with here. But it has a direct bearing on the nature of crime in a so-called free industrial society.

To return to more obvious sociological concepts, Shaw and McKay emphasized the group character of most delinquency. They found that nearly all of the juvenile offenders had committed their crimes in the company of their peers. Sometimes this meant being in the company of a small group of cronies, at other times it involved being a member of something more akin to a gang. Usually we mean by a gang a group who meet regularly for specific activities and who, as a result of their interaction, have developed a fairly formal pattern of relationships, perhaps with one boy acting as a leader. But not all juvenile gangs are delinquent. Nor are all delinquent gangs delinquent all the time. Clearly the friendship set merges into the criminal gang and most juvenile groups located in the older and poorer parts of big cities will be found to be indulging in illegal behaviour from time to time.

[1] Ibid., p. 438.

II

The gang proper had been made the object of an important study by Frederic Thrasher in the early 1920's.[1] In Chicago alone he discovered as many as 1,313 separate gangs operating in what he termed the 'interstitial' areas, that is to say in residential districts lying close to the business and commercial centres and adjacent to somewhat better districts, the same localities that Shaw described as 'delinquency areas'. Thrasher defined the gang as 'an interstitial group originally formed spontaneously, and then integrated through conflict. It is characterized by the following types of behaviour: meeting face to face, milling, movement through space as a unit, conflict and planning. The result of this collective behaviour is the development of tradition, unreflective internal structure, *esprit de corps*, solidarity, morale, group awareness, and attachment to a local territory.[2] A similar recipe indeed to the gangs of present-day Camberwell or Liverpool dockland. Their activities were also depressingly similar: 'Games of chance, like many athletic sports, may be regarded as one form of conflict behaviour involving risk. In gambling the gang simply follows a social pattern prevalent among all ages in gangland'.[3] Thrasher regarded 'Stealing, the leading predatory activity of the whole adolescent gang . . . as much a result of the sport motive as a desire for revenue. It is regarded as perfectly natural and entails no more opprobrium for the ordinary gang boy than smoking a cigarette. "C'mon, lets go robbin" is the common invitation. The response might be, "Naw, too tired" or "Too busy", but never "Taint right".'[4]

Thrasher believed that gangs offered substitute 'for what society fails to give' and 'a relief from suppression and distasteful behaviour'.[5] They indicated for him 'a symptom of disorganization in the larger social framework'. In this view he is close to Shaw and McKay, and very much in sympathy with later commentators who have thought of the gang as the inevitable outcome of the failure of the family or the school to provide a youngster with a stable and absorbing group life.

[1] *The Gang*, Chicago University Press, 1927.
[2] Ibid. Second Revised Edition, 1936, p. 57.   [3] Ibid., p. 89.
[4] Ibid., p. 92.   [5] Ibid., p. 38.

PARTICULAR SOCIOLOGICAL THEORIES

While it is easy to exaggerate the importance of the gang as a cause or precondition for crime, it is important to remember, as Sutherland reminds us, that the existence of juvenile groups can exert a criminogenic influence in two separate ways. 'To be left out of groups,' he maintains, 'may be just as productive of delinquency as to be included in them . . . rural and small town delinquents are frequently rejected isolates rather than gang members.'[1] Moreover, as I discovered in my Liverpool investigations, lads sometimes commit offences in order to get recognition from or to qualify for membership of some highly regarded neighbourhood gang. In my sample there was one boy who went so ineptly about the job of seeking admission to the 'Peanuts', a notoriously violent and criminal gang which flourished in South Liverpool towards the end of the Second War, that he got himself permanently excluded. He told me how one day in order to impress their leader with his own toughness he went up to him in the street and offered to fight him. The outcome was an angry beating up and permanent disqualification!

III

So far the theories we have been examining have dealt with what we may term a conflict between local cultures and the wider community. They have underlined, even when not always appreciating the fact, the importance of solidarity amongst disadvantaged members of society as a reaction to their inability to achieve social status and financial rewards in recognized and generally acceptable ways. Edwin Sutherland's theory, or rather his combination of theories to which he gave the generic title of 'Differential Association', includes this sort of explanation while, at the same time, endeavouring to present an inclusive theory which is capable of explaining all criminal behaviour. The following extracts from his major work on *Principles of Criminology* summarize his viewpoint.

'Criminal behavior is learned. Criminal behavior is learned in interaction with other persons in a process of communication. The principal part of the learning of criminal behavior occurs within intimate personal groups. When criminal behavior is

[1] Edwin Sutherland and Donald Cressey, *Principles of Criminology*, 5th edition, Lippincott, New York, 1955, p. 165.

85

learned, the learning includes (a) techniques of committing the crime, which are sometimes very complicated, sometimes very simple; (b) the specific direction of motives, drives, rationalizations, and attitudes. The specific direction of motives and drives is learned from definitions of the legal codes as favorable or unfavorable.[1] A person becomes delinquent because of an excess of definitions favorable to violation of law over definitions unfavorable to violations of law. This is the principle of differential association. Differential associations may vary in frequency, duration, priority and intensity. The process of learning criminal behavior by association with criminal and anticriminal patterns involves all the mechanisms that are involved in any other learning. While criminal behavior is an expression of general needs and values, it is not explained by those general needs and values since non-criminal behavior is an expression of the same needs and values. Thieves generally steal in order to secure money, but likewise honest laborers work in order to secure money. The attempts by many scholars to explain criminal behavior by general drives and values, such as the happiness principle, striving for social status, the money motive, or frustration, have been and must continue to be futile since they explain lawful behavior as completely as they explain criminal behavior.'[2]

Sutherland's principle of differential association, which means, in effect, that if the number of criminogenic influences exerted on an individual is greater than the strength of anti-criminal influences then that individual will violate the law, has been criticized as tautologous and question-begging. Psychologists dismiss it as superficial. Other criminologists, while agreeing that it has a general usefulness, would no doubt say that it throws up as many questions as it answers. Its weakness is undoubtedly the fact that it fails to distinguish adequately between motive and behaviour, between what a crime means to an individual and what it means to the rest of the community. It takes no account of hidden or unconscious factors influencing behaviour. It assumes that all crimes of theft are identical and therefore can be treated alike. It is legalistic in this sense, inadequate and unsubtle. It takes us a little way and then abandons

[1] i.e. mixed and hence confused and confusing definitions.
[2] A summary from Sutherland and Cressey, op. cit., pp. 77–9.

us to doubt. Sutherland was, I think, not unaware of this weak side to his theory, and for that reason he embraced the social disorganization hypothesis, adding to it his own individualistic touch by calling it 'differential social organization'. Most communities he averred are organized both for law and law-breaking, so that differential crime rates reflect this fundamental distinction and may be said to validate the main hypothesis.

While one cannot fail to be critical of Sutherland's position and his claim to have developed a general theory to cover all crime, nevertheless his writings are of considerable value in their stubborn insistence on the importance of social causal factors. Like Durkheim, crime for him is a social artefact, a phenomenon deeply grounded in the structure of society and not merely due to the idiosyncrasies of individual citizens. For Sutherland, as for Shaw, the characters of persons are, in the final analysis, of less importance than the nature of the social group. Crime is a basic aspect of social organization or disorganization, not an epiphenomenon to be exorcised by moral pleas or even the dedicated missionary zeal of social workers and teachers.

IV

More recent sociological attempts to account for the facts that the majority of offenders are located in particular sorts of urban localities and are under twenty-one years of age have been concerned with the development of the concept of the 'delinquent subculture'. A subculture means something very much akin to a sub-community existing within the framework of a large society. Culture, in the sociological and anthropological sense, is a loose yet very useful term to connote the distinctive way of life of a comparatively small group. It was made much of by anthropologists in the study of small, compact and relatively stable communities such as are, or rather used to be, found in the South Seas and other remote parts of the world. Culture is a portmanteau word to cover every important aspect of social life, from the ways in which natives built and sailed their canoes to the spirits they worshipped and the way they organized their economic affairs.[1] In terms of modern societies

[1] Malinowski defined it as 'a system of objects, activities and attitudes in which every part exists as a "means to an end"', i.e. it is broadly functional, *A Scientific Theory of Culture*, University of North Carolina Press, 1944, p. 150.

the concept has been loosely used to describe the way of life, the group attitudes, values and standards of behaving, as well as the institutions which differentiate one society from another. A subculture, therefore, may be described as the distinctive pattern of life shared by a small and distinctive group which is part of a wider group but which has evolved some typical and different ways of behaving and believing. Examples of subcultures still to be found in modern society would be, perhaps, a Hebridean village, a small Midland mining town, the dockland of a large seaport, a public school or an ancient university. Every group in fact tends to create its own culture, be it the officers' mess or the dockers' canteen. A subculture may be said to exist in parts of the older and deteriorated urban centres such as Shaw and Thrasher found in Chicago and which have also been located easily enough and described in Great Britain. Sometimes they correspond to areas of high crime and delinquency rates and in such cases it is theoretically proposed that the residents of such districts share a number of attitudes and ways of behaving in common which predispose them to illegal conduct. Or, in other words, they are members of a delinquent subculture. Academic argument is currently going on as to whether or not true delinquency areas or delinquent subcultures in the American sense exist in this country, or whether here it would be truer to say that the idea of small pockets of so-called problem families embedded within the lower-class district does not provide a more accurate description of the facts. The objection to the more general concept of the delinquency-producing subculture theory is that it fails to account for the fact that everyone living in the area is not criminally minded. While it must be admitted that our theoretical concepts are still very imperfect (since they were to some extent evolved from a study of small, compact and homogeneous village societies and have subsequently been used to analyse large, complex, heterogenous, urban communities, these imperfections seem unavoidable and to be expected) I find the concept of the subculture myself a very helpful one. Agreed that the lines enclosing the areas which the ecologist defined as criminogenic are inexact and require closer scrutiny and definition. Nevertheless, it must be borne in mind that, when we use such terms as 'delinquent subculture' or 'criminal area', we are not claiming that every person who lives close to known offenders is obliged to break the law or even sympathetic to the illegal behaviour of those neighbours who do. What we are saying is that, within a broad zone which can be drawn on a map, a very substantial number of people commit offences and there is a general tolerance extended towards their behaviour. There are a sufficient number of delinquents and people who are, if not sympathetic, then, at least, neutral in their attitude towards them, to make up a social climate that can fairly be called delinquency-prone. The same thing could be said regarding other forms of behaviour which are not accepted everywhere in our society. Illegitimacy is a good example. Some social groups treat the girl who has an illegitimate child as an outcast, while in other districts the sense of stigma would either be less or non-existent. The same could be said of co-habiting. In some areas if a man and woman live together without being legally united and produce a family they would be shunned, while elsewhere their conduct would be accepted without censure. We are, I believe, justified in describing a locality as a subculture when the residents as a whole seem to share a number of such generally deviant and unconventional attitudes. They accept illegitimacy, they do not frown on sexual relations outside the marriage bond, and they either take part in illegal acts or are sympathetic or ethically neutral towards those who commit certain kinds of delinquencies. The more one considers all the available facts, the more one is driven back to the idea that a crime-tolerant social atmosphere exists in certain socially underprivileged localities. Individuals may come and go, as Shaw showed in Chicago, and the rooming-house district of any big city reveals an exceptionally high rate of population mobility together with high crime and delinquency rates. What we have in such areas, I suggest, is not so much a community of individuals linked together by intimate bonds, as an abiding *community of ideas, values and attitudes* which have developed over the years into a social tradition and which are handed on, more or less intact, to the rising generation and to newcomers. We know that language and street games and play rituals are transmitted in this sort of way, so why not shoplifting and other types of larceny?

If it may be allowed that the existence of delinquent subcultures has been proved, we must next ask how they arise.

PARTICULAR SOCIOLOGICAL THEORIES

What is their origin and why are they apparently perpetuated? Robert K. Merton[1] and Albert K. Cohen[2] have concerned themselves with answering these fundamental questions. Merton, who took over Durkheim's concept of anomie, used the idea to depict how in a large society some social groups get, as it were, cut off from the general culture. The deviant, i.e. criminal, behaviour is thus linked with the social process as a whole. Anomie, that is to say in this case the dislocation between various social groups and the consequent sense of social frustration and absence of agreed standards, is not the result of historical accidents but derives from the way in which the society operates at the present time. It is a concomitant of social processes at work now and which, unless the structure of society is drastically altered, will operate in the future. Criminal and deviant behaviour, therefore, which arises from this acute form of social disorganization will not be eliminated by the application of palliatives or by the administration of psychiatric and other individually therapeutic services.

Why are the members of delinquent subcultures cut off? Cohen, epitomizing his longer work, puts it this way. He argued that juvenile delinquent subcultures arise whenever young people in the lower socio-economic groups come together and through social interaction become aware of the fact that they are under-privileged.[3] Their lowly position in the social structure prevents them from achieving self-respect and status in ways which are generally acceptable to the wider community. They are frustrated in their aspirations because of poor education, inadequate homes, the lack of opportunities for advancement and so on, with the result that they develop the delinquent subculture as *a kind of substitute society*, in which in spite of their shortcomings, they can achieve the status they desire. It is a sort of social *pis aller*. Denied respect in one way, they take it by force in another. Cut off from the realization of legitimate ambitions, they make their mark in delinquency and other forms of anti-social behaviour. They have what is tradi-

---

[1] Robert K. Merton, *Social Theory and Social Structure*, The Free Press, Revised and enlarged edition, 1957, pp. 176–84.

[2] *Delinquent Boys*, Routledge and Kegan Paul, 1956.

[3] 'Research in Delinquent Subcultures', *The Journal of Social Issues*, Vol. XIV, No. 3, 1958.

tionally called a chip-on-the-shoulder mentality: Cohen describes this state of mind more technically as 'characteristics of non-utilitarianism, malice and negativism'. The non-utilitarian characteristic of much subcultural crime is of particular interest. It implies stealing things not mainly because they are valuable and desired for their own sakes, but as an end in itself. As Cohen puts it, 'In homelier language, stealing "for the hell of it" and apart from considerations of gain and profit is a valued activity to which attaches glory, prowess and profound satisfaction.'[1]

The subcultural juvenile delinquent steals very often to get his own back on society and to announce his solidarity with his mates. He derives positive pleasure from delinquent activities. The leader of the delinquent group is the boy who epitomizes these qualities of hostility towards the 'goodies' and who is exceptionally daring in discovering new and more vicious ways of venting their collective spite. Theirs is a society anti-society. They are not only deviant they are defiant, and consequently present an acute problem to the law-abiding majority with whom they are in a sense at war.

There is no better or more stirring account of the operation of juvenile gangs in the subcultural districts of New York and other American cities than Harrison Salisbury's book *The Shook-Up Generation*.[2] The picture he gives of the adolescent gang warfare that is still taking place in Red Hook, Fort Greene, Bedford-Stuyvesant, East Harlem, the lower East Side, the upper West Side and similar areas of New York where the social war reaches its apogee is incredible reading to people in this country where nothing so hopeless and terrifying has ever taken place. The war is tripartite. It is waged between groups of socially disconnected youngsters and between their gangs and the police. 'Nowhere,' wrote Salisbury, 'will you find a heavier concentration of police than in Bedford-Stuyvesant. Nowhere are the police quicker to wield their nightsticks on street-corner youngsters. Nowhere are more youngsters jailed for "unlawful assembly". And nowhere is there more gang activity.'[3] The three things are intimately connected. The gangs need the other gangs to fight against so that they can express their hostility in action. They also need the police to assure them of the hostility

[1] *Delinquent Boys*, p. 26. [2] Michael Joseph, 1959.
[3] Op. cit., p. 20.

of the big society and to weld them into a cohesive delinquent body. Each group exacerbates the others.

But one of the most surprising things which emerges from *The Shook-Up Generation* is the fact that the children of the upper-income suburbs are also infected with this aggressive and criminal virus. The mores of gangsterdom are observable even amongst better-off adolescents. According to Harrison Salisbury 'the slums are only reservoirs, and perhaps, tradition setters for anti-social adolescent conduct at all social levels. . . . Delinquency is a symptom, not a disease, and the disease knows no geographical and no social boundaries.'[1] The growing accent amongst young people throughout American society on viciousness and violence is due, according to Salisbury, to a breakdown in family life and to the growing emphasis on violence throughout society. Although he is not a sociologist, he is well aware that such changes are not merely the outcome of individual deviation or the product of personal breakdown. He knew that forces active within the framework of American society are responsible for nurturing these criminal and violent attitudes. The old frontier mentality with its accent on individualism, enterprise, ruthless and aggressive competition with others— epitomized perhaps even today by the widespread carrying of firearms in the U.S.A.—is no longer suitable to the complexities of a modern mass industrial society where no doubt the 'Organization Man' is more at home. The criminal and violent outbursts amongst the young people reflect then, to a large degree, the stresses and strains generated within the social structure. And young people are, as always, the first to experience and react to social stresses arising from whatever cause. Being especially vulnerable, they are usually the first victims of any disorders.

V

Further theoretical work on the topic of delinquent subcultures has been carried on recently by Richard Cloward and Lloyd Ohlin, both members of the New York School of Social Work at Columbia University. In their book, *Delinquency and Opportunity*,[2] they have refined previous work done by Sutherland, Merton and Cohen. Broadly, their thesis is that criminality is,

[1] Ibid., p. 24.　　　[2] Routledge and Kegan Paul, 1961.

in the final analysis, a property of the social systems in which criminals are located rather than of their personal psychological maladjustment. Criminal subcultures are generally identifiable in deteriorated social districts whose residents feel themselves to be excluded from achieving their full economic and status aspirations via legitimate channels. This thesis is, of course, substantially taken over from Merton and Cohen, but Cloward and Ohlin have taken their analysis a stage further by categorizing slum subcultures into three main types. These are: (a) criminal groups who compensate for failure to achieve in the free-for-all of normal capitalist society by creating their own under-world in which, through the development of criminal skills, they can gain both financial rewards and prestige. Such groups are characterized by their own internal organization and controls and by what may be termed an apprenticeship system which offers promotion to full adult criminal status of a few select juvenile delinquents: (b) conflict groups, usually composed of immigrants and newcomers to the society, who react to the indifference of the 'respectable' world by coercing attention by means of violence. These gangs are generally the 'boppers' and swaggerers who attain status by aggressive conflict behaviour which transforms social alienation into attention by the exercise of sheer brute force. They are characteristically made up of groups of youths and teenagers; and (c) retreatist echelons of the 'hipster' variety, who, convinced of their own fundamental inadequacy, no longer strive for acceptance by respectable society but are content to withdraw into a twilight zone in pursuit of the 'kicks' provided by alcohol, marijuana, drug addiction, unlicensed sexuality and the delights of both 'hot' and 'cool' jazz.

It is essential to Cloward and Ohlin's thesis that these three reactions to the same situation, that is to social frustration, are associated with different slum subcultures. When the local milieu is rich in opportunities for illegitimate access to status and reward, that is when organized crime, as Whyte described it in his Boston slum, is available, then the reaction of deprived groups is likely to be criminal but non-violent. For obvious reasons the retreatist group is not likely to cause violence, its vices and crimes being associated with drugs and sexual aberrations. The boppers or fighters are, of course, by definition aggressive and bellicose. They may be on the increase in American cities for the reasons Cloward and Ohlin suggest, i.e. the breakdown of organized rackets in slum communities, due to the decline of the local party political machine and the growth of the social welfare services, both of which have proved disruptive to slum subcultures. Unfortunately, as the authors point out, there is as yet little solid evidence to support their analysis. It is indeed the besetting sin of much recent American sociological writing that the gap between social theory and empirical research seems to be ever widening. As Cloward and Ohlin say, a reinvestigation of the 'Cornerville' society which Whyte studied and described some twenty years or so ago would prove or disprove the validity of their viewpoint. Such a study would indicate whether or not the prophecy that the breakdown of organized crime in the Boston slum has resulted in social disintegration has been fulfilled, or whether some other socially cohesive force has taken the place of political and criminal racketeering. According to their theory of 'differential opportunity' the local residents of Cornerville should be more violent and more retreatist than heretofore. But until somebody goes back to Boston to undertake the empirical investigation the whole thing remains a matter for speculation.

IV

It will be noted that the studies referred to in this chapter are all American in origin. The question people in this country are naturally eager to ask is whether theories derived from the study of transatlantic society can be utilized in studying our own social problems. Do criminal subcultures exist in Britain? Are there adolescent groups in particular localities whose actions are inspired by a defiance of conventional standards? If so, is this defiance a result of economic and status frustration or what?

In attempting to answer these questions we have to be very careful indeed. Very few studies have been made in this country which throw light on the social setting of crime in a sociologically meaningful way. Three perhaps should be mentioned. The first, carried out in Liverpool's south dockland by myself, has already been referred to in preceding chapters. This study, while suggesting that a juvenile subculture conducive to delinquency exists, does not lend any very substantial support to the idea of youthful frustration. The reasons offered to account for the prevalence of juvenile crime in that particular riverside community were (a) excess of leisure time (b) absence of adequate parental models and discipline in the home (c) young people's natural desire to indulge in daring and dangerous pursuits (d) the presence in the adult section of the population of a number of convicted offenders and of many whose attitude towards larceny and minor offences seemed to condone and encourage such acts. Historically, it was pointed out, this was a depressed neighbourhood where poverty and poor housing in the past had stigmatized the residents as socially inferior. But it did not appear that absence of legitimate outlets for ambition, for status seeking and other bourgeois rewards, were, in the comparative affluence of the post-war Welfare State, seriously motivating many young people into defiant delinquency. For the most part, a certain amount of petty thievery was the 'done thing'. In the University of Nottingham study of delinquency in the Midland mining town of 'Radby', similar traditional attitudes were observed on the part of residents occupying different streets in similar income-group areas, 'in one of which petty theft was taken for granted, while it was looked on with grave disapproval in the other'.[1] The Nottingham study accounts for the existence of the 'black' streets, the streets that is to say where the most delinquent and easy-going residents lived, by employing Merton's thesis that the people are cut off from the realization of culturally prescribed aspirations because of the lack of socially structured ways for realizing their ambitions. They failed however to show the peculiar relevance of this analysis to the social structure of Modern England.

Terence Morris's ecological study of Croydon also tackles the problem of the existence of delinquency areas in particular parts of the borough.[2] He accepts the view that the delinquent subculture is characteristically proletarian and lower-income group, and is sceptical of Sutherland's contention that, if the total volume of committed (as contrasted with detected) crime could be known, it would no longer be so easily concluded that delinquency is a proletarian rather than a bourgeois activity. He

[1] *The Social Background of Delinquency*, University of Nottingham, 1954, for private circulation only.
[2] *The Criminal Area*, Routledge and Kegan Paul, 1957.

suggests that the Commissioners of Inland Revenue in Britain whose 'vigilant eye' cannot be deflected by bribes keep down the number of white-collar offences to a bare minimum. Morris, following myself and the authors of the Radby study, makes more use of the concept of culture, or rather subculture, to account for the differential crime rates observed between the social classes. His view seems to be, and I would endorse it substantially, that working-class ways of living have arisen in the past as a result of the chasm dividing them from higher-income groups. They indicate not so much a hostile, negativistic and resentful reaction against higher income group ways of life as the development of an indigenous culture which met their own peculiar personal and social needs in a fairly satisfactory way. Working-class culture is then not so much deviant as merely an alternative pattern. It has embodied the socialization of children, their discipline, training and induction into adulthood in rather special ways. Cohen also saw this as a significant factor in the creation of delinquent gangs in America. The traditional middle-class way of bringing up children is to set standards, to demand the child's adherence to these standards, and to carry out training in a deliberate, rational and demanding manner. Working-class children, by contrast, have been unaccustomed to restraint, they have not been spurred on by rewards and punishments in a consistent endeavour to comply with high personal and educational standards. The result is that, when confronted with a difficulty or obstacle, the working-class boy is less able to restrain himself from a violent or anti-social solution. Less inhibited and more spontaneous than his middle-class counterpart, he is easily irritated and erupts more readily into delinquency.

All three British studies agree that the delinquent subcultures in this country are less serious phenomena than those portrayed by Professor Cohen in the United States. This is almost certainly because British society is very different from American society, both in its actual organization and in the goals pursued and the attitudes of the population towards these objectives. Criminological theories derived from a study of American culture are therefore of only limited value here. Their lead must be followed with caution. It would be quite unrealistic to take over the concepts and theories evolved by American sociologists and to apply them uncritically and without modification to Britain. The nature of these differences between British and American society will be discussed more fully in a later section.

At this point, it is perhaps only necessary to say that British society is much less dynamic than American society, and that, curiously enough, the differential class structure has itself probably helped towards creating sufficient stability in the social structure to preclude the development of excessively criminalistic and violent sub-groups. In other words subcultural juvenile delinquency in Britain is more historical in origin and due to class differences which have thrown up traditionally variant ways of living. In the U.S.A. the criminal subculture is much more explosive in nature and arises much more from the fact that aspirations have been blocked, not only by class divisions, but because some individuals and groups have been able to get ahead at a more rapid pace than others and so oblige their less fortunately placed fellow citizens to climb the ladder of success by illegitimate means.

Chapter 7

THE PSYCHOLOGY OF CRIME

I

Before dealing with psychological theories proper, something ought to be said, by way of clearing the ground, about heredity. The old idea that a criminal is born not made dies hard. In its slightly more sophisticated form, garnished and fitted out with all the paraphernalia of pseudo-science, the idea of innate criminality formed the central theme of the Italian school of criminologists which stemmed from the work of Lombroso towards the end of the nineteenth century. In some parts of Europe this concept of the born criminal is still influential, but it has generally been dropped by most psychologists in Britain and America. This is mainly because such a view would involve the inheritance in ordinary law-abiding people of something like a 'moral sense' or instinct, a sort of built-in conscience that would guide the individual into the straight and narrow course of righteousness.

It is sufficient to say that, although some laws embodying the idea do exist, the concept of moral deficiency as an inherited quality of the individual mind is wholly unacceptable nowadays. Says Sir Cyril Burt in a famous text: 'The born criminal—*il renato*—is mere a pseudo-scientific myth.'[1]

While, however, the idea of inherited criminality is ruled out, there are still some scientific grounds for claiming that what might be called 'constitutional tendencies' to behave in a particular way could account for, or at least contribute towards, the commission of certain kinds of offences in some cases.

[1] *The Causes and Treatment of Backwardness*, University of London Press, 1952, p. 95.

Sheldon and Eleanor Glueck place bodily physique or soma-types amongst their list of causal factors. They have some interesting things to say comparing a group of juvenile delinquents with non-delinquents, which tend to contradict certain popular illusions. For one thing, they found as a result of medical examinations that there was no support for the idea that delinquents are generally in a poorer state of heath than non-delinquents. There was, in fact, no significant difference between the two groups. As far as bodily size and structure were concerned, the delinquents seemed to be the superior, 'this superiority being expressed especially in the shoulders, chest, waist, and upper extremities, and outlining the picture of the masculine physical type with tapering torso, heavy arms, small face, strong neck, and wide shoulders'.[1] Physically considered, the delinquents were more homogeneous than the non-delinquents. They tended to be somewhat retarded in growth until about the fourteenth year when they spurted forward and often outpaced their non-delinquent counterparts. As a group, the delinquents were characteristcally mesomorphic, that is to say in bodily constitution they tended to be solid, closely knit and muscular. In temperament they were often 'restlessly energetic, impulsive, extroverted, aggressive, destructive (often sadistic)—traits which may be related more or less to the erratic growth pattern and its physiologic correlates or consequences'.[2]

While the Gluecks do not press these findings too far, and would only quote them in association with other personal qualities as being in some way causally associated with crime and delinquency, William H. Sheldon advances the idea that what he calls a 'predatory factor' is probably present in the constitutional make-up of many criminals. This view, which owes much to the earlier work of Kretchmer, is somewhat esoteric, being based upon the rather dubious theories of what has been called 'constitutional psychiatry'. Predation is so common amongst human beings, Sheldon argues, that, *for some members of the species* it may constitute the normal[3] outlook on

[1] Sheldon and Eleanor Glueck, *Unraveling Juvenile Delinquency*, New York, 1950, p. 196.
[2] Ibid., p. 281.
[3] Normal in this sense means relative to the individual himself, not to the social group.

life. Some men and women are so endowed, morphologically and temperamentally, that 'it is quite normal for them to seek to prey upon others and to seek to live off others without "contributing" as it is normal for the rest of us weaklings'.[1] Such personalities he calls Dionysian, and he argues further that western forms of social organization are in fact based to a large extent on their necessary existence. Our societies are organized so that the predatory dionysian types can flourish and trample upon us, not only as criminals but as political and military leaders, dictators and big business bosses. The idea, while excessive, is not merely fanciful. It serves to indicate the way in which the constitutional and inherited factors in explaining delinquent and criminal careers are far from being utterly outmoded. Some further support for the inherited tendency concept is derived from the study of one-egg twins which Professor Lange conducted in Germany in the early nineteen-thirties. In the words of C. D. Darlington this research 'although . . . not at all well described, has shown that where one twin has a criminal record, with few exceptions the other has also.'[2] 'Moreover', he adds, 'the type of crime is similar. The first occurrence of crime is at a similar age, even when the twins have been separated. The frequency of conviction is similar. But we have to allow for the fact that different judges may give different sentences for the same crime—for the judges are not usually one-egg twins—and a prison sentence stops further offences for the time being.'[3] Darlington then adds a delicious coda to these comments which I cannot refrain from quoting, even though it may not be entirely relevant to my own argument in this chapter. 'Indeed,' he says, 'one may ask: is there anything else that will stop further offences? The German enquiry shows that there is one other circumstance that will stop a criminal career. It is if a weak-minded criminal man marries a strong-minded non-criminal wife'.[4]

---

[1] William H. Sheldon, *Varieties of Delinquent Youth*, Harper Brothers, New York, 1949, p. 828.
[2] 'The coming of Heredity', *The Listener*, 3rd January, 1952, p. 17.
[3] Ibid.   [4] Ibid.

THE PSYCHOLOGY OF CRIME

II

The psychological approach to crime may be divided into two main categories. First, there is the approach of the general and educational psychologist, and secondly, there is the ever-growing body of theory, speculation and clinical experimentation associated with psycho-analysis and psychiatry. On the whole the psycho-analysts, who originate in the work of Sigmund Freud, have proved most influential in recent years and they may be said to be in the forefront of so called 'expert' thinking about the nature and treatment of crime. But before we have a look at psycho-analytical and psychiatric explanations it is worth while saying something about the work of a more general psychologist like Sir Cyril Burt, a pioneer in Great Britain, whose main orientation is still, to my mind, outstandingly important. For Burt a criminal act is conscious. It arises from a complex of connected causal factors which combine together to produce the offending behaviour. Innate mental qualities, the events of the individual's past life and the actual circumstances in the environment interact to precipitate the specific delinquency. Instinctive impulses, which are inborn, are, according to Burt, 'adapted to life in primitive uncivilized conditions', whereas the 'sentiments we acquire are adjusted to life in civilized society. What else is to be expected but that at times the two should violently collide?'[1] Delinquent behaviour, then, can sometimes be categorized as normal behaviour which is carried on in an inappropriate setting, conduct suitable for a jungle or frontier but out of tune with the highly artificial urban habitat with its bewildering complexity of laws and vetoes, its excitements and compulsions, restrictions and alluring possibilities ranging from the eleven-plus examination to contraceptive pills, from commercial television to cathedrals, from car parking offences to compulsory military service —the astonishingly heterogeneous world, in fact, which we all take for granted.

Burt found that actual mental deficiency accounted for only a minor proportion of the offenders he studied. But congenital factors, he thought, were crucial in a substantial minority, about 36 per cent of the boys and 41 per cent of the girls—well over

[1] *The Young Delinquent*, London University Press, 1925, p. 558.

one-third of all his cases—'some deep constitutional failing' appeared to be the 'primary source of misconduct'.[1] It is important, however, to remember that he never speaks of these causal factors in isolation but always in association with one another. It is constitutional proclivities in conjunction with environmental stimulation that precipitate the final offence. As far as children go, it is their immediate social circle, their friends and relatives and especially their parents whose influence, operating on their basic mental constitution, determines whether or not they are law-abiding. While he says that as many as 'Three-quarters of our young delinquents and five-sixths of our habitual criminals are educationally subnormal as well as morally unstable',[2] it is clear that he does not regard this state of affairs as necessarily irreparable and certainly it is far from being inevitable. Treatment is to be thought of rather as a process of re-education than of medical therapy or even of psychotherapy. 'To strengthen the character of the dull and backward, and implant moral habits if we cannot successfully inculcate moral ideas, will be one of the surest ways to diminish crime',[3] he wrote. Crime is therefore to some extent learned behaviour, often the wrong sort, and is open to remedial action by training in fresh habits. Usually crime is normal in this sense, 'the result of a perfectly natural if undesirable reaction in a perfectly healthy and normal individual to what may be regarded as an abnormal or undesirable situation'.[4] Training involves education of the emotions. Devotion to and identification with human models is characteristic of the formative years of childhood. Thus it is important that the ethically right models in the way of parents, siblings and playmates should be available if the child is to grow up safely in the often temptingly dangerous environment of a modern city.

III

The borderland between the normal and abnormal or unusual may be found in cases where individuals possess emotional instabilities to an unusual degree. When faced with conditions of

[1] Ibid., p. 605.   [2] *The Causes and Treatment of Backwardness*, p. 123.
[3] Ibid.
[4] 'The Psychology of Crime', *The Listener*, 30th November, 1950, p. 639.

stress or conflict, emotionally inhibited introverted people tend to develop anxieties to the point of neurosis. One of less inhibited extraverted temperament is more likely to seek relief in wild, aggressive, impulsive conduct which will very likely bring him into conflict with the law.

Since we can do little to undo hereditary factors as such, obviously control of the social environment becomes increasingly important in any attempt to prevent delinquency arising. 'Normal' delinquency is in theory at least re-educable. It is based upon habit which is the result of conditioning processes. Abnormal criminal behaviour, on the other hand, may be said to arise from a pathological fixation which arises as a result of the individual finding a forbidden or illegitimate way around his difficulties. Like a river which is impeded by a fall of rock, the impulse creates a new channel for itself which thereafter becomes essential for its life. A particular type of temperament under conditions of acute stress or frustration discovers, as it were, a substitute outlet for discharging his emotions and achieving his psychic purposes. Any disturbance of this fixation, therefore, is liable to produce serious psychological disturbances in the individual, with possibly grave consequences both for him and for society.

I think it is fair to say that the distinction between the work of the psychologist and the work of the psycho-analysts in the field of criminology is that the former is in the main concerned with ordinary minds which have developed anti-social habits while the latter is more interested in pathological mental states which have arisen as a result of some psychic wound in the past or of some illegitimate fixation arising from deep-seated and often unconscious causes. Somewhere in between hover those eclectic psychiatrists, who cover the dubious border country between something which may be more realistically termed a mental illness, on the one hand, and sheer bad habits and egoistic self-indulgence, on the other.

Most psychologists, and here I include psychiatrists and analysts, would agree that much delinquency in juveniles has a social origin. 'Everyday observation,' wrote Lucien Bovet, 'confirmed by numerous studies from the U.S.A., Great Britain, and Germany after the first World War, points to the etiological significance of the environment, without the intermediary action of complex psychological mechanisms. A large proportion of children and adolescents appearing before the courts have no major physical or psychological abnormality. They are simply the victims of adverse external circumstances, characterized by social insecurity, or a too low standard of living, or a combination of both.'[1] To be sure, the reaction of the individual to such adverse conditions has a psychological basis, and no two people will react to them in the same way. But, basically, the major causal factors lie *outside* the individual mind. This is a most important point to which we will have to return in a few paragraphs when we try to distinguish between so-called 'real' and 'pseudo' delinquency. The common psychological denominator in most cases of delinquency seems to be some kind of emotional insecurity which gives rise to a state of anxiety. This must not be taken to mean that anyone who feels insecure or anxious must seek a delinquent solution to his problems. But many individuals seem to be so constituted emotionally, and already so disturbed by what has happened to them in the past, that they react to anxiety by some kind of aggression. This, in the case of a neurotic, may be aggression turned inwards upon the self (intropunitiveness), resulting in some kind of 'nervous breakdown'. Or, in the case of uninhibited personalities it may result in extrapunitiveness and delinquency. 'In most people,' Bovet says, 'this aggressiveness will give rise to feelings of guilt which, in turn, produce further anxiety. Thus the vicious circle is completed which is doubtless one of the most constantly found psychological aspects of delinquency, particularly of juvenile delinquency.'[2]

IV

We all experience stressful situations in the ordinary course of our daily lives. We all feel resentment, anxiety and aggressiveness to some degree, but most of us have sufficient self-control and have acquired, through experience and education, techniques to cope with these exacerbating situations without breakdown or disaster resulting. But the delinquents and criminals either lack these mechanisms or their powers of adjustment have

[1] *Psychiatric Aspects of Juvenile Delinquency*, W.H.O., 1951, p. 80.
[2] Ibid., p. 82.

been damaged by emotional shocks and deprivations to such an extent that they are incapable of coping with any further stress. The well-behaved Borstal boy who fits easily into the regime and seems to be making progress is often the boy who breaks down very quickly after he is released and returned to the stress-creating situation from which his period of routinized detention protected him. While, on the other hand, the inmate who fights the regime to some degree and asserts his individuality by indiscipline may settle down much more easily on release. Those who cannot withstand stress ultimately cannot live in the workaday world, and must retreat from it either as criminal recidivists, inmates of mental hospitals, drug addicts, tramps or recluses.

In most cases the difference between the average man and the criminal is quantitative rather than qualitative. 'If we go to the depths of the unconscious we are all alike.'[1] Delinquents are people who, like everyone else, have experienced frustration, particularly in their human relationships, but their reactions to it are abnormal. Why should this be so? What factors in the psychological make-up of the offenders distinguish them from those who are more or less successful at keeping their behaviour within legal bounds?

There is widespread agreement amongst psychologists and psychiatrists that the answer to these questions is to be found in what happens or fails to happen to a child in the prepubertal stage, and especially during infancy. Aichhorn based his pioneer work with severely maladjusted and delinquent boys on the principle that the love life of his inmates had been gravely disturbed during early childhood by lack of parental affection or an excessive amount of it.[2] Following Freud, he believed that an individual's emotional relationships with his parents in the early years of life set the pattern for all later relationships. If these primary relationships go wrong for any reason, the developing child is emotionally warped. His basic needs are for affection and discipline, or, if we want a comprehensive term, which includes both facets in the same concept, Love. Through love the socialization process is carried out. His parents teach

[1] Tadeusz Grygier, *Oppression, A Study of Social and Criminal Psychology*, Routledge and Kegan Paul, 1954, p. 240.

[2] See *Wayward Youth*, Putnam, London, 1936.

and help him to control his basic drives and urges in an acceptable manner. According to Dr. J. D. W. Pearce, 'The acquisitive, aggressive, sexual and escape instincts underlie almost all delinquency'.[1] Delinquency can satisfy one or more of these instinctual drives at one and the same time. It may, in larceny for instance, satisfy acquisitiveness, relieve sexual tension and gratify aggressiveness simultaneously. In a case like this, it would be fair to say that the individual has invested a considerable amount of his psychic capital in crime, and will accordingly be the harder to deflect from his illegal practices. It is the task of the parent and educator, or, at a later stage, of the therapist and re-educator, to assist the delinquent to master his instinctive urges or, as we would say in ordinary terms, learn self-control.

V

Such a view as outlined above suggests that delinquency is a natural form of primitive self-expressiveness and that, being a little savage, the child, if left to his own resources, will aggress against the world in an uninhibited orgy of self-gratification. The only thing that restrains it from so doing is its helplessness and dependence upon its mother. And, in order to receive the loving ministrations of the mother, the child accepts certain constraints which he comes to internalize and make his own. He forms his conscience in relation to his parents, or, in psychoanalytical jargon, his super-ego is an internalized parent. The morality of the parents is then of crucial importance. A loving, but criminal, parent can create a criminalistic offspring by transmitting what the analysts term a defective super-ego. For the Freudians, what happens in the family situation, the relationships between parents, and especially mothers, and their children in the first five or six years of life, are the crucial determinants of subsequent character and conduct. William Healy and Augusta Bronner, in their famous study of 105 delinquents and their 105 non-delinquent siblings treated over a three-year period in three Boston clinics, found that no less than 91 per cent of the delinquents as compared with only 13 per cent of their non-delinquent brothers and sisters were suffering from deep emotional problems related to their parents or parent

[1] *Juvenile Delinquency*, Cassell, 1952, p. 340.

surrogates.[1] While this research has been open to the criticism that it was carried out by psychiatrically trained workers on the *qui vive* for symptoms, it remains an impressive and suggestive piece of work. What is, of course, more difficult to prove— and this is a weakness of all retrospective as well as mainly clinical studies—is that there is a direct causal connection between emotional disturbance and delinquency. As Sutherland suggested, 'the delinquent behaviour may cause the emotional disturbance'.[2]

The work of some more recent psychiatrists has tended to concentrate on what Ian Suttie called the 'separation anxiety' which also seems to be most influential in the early years of infancy. John Bowlby has most notably in this country applied this concept to the etiology of chronic criminality and recidivism. Both Bowlby and Suttie were associated with the pioneer work of the Tavistock Clinic, and Bowlby's first major study of delinquents, *44 Juvenile Thieves*,[3] was based on a sample of cases referred to him at that institution. In this particular study he compared his thieves with a similar number of non-delinquents as like to them in mental endowment and social characteristics as possible. Bowlby's findings considerably modified earlier thinking on the causes of serious crime. The 'broken home' theory, which had long held sway in a general way, was narrowed down to homes broken in particular ways, when the child had been separated from his mother or mother-substitute for long periods or permanently during his first five years of life. Burt, who Bowlby claimed had earlier stumbled upon this important fact and failed to realize its significance, had erred by putting early separation of parents and children among the minor factors making for delinquency when his actual findings demanded that it be placed among the major determinants. Burt, in fact, showed that 23·5 per cent of the boys and 36·5 per cent of the girls in his sample had undergone prolonged separation from their parents in early childhood, as contrasted with only 1·5 per cent and 5 per cent for the control group.

Bowlby claimed that his theory of maternal deprivation in the first five years of life accounted for chronic criminality in a significant number of his cases and was highly characteristic of

[1] *New Light on Delinquency*, Yale University Press, 1936.
[2] *Principles of Criminology*, p. 130.   [3] Baillière, Tindall and Cox, 1947.

the persistent offender. This loss of maternal love at the most vital stage of human development could be brought about by a number of accidental causes, including death, hospitalization of either mother or child, as well as by rejection, desertion or divorce. A child so cut off from his mother's affection at this critical stage of development might thereafter be unable to form a loving relationship with any other person. It is as though a potentiality were forever denied fulfilment because the right things were not present at the right time. The deprived child not only has its source of love fouled by the poisons of rage, but also seems to become determined, at all costs, that the risk of such a profound disappointment should never again be taken. He becomes withdrawn, capable only of superficial response to any advances, impervious to praise or blame alike, lacking real friends, rootless and undemonstrative. Bowlby terms this the 'affectionless personality' and he found fourteen such characters amongst his delinquents and none amongst his control group. Its association with criminality is thus statistically clear. 'I am doubtful', he declares, 'whether the law-abiding affectionless character exists.'

VI

Both Suttie[1] and Bowlby have put the concept of love right back into the middle of the family picture as the most important ingredient of a successful parent-child relationship. Both fear and hatred in the child stem from the same source—attachment to the mother—as do love and affection. To be deprived of her love is to experience rage and fear. Unlike Freud, Suttie denied that the child is born with a set of instinctual drives all struggling for assertion. His concept of love is a spiritual one, in contrast to the Freudian idea of the *libido* which is always associated with genital sexuality. In place of the *oedipus complex*, and the conflict of love and hate generated by the child's ambivalent attitude towards his parents, Suttie emphasizes the all-importance of a simple and secure attachment between child and parent as the growing point of personality. It is an elegant and morally satisfying theory with which to replace the somewhat sordid and offputting complexities of Freudian psychoanalysis. It has,

[1] *Origins of Love and Hate*, Penguin Books, 1960.

moreover, the advantage of being essentially compatible with the teaching of religion. It springs from Christian and not from pagan origins.

The theory of emotional deprivation in early infancy as stated by Bowlby undoubtedly tended to exaggeration. Like any fresh insight, such as Freud's development of the idea of the unconscious, it tended to become an all-embracing theory, and there has been a justifiable reaction against it. Edelston[1] finds it, as a theory to account for criminality, as misleading as the old 'broken home' explanation. Hilda Lewis[2] has illustrated its shortcomings in her study of deprived children at a Kent reception centre and shown that separation in the early years need not necessarily lead to emotional stunting. As Edelston maintains, the way in which a child deals with its problems and difficulties is to some extent 'predetermined by the innate mental endowment and the stage of its development at the time of the separation'. He stresses the importance of the concept of 'emotional maturation.' Dr. Roper,[3] in his study of prisoners in Wakefield, lends much support to this notion. 'The question presents itself: if criminality and immaturity are so closely associated, may they not be much the same thing?' he asks. 'We know that young children can be seen, in any not too tidy nursery, assaulting each other, taking the belongings of others, and even engaging in sexual exploration, in a way which would be criminal in adults. No sensible person worries about these things because he knows that it is a normal phase of development which will disappear with training. May it not be that criminality is merely the persistence or reappearance of this nursery stage of development, which becomes ugly and dangerous because of the greater strength and sophistication of the adult?'

Roper reiterates a point of view, which we frequently find emerging from both psychological and social studies, that criminality is indeed the natural state of man. We are all potential if not actual criminals. Probably during childhood we are criminals in so far as we are egocentric animals greedily

[1] *The Earliest Stages of Delinquency*, Livingstone, 1952.
[2] *Deprived Children*, Oxford, 1954.
[3] 'Survey of Wakefield Prison, 1948–49', *British Journal of Delinquency*, Vol. I. No. 4.

seeking our own ends, epitomized in the 'I see, I want, I take' mentality. Dr. Emanuel Miller,[1] the psycho-analyst, speaks of 'larval delinquency' in a most interesting article. The phrase makes one shudder, evoking, as it does, an image of a human mind crawling with maggots, but it expresses a similar insight into the nature of criminal behaviour. 'There are,' he writes, 'in the experience of psychiatrists and their co-workers persons who, while conforming to the criteria of normality . . . do betray in character, in fleeting conduct, in confession, and in analysis intimations of delinquent undertones. . . . Not merely in overt behaviour, in sudden rages, periods of unreliability, the sailing-near-the-wind type in economic relations and in sexual expressions, but in character nuances and conduct suggesting rigidities, and (may one style them) hypocrisies which arouse suspicion. In addition to these are the occasional manifestations of our time expressed in the Arts: music and literature, entertainment and sport which might call for special attention. . . .'[2]

A leader by the editor of *The Lancet*[3] indicates a similar view. Discussing the class bias shown by the sentencing policy of the courts, the author writes: 'We can indeed ask whether there is any valid qualitative difference between a "carve-up among the Teds" and the great range of deviant behaviour exhibited by the average rugby-football club, which starts its activities with the scrum (assault, and even grievous bodily harm), goes on to the communal bath (indecent exposure), the enormous consumption of beer (drunken and disorderly behaviour), and the singing of songs (obscene language), and ends on the way home with the collection of inn-signs, road-names, and bus-stops (larceny).' The fact that one group of behaviour norms is socially condemned and other free of such opprobrium suggests that in contemporary society what is defined as criminal behaviour is often arbitrary and irrational, betraying in fact class bias. While one might not be able to go all the way with either Dr. Miller or Dr. Fox (the latter's idea for instance that communal bathing is indecent seems unnecessarily perverse), the point that is worth emphasizing at this stage is that both psychological and sociological interpretations of crime fre-

---

[1] 'Delinquent Traits in Normal Persons', *British Journal of Delinquency*, Vol. X, No. 3.
[2] Ibid., p. 168.   [3] *The Lancet*, 4th June, 1960, pp. 1238–42.

quently converge. The two disciplines need not lead to dichotomous viewpoints. There is a wide measure of consensus regarding what may be termed 'normal delinquency'. It is essentially ordinary human behaviour in an inappropriate context; behaving like a child when one should act as an adult. The thing that seems to distinguish the normal person who is not an offender from the one who is would seem to be something akin to *savoir faire*, a higher degree of sophistication and discrimination arising from early training and learned judgement, which enables the individual to choose the appropriate setting in which to give vent to his infantile, childish or primitive impulses. This leads one to ask whether or not basic intelligence has any contribution to make to this kind of normal misbehaviour. Does a richer intellectual endowment prevent one from committing social atrocities?

The relevance of low intelligence to delinquency, often assumed by unthinking people, is by no means settled. On balance the evidence seems to suggest, apart from actual mental defectives who might get into trouble as a result of their stupidity, that there is very little correlation between intelligence and crime. If low intelligence plays any part in delinquency causation it is probably no more than a minor factor. Of much greater moment, says Mary Woodward,[1] who made a comprehensive study of this topic, are 'emotional attitudes, social standards and methods of training of those dealing with the child'. Any tie-up between so-called 'problem families' moreover is largely fortuitous. The delinquent population appears to correspond to the non-delinquent group intellectually with a normal distribution of intelligence. The fact that certain artificial groups of offenders, e.g. boys in Approved Schools, have lower I.Q.'s than would be normal for their age group in the population at large is a function of other related conditions rather than an index of causal connectedness. The low I.Q.'s in these selected groups for example could very easily be a result of educational retardation, emotional lability and sheer social deprivation.

[1] *Low Intelligence and Delinquency*, I.S.T.D., 1955.

VII

We may sum up what appears to be the most generally agreed contribution that psychology and psychiatry have made to our understanding of the nature and origin of crime by saying that potentially anti-social urges exist in every human being and what determines whether they develop or not is what happens to us in infancy and childhood. In these early years the basic personality patterns are laid down, for good or ill, by our emotional relationships with our parents or parent surrogates. If all goes well and loving relationships are established, and if our parents discipline us by example and ethical instruction, we should live through the important formative years with little difficulty. If emotional deprivation occurs, for whatever reason, however, the risk of our becoming delinquents is intensified but not made certain. Natural endowment and our experiences before emotional shocks beset us will determine how far such slings and arrows of outrageous fortune prove overwhelming. The possession of a mesomorphic physique, an extraverted and excitable temperament and a love of thrills and adventure are further predisposing factors. Above all, we must learn and be taught how to deal with stress situations in socially acceptable ways. Most of us are liable to petty and occasional loss of control, and hence may become classified as official delinquents if we are unlucky enough to be apprehended. Such delinquency is a normal phenomenon. Its nature is benign, and, while it needs handling with care, need not create serious social problems. If, however, all does not go well and at any vital stage of our development emotional shocks and traumatic experiences prove too much for us, we may become psychologically maladjusted. That maladjustment may express itself either externally in criminal acts, or internally in neurotic breakdown. If it is expressed through delinquent acts, these acts are to be thought of as distress signals, and if one form of communication fails to elicit attention another will be utilized to attract attention to our problem. Delinquency in such cases is chosen for individual ends rather than accepted for social and other normally explicable reasons. Some writers describe the latter as 'real' and the former as 'pseudo' delinquents. These epithets seem to me to misrepresent the situation and to be arbitrary and confusing.

To my mind both kinds are genuine delinquents, but they are basically different types. The psychologically maladjusted delinquent often presents deepseated and intractable problems which prove intransigent to known forms of treatment. The second type is more benign in nature and much more amenable to restraining and educational techniques. I believe that scientific classification of offenders begins with this important analytical distinction of the two main types of delinquents.

VIII

So far in this chapter we have not mentioned some of the more extreme kinds of mental abnormality which may be associated with criminal behaviour. Criminal psychopathology is a topic to be approached with care and is more the concern of the professional forensic psychiatrist than the sociologist.

We have, however, touched on the criminal psychopath in Bowlby's concept of the Affectionless Character, but there are other kinds of psychopathy which arise from rather different causes. Three main groups have been described; the mainly aggressive, the mainly inadequate and the mainly creative. The last are an interesting and debatable group made up of those gifted individuals whose lives are so unbalanced that they ultimately prove incapable of achieving the distinctions that their talents seem to indicate.

It is not always easy to distinguish the true psychopath from the normal individual, partly because we know so little about the processes whereby so-called normal personalities are formed. As the editors of the *British Journal of Delinquency* put it: 'psychopathy in fact provides an exception to the general psychiatric proposition that one learns the normal through the study of the abnormal; to understand the psychopath one must grasp the larval abnormality of the normal.'[1]

Not all psychopaths, of course, turn out to be criminals. Nor is the term psychopath one that is as yet subject to a generally agreed definition. But it may be said that psychopathy arises either from constitutional predisposition or a severe traumatic experience or, most likely, from both. Psychopaths are essentially maladjusted and abnormal personalities but they are not,

[1] *British Journal of Delinquency*, Vol. VI, No. 1, 1955, p. 1.

in the legal definition, insane. Norwood East, who spent a lifetime devoted to what he termed the 'non-sane non-insane offender', described him in these terms: '. . . the criminal psychopathic personality may be defined, tentatively, as a person who, although not insane, psychoneurotic or mentally defective, is persistently unable to adapt himself to social requirements on account of abnormal peculiarities of impulse, temperament and character which may require specialized medical and rehabilitative treatment instead of, or in addition to, the ordinary methods of punishment before his social reclamation can be effected.'[1] This is a definition which leaves us a little fogged. The very concept of the psychopath has indeed been dismissed as a circular definition and its nature said to be derived from the behaviour it pretends to explain.

There would be much less dispute about offenders psychiatrically de ined as mental defectives. Straffen, the killer of little girls, mc t people would agree was a thoroughly abnormal individuaı and could fairly be regarded as being less responsible for his actions than many other homicides. Yet he is reported to have been an affectionate son, concerned for his mother's welfare. But he had what the layman calls a 'kink', some twist to his mind that led him into compulsive killing so that as soon as he escaped from Broadmoor, where he was incarcerated for having murdered two small girls, he killed a third. Undoubtedly there are some criminals whose behaviour is of such a nature that they are much less in charge of their own lives and hence much less responsible for what they do than the vast majority of people.

It would probably also be generally agreed that offenders suffering from some organic disease of the brain, or who have had a lesion, form a special category, as do epileptics. As far as the latter are concerned, it seems to be clinically well established that in the aftermath of a seizure they do things without being conscious of what they are doing. But by no means all epileptics or all mental defectives commit offences. In fact, there is no close tie-up between the medical and the legal definition of insanity. Broadly speaking, the psychiatric term for insanity is psychosis, and psychotics usually suffer from some form of total mental derangement which serves to distinguish them from

[1] *Society and the Criminal*, H.M.S.O., 1949, p. 41.

psychoneurotics who are only thought to be suffering from partial disabilities. Many psychotics seem to experience hallucinations and to harbour delusions about themselves. They may claim to hear voices and see visions. They may believe themselves to be reincarnations of historic characters or to be poached eggs on toast. Other psychotics may be callously detached to the point of being 'split' minds. As the late Sir Norwood East indicated, the various psychopathological groups often overlap and are far from being clear. He admitted that 'no psychiatric classification is likely to give entire satisfaction until the dividing line between mental diseases and character anomalies is established with some degree of precision apart from personal estimates'.[1] It does not seem that we have yet reached that stage of psychological sophistication, hence the discrepancy between medical and legal definitions which Barbara Wootton has discussed in a famous text. The whole divergence between medicine and morals in the criminological field seems to centre round the idea of culpability. Criminal responsibility in Great Britain was until 1957 defined in the terms of the McNaughton Rules[2] which laid it down that juries could bring in a verdict of guilty but insane if it could be shown that the offender was suffering from 'some defect of reason due to disease of the mind, in consequence of which he either did not know the nature and quality of the act at the time he performed it, or did not know that the act was wrong'. The Homicide Bill, 1957, is a slight variant on this, and reads that a person shall not be convicted of murder 'if he was suffering from such abnormality of mind (whether arising from a condition of arrested or retarded development of mind or any inherent causes or induced by disease or injury) as substantially impaired his mental responsibility for his acts and omissions in doing or being party to the killing'.

The admission of the concept of 'diminished responsibility' has probably not made things any easier. As a result, in almost every trial for homicide we see expert medical evidence given both for and against the accused as part and parcel of the legal tussle that goes on between prosecution and defence counsels. It is not an edifying spectacle nor does it bring much credit to psychiatry. It is only in murder trials that the cleavage between

[1] Op. cit., p. 6.　　　[2] Set up in a famous trial in 1843.

medicine and morals reaches such a pitch. Strictly speaking, medical witnesses have no right to make categorical statements about the accused's culpability or responsibility. However, they frequently do. But, as Lady Wootton has cogently argued, 'the presence of a psychiatric syndrome or of a disturbance of part-functions does not, of itself, necessarily explain, still less does it necessarily excuse, disregard of social norms. Even at the level of mere explanation, the link between the two needs to be demonstrated. Many anti-social persons may prove to be suffering from anxieties or depressions, or even from delusions or hallucinations.'[1] She goes on to argue that 'it is far from self-evident that these mental peculiarities explain their violence or their thieving, their casual attitude to domestic ties or their general social incompetence. Many anti-social persons may prove to be suffering from high or low blood pressure, from incipient peptic ulcers or even from malignant tumours; but we do not assume, and we are not entitled to assume without evidence that these morbid conditions have anything to do with their standards of social behaviour.' To Lady Wootton's mind the psychopath is the extreme example of such special pleading, 'he is *par excellence* the model of the circular process by which mental abnormality is inferred from anti-social behaviour while anti-social behaviour is explained by mental abnormality'.[2]

This point of view is, I think, somewhat extreme but very salutary. It puts the brake on an already accelerating process whereby we tend to assume that, if one part of the individual mind is seen to be malfunctioning, therefore other parts must also be pathologically disarranged. On the other hand, until psychiatric knowledge becomes more exact, we have to be content with legal definitions which are broad enough to allow room for expert argument, discussion and, I am afraid, disagreement. As the editor of *The Lancet* put it, 'The decision in the Mental Health Act, (1959) to define psychopathic behaviour in terms of "abnormally aggressive or seriously irresponsible conduct" cannot be expected to still dispute'.[3] On the other hand, we cannot leave things as they were. It is surely not suggested that all psychological and psychiatric theories are entirely without foundation. That they will change is certain.

[1] *Social Science and Social Pathology*, Allen and Unwin, 1959, p. 239.
[2] Ibid., p. 250.   [3] *The Lancet*, 4th June, 1960, p. 1241.

It may be that they will, in the end, be found to be connected with physiological conditions at present unknown. But the man in the street, the average citizen, the Member of Parliament and the member of a jury as well as the legal expert, should be given what help they can get in carrying out their difficult and different jobs. Psychiatrists ought to be allowed to offer diagnoses tentatively accounting for the accused's conduct, but they should make it plain that the decision as to culpability is not theirs but properly belongs to the court. An explanation is not an excuse and any statement as to why an act occurred must not be given or heard as though it implied that no other outcome could have eventuated. However much we may disagree as to where the line should be drawn, most people would, I fancy, accept the view that a line should be drawn somewhere between behaviour that is normal, and hence treatable by conventional disciplinary and punitive means, and behaviour which is abnormal and hence treatable, if at all, by rather different means. Most of us would agree that, while all people are to a degree responsible for what they do, short of complete insanity (to be defined operationally and clinically) there are other cases in which the individual mind has undergone such stress and been submitted to such extreme conditions of privation and emotional upset, that they cannot in all fairness be treated as normal. As we have already said, some people can bear stress more successfully than others, and this may be due to basic constitutional factors. The breaking point is not the same for everyone and therefore, although the law must in the main be the same for all, justice demands that it be tailored to take cognizance of certain peculiar circumstances. It is a well-known fact that in the frustrating and often terrifying conditions of prisoners of war and concentration camps, some individuals put up a stiffer resistance to the malign pressures than others. Grygier claims that after World War II, the delinquency rates for those who had been in Nazi concentration camps was 'about forty-five times greater than for the whole displaced person population'.[1] Oppression, he believes, conduces to the formation of anti-social character structure for the unfortunate inmates. The excoriating experiences, as it were, break them down and educe their worst tendencies. Inmates of horror

[1] Op. cit., pp. 122–3.

camps are found to be unduly prone to conflict and to crime. Their behaviour is frequently characterized by egocentricity and projection and the development of acute feelings of distinction between their in-group and the rest of the hostile world. In other words, one might say that they have gone through experiences which have warped their personalities. Henceforth they are sick men, damaged beings. So, it may also be just to make allowances for criminals in ordinary society who have lived through extremely distressing experiences. This does not mean that we should not take any action when they break the law. But it does mean that, having offended, past traumatic experiences should be taken into account in deciding treatment and disposal. Punishment in any other terms, based merely on principles of retribution, is repugnant to modern sensitivities.

CHAPTER 8

THE SOCIALIZATION PROCESS

I

In the preceding chapter reference was made to the important role of the parents in bringing up their children in such a way that they gradually become reasonably well-adjusted members of the wider society. Children may be regarded as essentially asocial creatures, concerned with the gratification of their own immediate desires without regard for or even real awareness of, the needs of others. The primary educative instrument is the child's capacity to feel and reciprocate affection. He learns what he must do to please his mother or father and such actions, because they are rewarded by kisses and other indications of approval, come to be defined as 'good'. Thus what pleases mother and delights father is made the basis of primitive moral valuation. Conversely, what displeases them is defined as bad and prohibited, regardless, at this early developmental stage, of what society at large considers right and wrong.

Small children are far from being passive recipients of affection. From a very early moment they not only respond but actually initiate relationships with their parents. They seek love and derive pleasure from association with their mothers and fathers. At the emotional level the parent-child relationship is reciprocal, but in one important respect, the child is helplessly at the mercy of the parental ethical viewpoint. He lacks knowledge of the outer world and must therefore accept his parents' definitions of good and bad, right and wrong, proper and improper, uncritically. For this reason it is crucially important to have as one's parents men and women whose definitions coincide with the culturally prescribed norms of the society that one is about to enter. If one has the misfortune to have a Fagin or a Sykes as a parent, one might conceivably receive sufficient emotional warmth to develop into a psychologically healthy individual, but one would certainly turn into an enemy of society. In psychoanalytical terms one would have a criminal super-ego. Socially one would be maladjusted because one's conduct would be at variance with the mores and codes to which the majority of other people are bound. The only lasting friendships one could thereafter hope to make would be with the criminals and social outcasts.

Fortunately not many children belong to criminally oriented families. Even those whose parents are habitual offenders are not necessarily exposed to overt criminal indoctrination. A prostitute who has a child might bring him up in complete ignorance of the nature of her professional activities and train him to be a law-abiding, conventional member of society. And a burglar father might be equally discreet! I do not think that there are many cases of children whose outlook is deliberately perverted. There are, however, many gross deprivations in home and family life which have a marked criminogenic effect. We cannot leave the topic of how criminal behaviour comes into existence as a result of social influences without examining the nature and quality of family relationships. Such an examination involves making use of both sociological and psychological concepts and theories. This is both inevitable and desirable. Ultimately sociology and psychology must come together if they are to illuminate the origins of human behaviour and help us to unravel the complicated issues involved in social problems such as crime and delinquency.

It is pre-eminently in the study of family life and the nature of the relationships between the various members of the home circle that a fusion of the concepts derived from these two branches of learning is most fruitful. As the child develops in his early years under the influence of his parents and siblings and other intimate relatives we can study the way in which individual psychic factors are conditioned by social and extra-familial cultural influences. This is the point, as the Gluecks have persistently emphasized, where social and biological processes make contact, where environment and organism interact, to which we must turn our attention if we are to understand the way in which delinquents evolve. The parents not only meet the child's needs for physical and emotional security; to do their job properly, they must also mediate the culture of the wider society. The child must learn how to behave in socially acceptable ways. He acquires from his family an understanding of how to live up to an objectively defined standard so that, as he progresses from one stage to another, he knows more or less what his appropriate social role involves and necessitates.

Successful social conditioning is closely associated with the way in which the child accepts and deals with frustrations and prohibitions and how he reacts to the authority of the adult world vested in his parents. If he is sure of parental love and support, he will come to accept limitations on the freedom of his behaviour without experiencing intolerable stress. If he is not thus assured, the outcome of frustrations may prove more serious. He may test the length of parental indulgence and affection to the point at which the law is broken. And, if he feels that his parents are constantly cold towards him or positively reject him as a recipient of their care, he may react by increased aggressiveness to signal his distress and relieve his bitterness.

In their account of the work of the Wallingford Farm Training School, Menday and Wiles give a heart-breaking analysis of the home backgrounds of their inmates:

'Seventeen of the 170 boys at Turner's Court were abandoned by their parents at birth: another eighteen were sired by "unknown" fathers. In twenty-three cases the fathers deserted the home during the child's infancy; in twenty-seven cases the mothers deserted the family leaving the child to the care of the father or neighbours. In a number of other cases, almost impossible to determine, both parents walked out on their responsibilities, abandoning the children to the tender mercy of anybody who happened to be around at the time.'[1]

There seem to be two vital aspects of the parent-child relationship which, in combination, determine the sort of discipline existing in a family. These are affection and authority. Parents need to represent both to their children if they are to do their

[1] *The Everlasting Childhood: The Predicament of the Backward Boy*, Gollancz, 1959, p. 124.

job effectively. The acceptance of authority is only tolerable when mediated through a loving parent or adult figure. But authority is something that every one of us has to come to terms with. It is a social fact; a reality which exists irrespective of and external to the relationships of the nuclear family. An essential element in all training is to assist the child to accept external authority without being overwhelmed by it. He must be able to participate in social life without loss of individuality and be capable of assuming responsibility while, at the same time, coming to terms with those in whom society has vested authoritative powers. All this means, I think, in simple terms, that a child has a right to be loved by his parents and he has equal right to be disciplined by them. Love and discipline are inseparable elements in good child care. Psychiatrists have, in recent years, paid a good deal of attention to the need for parents to express their love for their offspring, but there has perhaps been a danger in some quarters of mistaking affection for sloppiness. In some homes, and these are by no means exclusively lower-class, affection has become so permissive that few limits have been put on the children's egotism. The result is a number of rude, ill-disciplined, greedy, bossy children, who, while they may not be delinquent, are not amenable to control and are, therefore, in greater risk of becoming offenders.

II

In this chapter I want to consider the importance of the training aspects of family life rather than their emotional significance. For both training and discipline are nowadays somewhat suspect words, smacking of authoritarianism and hence to be eschewed. But it is interesting to note that some recent research workers in the criminological field have thought fit to return to the apparently outmoded concept of discipline. Sir Cyril Burt,[1] writing his famous book in the mid-nineteen twenties, placed 'defective discipline' first in his long list of the various conditions associated with the origin of delinquency in the group of London children he was studying. 'Defective family relationships', by which he meant the absence of the father or the presence of a step-mother, he only placed tenth. While influences

[1] *The Young Delinquent*, pp. 606–7.

outside the family such as the lure of street associations and lack of healthy facilities for recreation came eleventh in his list.

Child delinquency is generally associated with a poor quality of home life. This is both the popular view and one that is substantiated by many academic researches. Sheldon and Eleanor Glueck found that this was 'the case as regards the relationships between the parents, the supervision of the children, provision for recreation outlets in or outside the home, and finally the cohesion of the family as a group'.[1] Many more 'broken homes', those, that is to say, deranged by separation, divorce, death or the prolonged absence of either parent produced delinquents than did unbroken homes. And 'only half as many fathers of the delinquents as of the non-delinquents (40·2 per cent : 80·7 per cent) evidenced warmth, sympathy, and affection toward their boys'.[2] Moreover, they found that 'a far higher proportion of the mothers of the delinquents were frankly indifferent (21·2 per cent : 3·4 per cent) or openly hostile and rejective (6·7 per cent : 1 per cent)'.[3] Nine-tenths of the entire group of the Gluecks' delinquents showed difficulties of social adjustment before puberty, from which they deduced that what they call the 'under-the-roof-culture' and the quality of relationships between parents and children in the home circle are more important factors in the development of criminal attitudes than are the social influences operating in the local milieu. So impressed were they by this discovery that when they came to prepare the social background prediction tables (i.e. simple statistical formulae for gauging whether or not an individual child is likely to become a delinquent in the future) they made use of factors associated with the intimacies of home life rather than employing such indices as gang association or residence in a slum or other sociological notions. The five factors they used for their table were: discipline of child by father, supervision of child by mother, affection for child by father, affection for child by mother, and general cohesiveness of the family. Subsequent applications of the Gluecks' prediction tables to actual case material has indicated that their methods seem to be more successful in predicting what happens to individual children (both delinquents and non-delinquents)

[1] *Unraveling Juvenile Delinquency*, p. 115.
[2] Ibid., p. 125.   [3] Ibid.

than either the judgement of social workers or the forecasts of clinical psychologists and psychiatrists.[1]

A more recent and very important American publication by William and Joan McCord, which consists of a re-examination of the case records left over from an earlier piece of research, has powerfully endorsed the Gluecks' and other criminologists' emphasis on the importance of home life. They conclude: 'our investigation of the origins of criminality reveals that the roots of crime lie deep in the early familial experiences—so deep that only the most intensive measures, applied very early in life, can offer hope of eradicating them.'[2] It is a gloomy conclusion, based upon a careful scrutiny of the facts, and one with which most, if not all, psychiatrists, psychoanalysts and psychologists would agree.

The McCords have some significant points to make on the topic of discipline in the family. One of their most important findings was that 'lax discipline or erratic discipline involving punitiveness had a strong relationship to high criminality'. Their figures indicated clearly 'That the consistency of parental behaviour is more important than the methods parents use for enforcing their demands'.[3] In fact they discovered that children who had been severely but consistently disciplined had the lowest crime rate of the whole sample—a tonic to diehards but a bitter pill for more tender-hearted reformers!

The McCords, like the Gluecks, stress the importance of family cohesion, and concluded that 'The highest crime rates appear in poor neighbourhoods among families which are not cohesive'.[4] In poor neighbourhoods, as they point out, in spite of all environmental temptations, the cohesiveness of the family can save the child from becoming a delinquent: 'significantly fewer boys from cohesive families than from non-cohesive families became criminal—even though their immediate neighbourhood contained a delinquent subculture.'

Like the Gluecks, the McCords found that many delinquents had been emotionally deprived and stunted in personality development as a result of experiencing unsatisfactory relations with their fathers. Warm-hearted fathers, they found, did best

[1] See Appendix II.
[2] *Origins of Crime*, A new Evaluation of the Cambridge-Somerville Youth Study, Columbia University Press, 1959, p. (viii).
[3] Ibid., p. 77.　　　　[4] Ibid., p. 86.

for their boys. However, the father's influence was only secondary. Providing the mother was loving, the impact of the father's personality seemed unimportant, but, in cases where the mother lacked affection, the significance of the father's attitude became correspondingly more vital.

It is extraordinary how many complex academic investigations have ended up by reiterating ancient saws. We all know that home life is crucial in determining what sort of characters children develop. We all know that the unquestioned love of a mother is the basis of sound psychological growth, and that fathers, too, have a job to do in training, disciplining and loving their offspring. 'This study of parental influence,' the McCords concluded, 'points to the fact that maternal love is a primary socializing force. However, paternal warmth is generally effective as a substitute for maternal love . . . rejection is likely to cause criminality.'

Mr. B. Marcus, Principal Psychologist, H.M. Prison, Wakefield, in a fascinating article summed up his investigations in this way:

'The common criminal has quite clearly come from a highly inharmonious home background. As a child he was rejected by his mother, he grew up against a background of constant bickering between his parents, he strongly resented his father, who was a heavy drinker (itself a fact substantially correlated with the quarrelling between the parents), and he himself frequently quarrelled with his brothers and sisters—in short, a degraded background in which love and mutual respect were at a minimum or totally absent, and in which fierce hostilities raged between all the members of the family. A glance at the original matrix shows that all these variables are associated with each other, not always highly, but always positively, indicating a veritable *gestalt* of unfortunate influences.'[1]

It is encouraging that common sense, experience and the researches of the social scientists so readily concur in indicating the value of a happy and affectionate home life for the development of what, in our culture, may be termed well-adjusted normal personalities. It would be surprising and alarming if they did not. The common denominators of criminality, as of

[1] 'A Dimensional Study of a Prison Population', *British Journal of Criminology*, Vol. I, No. 2, 1960, pp. 130–53.

many other disorders, are parental neglect, quarrelsome spouses, and erratically punitive discipline of the children. There is general agreement on this. But where I would myself part company with the McCords and with the Gluecks is on the score of neighbourhood influences, which, in my opinion, they seriously undervalue without adequate consideration. Here again I revert to the important insights to be derived from a sociological approach to crime as to any other kind of human behaviour. I do not wish here to press the disagreement very far in a chapter on the socialization process. All I would point out is that the way in which parents behave toward their children, how they discipline them, whether or not they supervise their leisure time and vet their associates, and how they relate to one another as husband and wife are subject to profound social influences, and that these influences are mediated through the local environment. Erratic and punitive discipline is not only the outcome of the psychological condition of the parents, it is also a social tradition. The failure to express, if not to experience, affection for children is also, in my view, powerfully conditioned by the locality in which particular families live. Or, to put it more academically, the way in which parents interpret their roles is as much a function of the neighbourhood as of their own personalities.

We cannot, I believe, rule out the importance of the subculture either in analysing the origins of delinquency or in examining the network of relationships within the family itself. The fact that a father leaves the supervision of the children substantially to his wife is not merely due to his own mental inclination or laziness or indifference, it is also a result of the fact that that was how his own father behaved and is the way in which the majority of other men in the district seem to interpret their role.

Mr. Marcus, in the article already quoted, draws attention to the importance of the father's role and goes so far as to claim that 'it would appear that the personality of the father has had far more to do with the prisoner's social maladjustment than has the rejection by the mother'.

Two recent books[1] have further highlighted the importance

[1] Robert G. Andry, *Delinquency and Parental Pathology*, Methuen, 1960, J. B. Mays, *On the Threshold of Delinquency*, Liverpool University Press, 1959.

of the father in the etiology of delinquency. Dr. Andry submitted a questionnaire to two groups, each consisting of eighty boys coming from more or less the same type of locality and of roughly the same range of age and intelligence. He deliberately excluded psychopathic or neurotic cases from his sample and any children who derived from broken homes. One group were known delinquents, while the other group had never made an appearance at a juvenile court. He applied a modified version of the same questionnaire to a sub-sample of thirty of the parents of boys in either group, partly to check up on what the children had answered and partly to throw light on the ways in which parents as well as children perceived their roles. Among the many interesting findings that emerge from this investigation, those most germane to this chapter are those which concern the differences of parental roles between the delinquents and the non-delinquents. Delinquents were found to experience 'less open and strong love from their parents (especially from their fathers)' than non-delinquents. They also experienced 'less adequate communication (both environmental and psychological) with their parents (especially with their fathers)'. Their home atmosphere was described as being 'more tense (to which their fathers contribute a substantial share)'. The delinquents, moreover, experienced 'less adequate parental training (especially from their fathers)' and their deviant behaviour 'was less known to and less adequately dealt with by their parents' than was the case with the non-delinquent group.[1]

Dr. Andry's major contribution to our thinking about family life is his insistence on our need to study the attitudes of both parents if we wish to understand why the children behave as they do. He has brought out with convincing clarity the importance of the hitherto neglected roles of fathers in the etiology of delinquency and in this way has valuably modified the almost exclusive preoccupation with maternal roles which followed upon the publication of Dr. Bowlby's investigations at the Tavistock clinic. But his conclusions are somewhat at variance with the findings of the McCords already mentioned. The latter insist, like Bowlby and many other psychiatrists, on the primacy of the mother-child relationship, regarding the role of the father as supportive and of crucial importance only if the mother

[1] Andry, op. cit., p. 126.

proves inadequate or rejecting. Now Andry's families were all normally-structured and none of the children were judged to be either psychopathic or psychoneurotic. But Bowlby's famous forty-four juvenile thieves were. The latter had, moreover, undeniably been deprived of maternal care during their early years. There is a clue here, I think, to the origin of different kinds of delinquency. In the case of the severely deprived child who eventually becomes a delinquent the precipitating cause seems to be loss of mother love and care at the vulnerable infant and early childhood stages. Such a delinquent is gravely disturbed and a chronic recidivist, offering the most stubborn resistance to treatment or punishment alike. The delinquents in Andry's sample seem to be rather different in kind. On the whole they are not what might be called 'psychiatric cases' but children, lacking discipline, guidance and affection, who developed character defects which frequently involved them in illegal activities. In such cases, I believe, the role of the father is of paramount significance at a particular stage of a delinquent boy's life. That is, round about the time of the onset of puberty when the boy has a positive need to identify himself psychologically with an adult figure of the same sex. Says Andry, discussing this point: 'the factor which may well make the major difference between malformation of character in a child and good mental health may be the extent to which father-child relationships have or have not been established satisfactorily.' There is no necessity to carry this idea to the extent that the Freudians do and postulate the presence of an oedipus complex in every case in the pubertal child. As Andry argues, 'a child who perceives his father in a negative way over a period of years may gradually not only develop hostility towards the father but may also at a given time start to project such hostility beyond the family scene on to the world at large.'[1]

III

My own work in connection with a boy's club specially designed to prevent and treat early delinquency, tends to confirm this view of Andry's.[2] We recruited our members in the main

[1] Op. cit., p. 128.
[2] *On the Threshold of Delinquency*, Liverpool University Press, 1959.

from children recommended by teachers and social workers as being either actually or potentially delinquent or in some other way in need of attention. Over the experimental four years' project we serviced in all sixty-six families or households. The lack of adequate male support in most of these homes was one of the most striking outcomes of the enquiry. The table below indicates the incidence of the absentee or incapacitated father most vividly.

'Parents' in Households or Families not carrying out their Responsibilities

Fathers		*Mothers*	
Away at sea or working outside the city	8		
Deserted the home	8	Deserted the home	1
Deceased	4	Deceased	1
Chronically ill or invalids	5		
Legally separated or divorced	6		
	31		2

Nearly half of the fathers of our members (48 per cent) were incapable for one reason or another, even in terms of a very simple analysis, of carrying out their functions regarding the control and supervision of their children adequately. The mothers were, by contrast, paragons of dependability. We found in all too many cases that the father and husband was a marginal figure on the fringe of the family's activities, and flitting in and out of the children's lives unpredictably and undependably. Our evidence suggested, but, of course, did not prove, that there is a connection between delinquency-proneness and the absence or inadequacy of the father or father figure in the home life of boys living in an admittedly criminogenic slum environment. This clearly does not mean that every boy whose father is inadequate or absent at this critical phase of his development is bound to become a criminal. But it does, however, support the common-sense view that the risk is proportionately greater than for the boy who has a father to guide, discipline and support him on the threshhold of adolescence.

IV

We may summarize this chapter by saying that the family is the primary socializing institution in our society. In the give and take of adjustment to brothers and sisters the child learns something of the rights and needs of other people. From his parents he derives both affection and control; a broad code of ethics and the motivation to live by and up to their standards. Parents and the family mediate the outer world to the mind of the growing child. If the values and attitudes maintained in the home are in general accord with those of the wider community, the child is likely to grow up to be a law-abiding citizen. If they are contrary, then the child will very likely develop anti-social tendencies himself. If, for any reason, either parent is absent or incapacitated and thus unable to carry out his or her necessary functions (the mother in early childhood, the father in the pubertal phase pre-eminently) there is a grave danger that psychological maladjustments may result which may, in turn, be conducive to delinquency, especially amongst boys. David Wills, who had devoted his life to the institutional training of deprived and maladjusted children and given us several stimulating books describing the principles with which he works, has said that 'The main ingredients of a successful home (apart from physical necessities and conveniences) are a mother, a father, love and commonsense. And the greatest of these is love.'[1] It may seem ungracious to add a rider to so felicitously phrased a testament but, in the adverse social conditions of an urban slum it would seem advisable to give affection and common-sense equal primacy. Mere affection may not prove sufficient to safeguard the child, and especially the boy, who is always the greater risk, from developing some minor delinquent habits, which, if unwisely handled, may turn in the course of time into a much more seriously maladjusted attitude towards authority. In which case the socialization process may be said to have failed, and the child's delinquency will be a witness to its failure.

[1] *The Barns Experiment*, Allen and Unwin, 1945, p. 63.

CHAPTER 9

VANDALISM AND VIOLENCE

I

Very early on a January morning a few years ago, a peaceful and mostly sleeping Merseyside suburb was the scene of a most terrifying race. Two Jaguars, which had been removed from a city carpark and opened by means of duplicate keys, hurtled terrifyingly along a stretch of straight road at 100 m.p.h. As the second car drew out attempting to overtake the other, the youthful driver lost control. The car mounted the grass verge and struck the adjoining wall in two places, finally overturning and throwing two of the occupants clear. The driver was killed. The four youths who survived the race, two of them very dazed and shaken, drove off as the police arrived but were later charged with and convicted of unlawfully taking away a motor-car without the consent of the owner. One of the youths was further charged with driving while being disqualified. He was sentenced to twelve months' imprisonment and disqualified from driving for a further seven years. The others were all disqualified from driving for five years, one was sent to prison for twelve months, and the youngest, who was nineteen, was remanded in custody to await a report as to his suitability for Borstal training.

In passing sentence, the Judge said that it was one of the worst cases that he had known of a kind of offence which was becoming much too prevalent.

'In London alone in 1959', according to C. H. Rolph, '21,675 cars were either stolen or unlawfully "borrowed". 20,127 of them were recovered . . . but before "recovery" they had been driven through London streets by men or youths who, in many instances, were incompetent or disqualified drivers, caring nothing for the damage and injury they caused or for the consequences of driving without third party or other insurance.'[1]

Offences of this nature are comparatively new phenomena, and are part and parcel of the motorized world in which we now live. In former times, I suppose, the analogous offence was to gallop off on somebody's horse, and beat up the countryside that way.

Untended motors are apparently almost irresistibly tempting both for those who have been banned from driving and for reckless youths who are in search of a 'kick'. The craving for mechanized speed and a gusty delight in the thrills and spills offered by rapid acceleration and roadways abounding in difficult and curious cambered bends is a special affliction of contemporary youth, but one which is by no means confined to that age-group. Middle-aged business men who lick along with their bellies awash in alcohol are equally menacing and much more blameworthy.

In this chapter, however, I want to concentrate on young people and their thirst for adventure and what this appetite means in terms of illegal behaviour. I want to discuss the meaning of the violent conduct of a small proportion of young people which gets so much publicity nowadays and causes kindly and dismayed folk to wonder whether or not more repressive penal measures ought to be introduced. I want to relate this kind of behaviour to what may be called 'normally aggressive conduct', and, without excusing it, to try to throw some light on its nature and origin.

The local and national newspapers present us with an almost monotonous sequence of cases of juvenile hooliganism and youthful vandalism. One finds headlines or reports such as the following in almost every part of the country and for almost every day in the year:

GANG WAR AT DANCE ALLEGED

'Sheath knives, studded belts, bicycle chains, a pick handle and a cut-throat razor were shown to Havant, Hampshire, magistrates yesterday, when 24 youths faced charges arising from a dancehall fight. They were charged with causing an

---

[1] *Common Sense About Crime and Punishment*, Gollancz, 1961, p. 74.

affray, carrying offensive weapons, and maliciously wounding. The M.C. at the dance said that fighting started when about 60 youths came rushing into the hall. Several youths, some armed with knives, attacked some of the dancers. Some of the boys said that about 30 of them had come from Portsmouth by bus, taxi, in cars and on motor-cycles to fight the local gang.'

STABBED IN HEART, HE OWES HIS LIFE TO SURGEONS

'A young Liverpool man, stabbed with a knife which entered the muscles of his heart, owes his life to the skill of the surgeons who carried out an emergency operation at Liverpool Royal Southern Hospital. Five youths appeared accused of attempting to murder a twenty-two-year-old dock labourer and of making an affray. X made a statement admitting being in the fight and told police officers that when the struggle started he walked over, drew out a knife and held it to the chest of Y— who must have slipped and the knife went in.

RECORDER TOLD OF GANGS WHO TERRORIZE SPEKE

'Two gangs of youths are roaming the Speke district at night and terrorizing other boys, Judge Laski, the Recorder, was told at Liverpool Crown Court yesterday. The probation officer said he did not know if the five youths before the court were gang members but the probation service felt that they were on the fringe of a gang. A and B were found guilty of wounding P.C. M— with intent to do him grievous bodily harm and were remanded for a report on their suitability for Borstal. The other three were found guilty of unlawfully wounding and were put on probation for two years.'

TEENAGE GANGS ARE BLACKPOOL MENACE
POLICE ORGANIZING EXTRA SMALL-HOUR PATROLS

'Blackpool town centre is threatened by gangs of teenage rowdies, say local councillors and boarding-house keepers. They complain that many boarding-house rooms in the area are empty because teenage toughs have driven away peace-loving visitors. And they claim the teenagers—

Throw bricks through boarding-house windows;

Hold races on motor-cycles in the streets just before dawn;

Sing and shout in the early hours and threaten anyone who asks them to be quiet and;
Wander round in various stages of undress.

A private hotelier said last night "You would think we were in an Eastern port. We have seen girls walking about wearing nothing more than transparent plastic macs."'

The following headlines are equally typical of what appears every day in the press.

FANS WRECK CARRIAGES AFTER MATCH
BENCH RAP BOY SOCCER FANS
CITY GANG WERE SEEKING TROUBLE
DAY-TRIP BOY STABBED ON PROM
USHERETTES THREATENED BY CITY TEDDY BOYS
THOUSAND TEENAGERS RUN RIOT
MORE DRUNKENNESS AMONGST YOUTH
200 BOYS IN CITY STREET BATTLE

One of the most frightening things that have been happening in recent years is the amount of damage children have done on the railways in various parts of the country, particularly in the north-west. Deliberate attempts have been made to derail trains by placing metal blocks and rubble on the lines and by driving wood wedges between points. In addition, stones have been hurled at passing trains and debris dropped over cuttings on to engines and coaches. One engine driver lost an eye as a result of a stone flung at his cab by a child, and many more footplate men have had near misses from brickbats. In one case children broke into a signal box and altered signals. There have also been cases of juveniles trespassing on electrified lines and sustaining severe injuries themselves. In some places, railway embankments have become regular playgrounds for local children in out-of-school hours. And what is so revealing in these cases is the fact that very often the parents seem to know where they are yet take no action in the matter. They just let them go and do whatever they want, no doubt keeping their fingers crossed and hoping that no disaster will befall. I have a vivid memory of a small boy of perhaps eight who, when found sitting on a bank at the side of the Manchester–Liverpool line, told the T.V. interviewer that his mother 'didn't mind him trespassing on the railway but she would shout at him and hit him if he got his clothes dirty and torn while he was there'. Such is the basis of much modern parental discipline: it amounts to 'do what you like but don't give me any trouble'.

In an article printed in the *Liverpool Daily Post* in April 1956 there was an account of mass destructiveness on the part of school children of a kind which, while it may occur on a somewhat lesser scale in other parts of the country, epitomizes the organized destructiveness of many youngsters nowadays. I quote some highly relevant paragraphs:

'The Easter school holidays of this year will be remembered by many Liverpool people for one of the worst outbreaks of vandalism which Merseyside has ever known. A house and tennis clubhouse wrecked, cars smashed, trees uprooted and parks despoiled—for the unfortunate, unsuspecting people who have suffered from these destructive attacks it has been a reign of terror.'

'The series of incidents seemed to have been sparked off by the worst—the newly-renovated house in Hartington Road, Wavertree, which was broken up by seven boys, aged eight to thirteen. The owner said it looked as though a bomb had exploded in the house. Damage was estimated at £450. One of the boys, it was said in court, took his own pickaxe to help demolish the interior. A six foot hole in a brick wall between the lounge and kitchen was made, fireplaces were wrenched out and thrown downstairs, floorboards were ripped up, windows smashed and plaster ceilings ruined.'

It was the same sad tale of merciless destruction in the case of the cars and the clubhouse.

'All over the city, the corporation has been faced with the problem of children breaking and uprooting newly-planted trees along the roads and in the parks. Dam Woods at Speke looked as though it had been shelled by artillery. . . . All these cases have one thing in common; utter wantonness and pointlessness, etc.'

II

It is probably impossible to decide whether or not instances of the sort we have been describing have increased by fifty or a hundredfold in the last quarter of a century. But there can be little doubt that they are much more numerous and that the audacity and impudence with which they are carried out is something of a new social phenomenon. Tendencies which in the past may have to a considerable extent been inhibited have recently been given a much freer rein. And for this we must blame the indifference of the adult members of the community and the laxity and indulgence of parents in particular.

Not only are many of the acts committed by children and young people of great physical hazard to themselves and a danger to the public, they also cost the community a considerable sum of money. How much is not known, but if we take one item, viz. the replacement of street lamps in one provincial city in one year the cost to the public purse could be anything between four and five thousand pounds—enough that is to say, to pay the salaries of four youth workers or two psychiatrists.

How can we begin to explain this mounting tide of juvenile hooliganism? Until we know what causes it and what social conditions and psychological attitudes foster it, we will never be able to tackle the problem.

We must begin our explanation, I believe, of the increasing number of violent offences committed both against property and against persons by pointing out that these things are merely extensions of perfectly normal tendencies. Just as theft is rooted in the nature of our society, so is aggressiveness a necessary component of our human nature. We must not make the fatal mistake of assuming that they are in some way novel phenomena or, in essence, abnormal happenings.

We return to the explanation of crime which has been implicit and explicit throughout the foregoing chapters. Crime is normal. It is normal for several reasons, because society is organized both co-operatively and competitively. If an individual is to make any sort of success of his life he must learn at an early age to hit out at his environment, make his mark in the basic struggle for survival and eminence. As George Simmel argued, 'Conflict is a form of socialization'. Without some form of conflict or competition we would very likely to be much more inert personalities than our culture demands.

I have been tremendously struck by the way in which my own small son, during his pre-schooldays, was induced to bend his mind more assiduously to his academic labours to achieve literacy and numeracy. On his own, in the family kitchen and under the guidance of his mother, he made some rather painful and reluctant progress, scrawling his alphabet and learning their sounds. But as soon as a slightly older neighbour's child was introduced, who had already commenced formal education, he immediately quickened his pace of learning and execution. Not to be outdone by his slightly more advanced playmate, he responded to the stimulus of competition and began to aggress towards his own ignorance in order to be able to beat his friends at their own game.

This homely, and to some minds perhaps naive, illustration indicates the nature of group life and the way in which the individual is encouraged to develop his innate capacities by competition with other people.

From a small boy struggling with his alphabet to the violence of teenage gangs may seem a far and impossible cry. Yet I am convinced that we have here the clue to the normalcy of much aggressive behaviour. Aggression is necessary, nay even a good thing, within certain limits. It is individually and socially desirable. Beyond such limits, however, it tends towards an anti-social and pathological condition. It is a further example of the hoary classical tag, *corrupta optima pessima*.

We must now take the normalcy argument one stage further by pointing out once again that men and women are called on to play very different roles in our kind of society. Males are expected to be more active socially than females. They are to earn their own living, be the breadwinners, the strong arms of family and state, fighting our country's hot and cold wars. They are expected to be fearless and unflinching in the face of physical dangers, to be unperturbed by risky hazards, to undergo bodily strain without breaking down. In order to be like this, they must in their formative years be faced with difficult and even dangerous tasks. They must learn 'to strive, to seek, to find and not to yield'. Occasionally one hears of a young man being lost in Snowdonia, caught in a mist on a dangerous face when involved on some lonely exercise designed to test and strengthen his virility. His dead body is found two days later by the local search party, as he lies at the foot of a ravine silently witnessing to the logic of education for masculinity as it has been known and inculcated down the ages. His death in such circumstances is as sacrificial as is that of the astronaut in his unrecovered capsule or of Scott, Wilson and Bowers in the frozen snows of their antarctic tent. We do not say that such deeds are criminal, lunatic or even unnecessary. We salute their valour and mourn the fallibility of human strength pitted against unyielding natural forces. But, while men are men, we know that such things will happen if the race is to endure.

It has also been argued by some psychologists and sociologists that in societies where women have attained equality, even dominance, as to some extent in contemporary U.S.A., the male members of the society are obliged to reinforce their masculinity by exaggerated displays of their physical prowess. This is said to arise from an over-identification with the mother during childhood and to be associated with fears of homo-sexuality. While there may well be some element of truth in this analysis, I believe that more general social and psychological pressures account for the widespread phenomenon of boyish daring and love of adventure.

There are, of course, many other ways of showing prowess, avenues of useful aggression other than purely physical. There is the fight against disease, plague, ignorance, and fear—the epic of a Schweitzer or a Damien.

But to the young, physical courage has a special appeal. I would go further and claim that any youth or boy must, at some stage of his development, learn to come to terms with fear. He must know at first hand the dread of destruction. He must hang over his own precipice alone and feel his blood race with the arduous challenge to his skill and endurance. He must experi-ence fear on his own pulses, know it and face it in his own body if he is ever to be master of himself. I have no doubt that, at a somewhat less rigorous level, the same experience is necessary for girls. Only, in our culture, their target is set rather differ-ently, and they are called to psychological and physical courage of a special order in bearing children. God knows there are abysses enough in maternity!

Once again in attempting to grapple with this important topic I want to recall my own childhood. I am, I suppose, one of the most cowardly of creatures and from a fairly early age have been blessed or cursed (probably both!) by an acutely vivid imagination of what might happen in an extremity. Yet

I too remember a phase in boyhood when I had to experience and master fear at first hand. One summer holiday long ago, my family were staying at a seaside resort. Behind the boarding house where we were living was a high cliff which overhung deep water at high tide. For several days on end, all unknown to my parents, I went out and forced myself to climb the cliff from the safe shoreside and go right round the rocks until I hauled myself, wet with sweat and almost rigid with fear, on to the cliff top. For several minutes I hung over the pounding sea, gripping outcrops of rock and tough grasses. One slip would have shot me into the water below, where, even if no limbs had been broken, I would have drowned, since I could not swim and nobody was ever in sight to come to my rescue. I still shudder recalling that exploit. Yet, I forced myself to undergo this perilous climb for several days on end. Why I did it, at that remote time, I could not have said. But looking back, I can understand something of the fearful compulsion that was laid upon me.

III

We can now return to consider the violence and vandalism of teenage youths and children in modern urban communities. In the slums of our big cities life is highly artificial and tremendously cramped. Family life is somewhat unregulated and there is little effective parental control. Young people are left very much to their own resources and to the cramping limitations of their sterile environment. For them the back of a lorry bumping uphill from the docks is a challenge to dangerous endurance, and the very smallest will swing there close the the wheels with the greatest nonchalance. Swiftly moving traffic offers a fine spice of adventure. To get as close as possible to a passing vehicle without flinching, to cross the road at the most hazardous corner, to dart in and out of traffic forcing the drivers to brake and curse—here is the thrill and tonic of illicit danger which gives zest to the meanest life!

It is not possible for all to travel to the Himalayas, to traverse the Antarctic continent and reach the pole to gasp with Hillary on top of the world or stand with Joe Brown on the summit of Kangchenjunga. For the slum boy who has what the Services call 'guts', the side of the warehouse is his mountain chasm, the railway cuttings his adventure course; night watchmen, patrolling police and shopkeepers are worthy antagonists to test his steel against, and street football and forays among the limited outlets for competitiveness.

This is, I am aware, an oversimplification, an extreme picture. But it contains the kernel of an important truth. If home life is unsatisfactory, if there are no youth organizations to meet his need and challenge his initiative, if the substitutes of camping, boxing, swimming, organized games, and physical training, opportunities for the development of manual skills or mechanical interests are lacking or inadequately available, such substitutes for legitimate self-expression as those listed above will very likely be invoked. And if, in the neighbourhood, there are juvenile gangs to encourage and instigate lawlessness, the road to criminality is accordingly much more likely for the lad without discipline, leadership or the hope of a worthwhile future to work towards.

There is nothing inevitable about a boy's descent into crime. But in certain adverse circumstances the likelihood is increased. We cannot say that the five youths who knifed the man on the street corner, having apparently picked a gratuitous quarrel with him, had no alternative form of behaviour open to them. Nor can we say that the thirty youths who set out from Portsmouth with the set intention of beating up the local gang at Havant did so merely because their legitimate aspirations and their natural love of adventure were frustrated. Nor would I argue that the bands of young marauders roaming the streets of the new housing estate and terrorizing respectable citizens, or ripping cinema seats to ribbons and assaulting and insulting usherettes could have done no other. It is no service to youth to argue that their increased drunkenness, disrespect for law and order and lust for violent excitement are inevitable and wholly natural in origin. All I wish to do is to point out that many, if not all, the atrocity stories mentioned in this chapter have something in common with normal behaviour and spring, in however warped a form, from common and even desirable human needs and urges.

People who complain that 'young thugs' go about carrying weapons do not usually complain about scouts with sheath knives. Yet the habit is not so very different. Young people like to go armed. There is a genuine thrill and satisfaction in carrying a weapon. I well remember how horrified I was when I discovered that some of my older club members went on ferry-boat cruises every Saturday night and mingled with the dancing crowd carrying coshes in their pockets. I doubt if they ever used or even seriously contemplated using them. But they liked to feel them there under their jackets. This made me think again of my own boyhood and I was amazed to remember a phase through which I passed, probably round about the age of twelve, when I sallied forth night after night to walk alone in the darkness. I used to take the same track every time, alongside a deserted park and a cemetery—a lonely and rather frightening journey I had no ostensible need to make. Yet I went there night after wintry night and in my overcoat pocket I carried a home-made cosh, made out of an old drum-stick and a metal paper-weight. It was quite a formidable weapon, and, though I never had occasion to defend myself, it was a real reassurance. It is just another example of the way in which fear and the unknown exert a powerful compulsion on youngsters, and how, at a particular developmental stage, we are compelled by strong inner forces to expose ourselves to such experiences.

IV

The question responsible citizens should concern themselves with is why in particular does this love of adventure become pathological? How does this warping process take place and why? Need these fundamentally sound human impulses become perverted? Or is there something in society itself, something perverting in social experience, that fosters such malign attitudes and behaviour to which we should turn our attention instead of reacting by clamouring for more punitive treatment and stricter repressive measures?

We know that the measured amount of violence has gone up steeply in recent years. In 1938, 2·7 thousand crimes of violence against the person were recorded. The figure for 1959 was 13·9. Persons in 1938 found guilty of this offence constituted 1·6 in thousands, whereas in 1959 they totalled 9·1. While we have to acknowledge that this group of crimes covers a very mixed bag, such as abortion and concealment of birth, and while we must also be quite clear that an assault is sometimes no more than a verbal threat and can consist of the lightest of physical contacts, we must still admit that there has very likely been an increase and that the seventeen to twenty-one age group appear to be much more prone to violence (however interpreted) than their predecessors.[1] In so far as this is probably true, we must express concern about the trends. But, by way of understanding, if not of mitigation, are there any social factors peculiar to the present generation, which have made the general climate more conducive to physical brutality and encouraged recklessness and hooliganism?

Here we enter upon somewhat uncertain interpretations and subjective judgements. It is impossible to prove causal connections between two social facts without the most careful and detailed scientific study. Even then it is not always possible to show anything more than a strong probability relationship. Nevertheless I would myself be prepared to assert that the present generation has been brought up in a world of unprecedented violence, a world in which almost unlimited brutality has been unleashed and widely discussed and frankly publicized. The shadow of the swastika still lies across Europe and memories of concentration camps and their abominable practices remain vividly with us. The threat of total nuclear war is the constant background to our lives, and the possibility of annihilation is an immediate not a remote possibility. Strife and conflict are not new phenomena, but never before have the physical clashes between people and states seemed so close to us. The fighting in Algeria, the atrocities in the Congo are brought into our sitting-rooms and as we eat our suppers we can at the same time witness these appalling scenes on our television screens.

It is impossible to gauge the impact of all this on the psychology of youth. It is equally impossible to deny that it can have no influence whatsoever in conditioning their attitudes. In his

[1] At the same time it is salutary to point out that violence is still a fractional problem. As Lady Wootton said in her Clarke Hall Lecture, 1959, p. 11, 'The lurid prominence which the press gives to individual instances of violence fosters the belief that these are frequent incidents of everyday life: one cannot but be struck by the astonishment voiced by many members of the public on learning that the number of persons over the age of 17 convicted of crimes of violence amounts to less than 19 in every 100,000 of the population.'

book *The Seduction of the Innocent*,[1] Dr. F. Wertham has given us a horrifying picture of the sadistic violence served up for the enjoyment of American children (and until recently, when government banned their import here, of British youngsters) by the producers of the weekly comics. Dr. Wertham describes them as 'a distillation of viciousness'. 'The world of the comic books,' he says, 'is the world of the strong, the ruthless, the bluffer, the shrewd deceiver, the torturer and the thief. All the emphasis is on exploits where somebody takes advantage of somebody else, violently, sexually, or threateningly. . . . Hostility and hate set the pace of almost every story.'[2]

I have no wish to exaggerate these elements in cheap literature, the cinema and television programmes, or to suggest that children who are soundly brought up by firm and affectionate parents are unduly disturbed by what they see or hear. But those who derive from unsatisfactory homes, who are already moving towards psychological maladjustments of various sorts, are not so likely to be uninfluenced. Nor, it seems to me, ought we to take the risk that a single child should suffer unnecessary stimulation by the portrayal of violence in any shape or form. Robin Hood and his men against the Sheriff of Nottingham and bad King John, or the Lone Ranger and Tonto tracking down acknowledged 'baddies' are one thing. Pictures of girls being raped, blinded, flogged, of Negroes being hanged and other men being mutilated and assaulted in a hundred horrific ways are quite another kettle of fish. Children love and respond to action, but they are often horrified by watching anything abnormal or too close to the world of their own experience. Whatever the results, it seems to me that it is criminal to permit adult members of the community to sell in any shape or form stories which are allegedly designed for the child market which glorify physical torture and present examples of sadistic violence purely for commercial gain. Here we have a striking illustration of the way in which the values institutionalized in our society can at times be clearly seen to work against moral and ethical principles.

[1] Museum Press, 1955.   [2] Ibid., p. 94.

V

Violence in Britain, however, is played in a very minor key when compared with the horrific activities of America's so-called 'Kill-for-Thrill Kids', who do not stop at torture of people who have not harmed them nor even at murder, apparently, in order to gratify their lust for excitement. In 1953 half those arrested for burglary in the United States were under eighteen years of age. 17 per cent of the country's known drug addicts were less than twenty-one while that age group also accounted for 15 per cent of all homicide cases. Rape and assaults are also disproportionately high amongst American juveniles. The problem is now so gigantic that they can talk of having no less than a million juvenile delinquents on their hands by the mid-nineteen-sixties. In comparison with such figures our own youth problems pale into parochial insignificance.

Violence is indeed never far from the surface even in the most civilized of modern communities. At any moment, given the slightest encouragement, it will flare up volcanically, and the psychopaths and sadists will seize their opportunity to wallow in hate and conflict. In 1958 and 1959 the shadow of irrational violence, artificially stimulated and fostered by atavistic political interests, flared up in the notorious race riots of Notting Hill. Gangs of youths went out 'hell-bent', in their own words, on 'nigger-hunting', armed with iron bars, clubs and knives. In May 1959 a coloured man was murdered by white youths. The very name Notting Hill lingers thereafter as a stigma of national shame and degradation. But what was most disquieting in the many press photographs of the disturbances in that area was the obvious juvenility and youthfulness of the crowds who took part in and apparently seemed to enjoy the street meetings and mêlées that took place night after night.[1]

To look at another and more privileged section of the community, it is clear that the university student population is more irresponsible than ever before. The so-called rag days which have been institutionalized over many years, permitting the undergraduates to let their hair down a little by entertaining

[1] Similar recent racial riots in Middlesbrough which resulted in the death of a coloured youth are further evidence of the social volcano on which we so complacently sit.

the public in order to raise funds for some good cause, have recently degenerated in some university cities into demonstrations of blatant hooliganism. Processions through the streets have ended up in pitched battles and members of the public, including women and children, have been assaulted and injured. There is no doubt in some cases that the men students set out with the intention, not of amusing the spectators and raising money, but of having a damned good fight. University authorities in these instances have been forced to intercede and ban future street processions.

It is only one step from the organized street rag to the race riot. The same elements are involved and come to the fore, seizing their opportunity with both hands to break the peace and ventilate aggression. Children and youths who witness such incidents come to accept them as natural occurrences. And when they read that four of their favourite soccer stars have been prosecuted for squirting water over people's faces in the streets of Manchester 'for a lark' it is not surprising that they themselves get up to mischief on the railways and anywhere else they think they can get away with it.

The point need not be laboured further that the shadow of the Bomb hangs over us all, that violence simmers uneasily beneath the surface of our social life, waiting to erupt, and that there are many reckless and even pathologically-minded individuals eager to exploit any explosive situation for the sheer hell of it. The thrills of speed, the availability of cars and fast motor bikes are further exacerbating features of the contemporary scene. And children and young people are above all susceptible to example and prone to imitation. Yet aggression, as we have argued, is a necessary ingredient of human nature. But it must be understood, controlled and diverted into socially acceptable channels if it is to work constructively and not destructively within the body of society.

I cannot end this discussion better than by quoting wise words from the well-known psychiatrist, Dr. J. D. W. Pearce: 'Fifty years ago sex was taboo. Now it is aggression which is taboo. Yet aggression subserves good as well as bad purposes ... Society would be wise to examine its own aggressiveness and the aggressive needs of children ... the community usually answers aggression with aggression. .... Safety first in childhood means personal security first in later life. If society were to cultivate in children qualities such as endurance, loyalty, responsibility for others, their aggressive energy would be consumed in useful, healthy activities. . . . The real question is not what preventive measures are needed but why little or nothing is done.'[1]

[1] *Juvenile Delinquency*, Cassell, 1952, pp. 359–61.

CHAPTER 10

THE RACIAL FACTOR IN CRIME

I

Men and women, and to a much lesser extent, children, tend to think of other people, and particularly of strangers, in a stereotyped way. This desire to put people into pigeon holes, to affix labels to groups, seems an inveterate human habit. Undoubtedly bad newspaper reporting helps to foster this intellectual weakness. Thus any group of youths who are said to be causing any kind of disturbance are always labelled 'Teddy Boys', any group of political malcontents in remote parts of the world are 'Reds' or Communists, while at home they are decried as 'agitators'. Having affixed the condemnatory labels there is no longer any need to prove objectively that they are anti-social, dangerous or wicked.

The same stereotyping process has vitiated race relations throughout the world. Members of different ethnic groups are foreigners and suspected of ungentlemanly conduct on sight. Coloured people are obvious targets for racial prejudice and subsequent discrimination. The notion that Negroes are somehow biologically inferior lingers obdurately even in self-styled Christian communities. Various absurd myths, never put to the test of scientific validation, are still current in crude circles. For example, that Negroes are more sexually potent than white people, that Jews are misers, that Englishmen all play cricket and never smile except grimly through tightly compressed lips.

All this has its amusing side. But it is also deadly serious. In the modern world where most communities are racially mixed, where miscegenation is constantly taking place and ethnic groups mingle and merge to an extent unknown before, such prejudices foment trouble and lead to physical hostilities in addition to perpetuating discriminatory practices.

When things go wrong and social evils afflict a society, certain irresponsible and evil members make use of the existence of minorities of all sorts, racial, religious or class, as scapegoats to bear the burden of the general guilt and anger. Thus the Germans tended to blame the Jews for losing the first world war. In fact any minority group possessing conspicuous features may be singled out and blamed for the common failure. By projecting our shortcomings on to other people we relieve ourselves of the pain of responsibility and by persecution obtain the relief of action. By eliminating the minority we hope to dispose of our problems. On Merseyside, for example, attempts have been made to blame the Irish or the Roman Catholics for the high juvenile crime rates. Because three-quarters of the inmates of Remand Homes are said to be Roman Catholics, so the argument runs, Catholicism is the chief cause of delinquency! The fact that such a thesis can easily be refuted by the assembling of objective evidence does not prevent prejudiced people clinging obstinately to their opinion and giving it verbal expression.

Any criminological theory which is to be worthy of the adjective 'scientific' must take account of all the facts and not just a selection. Facts indeed should come first and theories follow after. If it can be shown statistically that there are differential crime rates between various groups or classes of individuals, it is not enough to pick on one distinctive feature and use that as a simple single causal explanation. In the case of the Liverpool Irish, to pick out their ethnic origin or religious affiliation and ignore their social rank or the type of neighbourhood they live in or their economic means is to blind our eyes to other much more significant factors. Criminology cannot be advanced by prejudice, hearsay or gossip. Pre-selective theories are not scientific. Yet the mere fact of biological and ethnic distinctions is still frequently taken as *in itself* sufficient evidence to prove criminality. In some parts of the United States there is a widely held belief that all Negroes are morally inferior beings, even degenerates. In South Africa the political structure is based on a similar wholly fictitious theory of the absolute inferiority of the coloured citizens which is as wicked and absurd as the Nazi doctrines of the purity of so-called Aryan blood.

II

In the criminological field, most of the work that has so far been done on the relationship between race, place of nativity and criminality has been carried out in the United States. For very good reasons. For one thing that country possesses a probably unique mixture of racial minorities and immigrants: Negro, Indian, Chinese, Japanese, Filipino and European. Secondly, in the United States there is a social tradition for tough honesty which demands the public facing of unpleasant facts, as the work of the Kefauver Committee well demonstrates or the meticulously detailed bulletins which are issued regarding the President's health. In Britain, alas, there is a less admirable social convention tending towards the glossing over of unpalatable truths. We miscall it over here good manners and gentlemanly tact and like to pretend problems don't exist by refusing to face them in the open.

Edwin Sutherland[1] has shown that the official arrest statistics in all American states reveal that Negroes, Indians and Chinese have rates about three times as high as for all the white population, although, interestingly enough, the Japanese have somewhat lower rates even than the whites. Commitment rates to Federal prisons showed that Negroes, Indians and Chinese are between four and six times as high as for the white members of the community. The rate for Filipinos is a little more than twice but the Japanese only half as much as the whites. But we have no reliable information about the relative numbers in the various racial groups at risk in the whole population. The figures available, which Sutherland quotes, are confined to those prosecuted and punished.

The homicide rate for Negroes in the American South is indeed several times higher than amongst the whites but lower than amongst the whites in New England—a most suggestive fact hinting at exacerbation and retaliation. Sutherland has shown also that, while Negro arrests for homicide and for assault are relatively more frequent than for whites, the arrest rate for rape is lower than it is for the whites, thus destroying a popular stereotype!

There may well be an element of discrimination against

---

[1] *Principles of Criminology*, especially Chapter 8.

coloured and in favour of the white people as far as arrests and prosecutions go. Police officers may on the one hand very well feel reluctant to charge members of their own ethnic group, while on the other, being over-zealous in prosecuting 'outsiders'. Thorsten Sellin has produced some evidence to show that this is very likely the case. He has shown that Negroes who offend against white people have a higher percentage of arrests and undergo stiffer punishment (i.e. imprisonment), than is the case for white members of the community who offend against one another.

The evidence available is extremely sketchy and fragmentary for this is a topic which, for obvious reasons, has attracted little attention. But such researches as have been undertaken support the view that the idea that certain racial groups are more criminal than others is illusory. All efforts based on scientific method to prove that coloured people are worse offenders and more criminally disposed than white people have failed. What remains is mere prejudice and unfounded suspicion. In any case there can be no valid reason for believing that skin colour or racial heredity is ever an important determinant of any kind of behaviour. On its own it is probably a neutral factor, and it is only when combined with other things, such as racial discrimination and residence in an underprivileged neighbourhood, that it even appears to have any criminogenic significance. Most criminals, as we have constantly argued in this text, are made by experience rather than born to be lawbreakers. General social influences seem to be quite sufficient to account for the criminal and delinquent activities of both white people and coloured folk.

There are indications that what may be called general social factors and patterning operate for the coloured as for others living in the large urban centres. The distribution of Negro juvenile delinquents, for instance, has been shown to be similar to the general trend. There is the usual bulge round about the inner urban core with a decrease in the suburbs and in the peripheral regions. Moreover, the ratios between the sexes are in line with the general picture; Negro girls, that is to say, are strikingly less delinquent than their brothers. Bernard Lander in his study of delinquency in Baltimore has shown that 'in areas of the city where the proportion of Negroes is below 50 per cent, there is comparatively more Negro delinquency than in areas with over 50 per cent Negroes, with the lowest delinquency rates in districts almost completely black.'[1] Lander maintains that tension and juvenile crime are highest in localities where the two groups, coloured and white, are nearest numerical equality, where, that is to say, more socially inflammable situations are likely to exist. Where the Negroes are in the majority or where they constitute a very small minority the crime rates are lowest. 'Lander's conclusion,' says Dr. Hermann Mannheim, Britain's most eminent criminologist, 'which seems to be well-founded, is that Negro delinquency is not a function of race as such but a reflection of social instability.'[1]

Similar findings and explanations have been published for Chicago, where delinquency amongst Negroes has risen on account of the influx of refugees from the south. According to Franklin Frazier the highest crime rates are located in areas of most recent Negro settlement and are lowest in districts where they have lived longer. Says Frazier:

'The widespread disorganization of Negro family life must be regarded as an aspect of the civilization process in the Negro group. It is not merely a pathological phenomenon. The stability of family relationships, which one finds among the isolated peasant groups in rural communities of the South, is not the same kind of stability which is achieved by the families in the areas of the Negro community in Chicago. In the latter case the Negro has learned to live in a more complex world. As the Negro is brought into contact with a large world through increasing communication and mobility, disorganization is a natural result. The extent of the disorganization will depend upon the fund of social tradition which will become the basis for reorganization of life on a more intelligent and more efficient basis.'[2]

According to Donald Taft[3] the general factor making for criminality is 'not a cultural, racial or individual one' at all. 'Rather

---

[1] *Group Problems in Crime and Punishment*, Routledge and Kegan Paul, 1955, pp. 198–9.
[2] Quoted in Walter C. Reckless, *Criminal Behaviour*, McGraw Hill, 1940, p. 52.
[3] *Criminology*, New York, Macmillan 1956, pp. 341–3.

it is a sociological factor of stability concerned with the maintenance of social regulation.' In his view opportunities for violation of the law are more frequent and common in unstable societies and in parts of a community where instability and rootlessness are rife.

III

Mere membership of a minority group is, however, not enough to explain the few facts we have. On Sutherland's showing the Japanese group are more law abiding than other low status groups and even than the host society. In Britain it is generally believed that the Jews and the Chinese minorities are exceptionally peaceable folk. The possible explanation is that, as far as the Japanese in America and the Jews and Chinese in this country go, they have no desire to lose their racial identity. For this reason it may be inferred they do not regard themselves as constituting a socially inferior status group. That they experience discriminatory practice cannot be denied. But it is their reaction to prejudice that is crucial. But in the case of Negroes, especially in the United States, there is a strong desire to be treated as normal citizens, a wish, that is to say, to be accepted as equals and to be identified with the mass. We may, therefore, deduce that where discriminatory practice is most damaging is when there is a group who are eager for absorption and who, at the same time, have reason to believe that they are regarded as inferior people. If they further experience real doubts and have secret fears about their own worthiness, then such a minority group is likely to be particularly unstable and aggressive. Hence, perhaps, more lawless in their behaviour. John Dollard in his famous study of *Caste and Class in a Southern Town*[1] put forward his theory of displacement to account for the fact that the Negroes were more physically aggressive and prone to attacks, not so much on the white population, as upon one another. According to Dollard's theory of displacement, aggression is built up over a period of time as a result of experiencing discrimination. But the Negroes feel themselves unable to hit back at their more powerful white fellow citizens and so fall to quarrelling and fighting among themselves. Aggression, once created by frustration, must find an outlet somewhere. In this

[1] New Haven: Yale University Press, 1937.

case it is vented upon less powerful peers who socially cannot do them much harm. In the same way, perhaps, in a somewhat repressive school, the outraged pupils may take it out of one another by bullying because they are afraid to aggress against their prepotent ushers. The bullies of the class, like the boppers of the low-grade subcultural locality, are aware of their inferiority and strive to attain some kind of status and to draw attention to themselves by swaggering and hooliganism for which alone they have some skill.

As we said a few paragraphs ago, there is insufficient evidence to enable us to make categorical statements about the relationship between race and ethnic origin and crime. But what we do know lends little support to the idea that some ethnic groups are inherently more criminally inclined than others. The consensus of informed academic opinion on the subject seems to suggest that the delinquencies of coloured children and the crimes of coloured adults are ultimately explicable in general psychological and sociological terms which are the same for all races and classes. That is to say, such factors as residence in an underprivileged neighbourhood, contact with delinquent behaviour patterns, together with feelings of frustration and inferiority, provide the most powerful criminogenic forces for white and coloured people alike.

IV

This view is further substantiated by study of a similar and related problem, that of non-coloured immigrants. The United States is, of course, *par excellence* the home of the world's refugees. Poles, Czechs, Irish, Italians, Germans, Russians, Sicilians, Finns have poured into America during the past hundred years seeking either political, economic or religious asylum. In their early days in the strange new society, these hundreds of thousands of immigrants and refugees must have found it difficult to adjust their minds and behaviour to the tempo of life and the conditions in an alien land. The clash of *mores* and customs between their former and their new manner of living must have been perplexing and at times disturbing, and no doubt many immigrants were so emotionally disoriented that they became mentally ill. Such an experience, while obviously conducive to psychological breakdown, would not be likely to make them more criminal or criminally disposed unless they were already so inclined before they arrived. In the main, immigrants reveal lower crime rates than the native born members of the host society.[1] It's rather as though the country cousins are not yet up to the wickedness and pace of city life and suffer from cultural lag. It is also true, as we have seen, that crime rates vary between the immigrant groups themselves, some settling down more easily than others. Evidence of the cultural hangover that they seem to bring with them from their previous lives is to be found in the types of offences which seem to characterize specific immigrant groups. The Irish are more frequently convicted of drunkenness than the Germans, while the Italians commit many more homicides and physical assaults than either of the other groups, but, for their part, the Germans are more prone to burglary. Chinese offences seem characteristically to be connected with the drug traffic and so on. In other words the immigrants, when they do offend, tend to commit the types of offences for which they are well known in the land from which they came rather than offences associated with the new culture.

The story is entirely different, however, as far as the younger generation is concerned. Immigrants' children have on the whole higher crime and delinquency rates than their parents and they also tend to commit the kinds of offences that they see being committed in their new environment. Their behaviour approximates more to that of the host society than to the traditional manners of their forefathers. This is what is generally known in the U.S.A. as 'the second generation phenomenon'. The young new Americans are more American than the Americans, in the same way that the new recruit to the crack regiment is more keen to maintain its traditional styles and rituals than even the older officers themselves. He falls over backwards to impress the world with his membership of an admired group.

The second generation tends to increase its criminal activities as its absorption into the host community proceeds. Indeed to some extent its acceptance of new types of crime and crime rates may be regarded as an index of successful absorption and assimilation. This underlines the significance of social tradition

[1] For a full discussion of these data see Edwin Sutherland and Cressey, *Principles of Criminology*, pp. 138–50.

in human behaviour and indicates the need, in every case, to study the criminal within the framework of the community in which he lives. Sociological understanding reinforces psychological analysis.

The association, then, between immigration and crime is explained in a similar way to the alleged relation between criminality and race. Immigrants and refugees are usually economically handicapped people and hence they tend to settle in the poorest and most dilapidated part of cities where lodgings are available and in the premises that members of the host society have vacated as unsuitable. They make invariably for the rooming-house district of the town, where social misfits and social failures and inadequate personalities also foregather to create the traditional slum subculture. Necessity drives the immigrants there, not choice, and most of them strive to get away from such insalubrious surroundings as soon as possible. In so far as they derive from different cultures and have been brought up to accept *mores* which are at times in conflict with those generally accepted in the host society, their presence may be said to increase the lack of homogeneity in the rooming-house district and make for social instability. Moreover, inevitable problems of inter-marriage arise with their resultant exacerbation of inter-racial prejudice and hostility. The race riots in Liverpool which broke out in 1948 were thought to have been triggered off by sexual jealousy. The white residents resented seeing their claims for female attention brushed aside in favour of coloured men and took the law into their own hands by attacking any coloured man they found in the streets. In times of economic hardship, also, when there is fierce competition for scarce employment, similar resentments are likely to flare up if some immigrants get jobs when the natives are refused. This hostility arises, of course, irrespective of the immigrants' superior ability or the relative incompetence of some of the natives.

V

The general findings on this topic can fairly be summarized by saying that membership of particular ethnic groups and the fact that people have newly arrived in a country have not of themselves any necessary criminogenic effect. They are only significant as ancillary influences contributing to the wider social problems which inevitably arise whenever there is instability and a confusion of standards and values (sometimes referred to by sociologists as a state of anomie). They contribute a little additional fuel to fires that are already smouldering and which may break out in riots and crime at any opportune moment when adverse economic conditions in the wider society create feelings of insecurity. As we have already noted, there is a psychopathic fringe in any large modern community waiting its excuse to erupt and aggress against law and order. Colour, racial and religious differences are used as excuses by the malcontents to foment trouble, but by themselves they can never be regarded as primary causes of crime.

CHAPTER II

HOUSING AND DELINQUENCY

I

We have no knowledge or proof of a direct causal relationship existing between the houses in which people live and their behaviour, although it seems reasonable to suppose that there is indeed some connection however hard to isolate and describe. Stuart Chapin[1] has produced some evidence to show that admission to a New Haven Housing Development effected a significant reduction in juvenile delinquency over the comparatively short period of time of four and a half years but few studies of this kind have been made elsewhere. We do know for certain, however, that inadequate accommodation is a characteristic of those slum areas where delinquency is deep-rooted and endemic and that it represents one aspect of the total problem. Professor Ferguson has epitomized the problems of the slum environment in a telling phrase as 'the co-existence of many adversities'. And one of these adversities is surely unsatisfactory accommodation.

Although a statistical correlation has been shown very frequently to exist between slums and blighted neighbourhoods and a relatively high crime rate, this is probably more a reflection of the general pattern of social life than the result of the mere physical environment. As Dr. Hermann Mannheim convincingly showed in his study of Cambridge during the last war, centrally situated and overcrowded wards are not inevitably more delinquent than the newer suburbs. I quote the relevant passage from his book:

[1] *Experimental Design in Sociological Research*, Harper Bros., New York, 1947, pp. 97–9.

'Here, one of the most central and most crowded wards, Market, has one of the lowest percentage figures, and for Petersfield and St. Matthews the position is also more favourable than for several of the residential suburbs. The most likely explanation may be the small size of the borough, which reduces certain differences between the centre and the outskirts to a comparative minimum. In particular, it has to be noted in a town like Cambridge, central position and high density of population do not necessarily mean complete absence or difficult accessibility of recreation grounds, playing fields and other open spaces. It is a significant feature, for instance, that Market ward possesses approximately fifty acres of such open spaces out of a total of about 170 listed for the whole town.'[1]

Thus the same thing may be said of the relation between overcrowding and crime as between crime and poverty. Neither is primary, yet neither can be lightly dismissed. They are integral factors in Ferguson's coalescence of adversities. The connection is probably of this order: poverty and bad housing serve to promote a subculture which is impervious to middle-class values and hence more susceptible to the commission of certain kinds of property offences. On their own neither of these factors would be sufficient to tip the scales towards delinquency.

Although we find many honest folk who are poor and who are obliged to live in unsuitable houses (sometimes in appalling physical conditions) this does not disprove the general argument or mean that we have to account for their less honest and law-abiding neighbours solely in terms of psychiatric illness or of psychological maladjustment. These more law-abiding folk are probably stronger than their delinquent brethren in having enjoyed such things as good parental example when young, and in the possession of imponderables such as a firm religious faith. Or they may merely have been lucky in that they were never brought into close association with delinquent contacts.

We can list the various aspects of housing conditions which, though not criminogenic as such, are certainly known to be factors closely associated with areas of high criminal risk.

(A) Cramped living quarters and overcrowding are likely to

[1] *Juvenile Delinquency in an English Middletown*, Routledge and Kegan Paul, 1948.

cause tensions and conflicts inside the household, especially if there is more than one generation cohabiting.

(B) Lack of essential privacy can have an influence on sexual ideas and behaviour and produce anxieties. The extreme prudery of slum children is probably a reflex of this condition and can be thought of as a form of protective reaction to promiscuity. Also, there are strong grounds for associating overcrowding with the incidence of incest.

(C) Recreative and leisure time activities become quite impossible in overcrowded homes and therefore young and old are obliged to seek their amusements on the streets or in the various kinds of commercial entertainment available. Lack of roomspace and amenity hence engenders inadequate home life and fosters the conditions of delinquent association on the streets.

Professor Ferguson in his thoroughgoing survey of the lives of some 1,400 Glasgow youths, who left school in January 1947, to which we have already referred, categorically stated that overcrowding in the home was a fundamental cause or precondition of child delinquency:

'Severity of crowding in the home is obviously an important factor in relation to the incidence of juvenile delinquency: the figures suggest that it may rank about equal in weight with a poor level of family assessment, as made by an experienced social worker, or persistence of the boy in stop-gap work.'[1]

Finally, he goes on to make the claim that residence in an overcrowded district *together with* frequent changes in employment produced the greater risk of delinquency for all his boys:

'Abatement of overcrowding of a severity of three persons or more to a room would apparently produce a reduction in the amount of juvenile delinquency equal to about one-fifth of the total, if it could be assumed that in their new setting the families at present severely crowded would conform to the standards of conduct prevailing among families not at present severely crowded: but this assumption is not likely to be realized within a generation.'[2]

That final proviso has the sting in it! How far can we expect people to change the pattern of their conduct just because they go to live in different sorts of houses? Is it not true to say that

[1] *The Young Delinquent in his Social Setting*, Oxford, 1954, p. 47.
[2] Ibid., pp. 150–1.

because they are the kind of people they are they live in substandard property? Many would argue in this way that slummies are always slummies, wherever you house them, and quote the hoary anecdote of the coal in the bath which used to be something of a sociological myth. I wonder how many people can honestly say they have ever seen coal in the bath in any case where a proper and convenient coal-bunker was provided?

II

The question of how far can we change people's behaviour and presumably their social character by administrative planning is one of prime interest to housing authority and academic sociologist alike. It happens that during the past thirty years or so large scale social experiments have been taking place which entitle us to give certain tentative pragmatic answers to these important questions. The new housing estates, which many municipal corporations have been building to accommodate bombed-out and slum-clearance families, are in fact as near as we can hope to get to laboratory conditions for conducting social experiments with human beings. What, then, do we know about new housing estates and the lives of the people who live there in relation to the incidence of delinquency? And are there any grounds at all for believing that improvements in the physical lay-out of homes has led to a corresponding reduction in criminal activity?

Unfortunately our knowledge of what has been taking place is partial and fragmentary. Few research workers have been available to study at first hand the results of these vital social experiments. But what we do know is not too discouraging.

The Cambridge figures we have already referred to indicate that in the new area the delinquency rates are higher than in the older wards, but Dr. Mannheim has suggested certain mitigating factors. It also has to be borne in mind that the residents of the new estates were ex-slum dwellers, and this fact may perhaps account for their higher delinquency rates during the interim period when the families were no doubt somewhat disturbed. It may well be that immediately following removal from an older neighbourhood families are so disoriented that their members commit more delinquencies for a limited period, that is to say until new roots are established in the reception area. Professor Ferguson has shown in his Glasgow enquiry that the crime rates for boys in the new estates approximate to those for his whole study group and that apparently little improvement is noticeable after migration. But he goes on to point out that the new estates are not identical in every respect and are seldom homogeneous groups. Some are occupied by former slum-dwellers while others receive a more mixed population, including families from inadequate homes in non-slum areas. When he considered the several types of local authority rehousing schemes separately, he found that the boys from the new areas used mainly to rehouse slum families had a much greater incidence of crime than boys whose families derived from other districts. The ex-slum boys were particularly prone to delinquency during their school days and this was true even after they had been living in the new area for upwards of ten years. It seems that these children carried with them the germs of delinquency already nourished in their early subcultural existence and that this tendency towards illegal behaviour stubbornly persisted in their lives in the new environment. But the boys from the more mixed areas did not deteriorate, which is a comfort.

It would appear that it is easier to change the physical environment than to change people's behaviour and general attitudes. Conduct norms become part and parcel of the group's way of life and take a much longer time to alter or eradicate. Delinquency seems to migrate with the people as a social tradition. It is habitual and habits we know are difficult to correct once they have got a grip. The process of re-education involves more than a mere physical change. The unlearning of learned behaviour and the substitution of different norms cannot be achieved in a few years! Even a decade is insufficient. But happily there is evidence, over a long term, that improvement does occur in rehousing estates which have been in existence for a generation or more. The only solid evidence for this that I am aware of is contained in Bagot's Liverpool investigation, carried out immediately prior to the Second World War. Bagot[1] tells us something of what was happening on the Norris Green estate, which was first occupied in the late 1920's, and

[1] J. H. Bagot, *Juvenile Delinquency*, Cape, 1941.

the Dovecot and Knowsley estates which were settled a little later. All the residents of these areas came from Inner Liverpool, from the worst slum districts where social conditions were chronically adverse.

Between 1934 and 1936 the total number of children in Norris Green decreased but the twelve to sixteen age group increased. These children, he claimed, were those most influenced by their former surroundings and this could be seen in the delinquency statistics for the two years cited.

However, when the figures for the younger children, i.e. those born on the new estate or removed at an early age were compared with the rest of Inner Liverpool it was apparent that this age group had begun to settle down to a more law-abiding way of life:

'Thus, whereas in the whole of Liverpool children aged 8 to 11 committed approximately one-third of all breaking offences in 1936, in Norris Green they were responsible for only one-tenth, although they had been responsible for only one-quarter in 1934. This suggests that the amount of delinquency is less in Norris Green than it would have been had the families remained in Inner Liverpool, and that this applied with greater force to the younger children who were not affected to the same extent by bad conditions in their most impressionable years.'[1]

Similar comparisons could not be made for the Dovecot-Knowsley estate for those years because of their more recent colonization. Most of the children living there were still very much influenced by the conditions of their former habitat and their delinquency rates were, hence, accordingly very high.

Bagot claimed in general, on the basis of the evidence in his book, that 'the effect of removing families from overcrowded areas to new housing estates is to reduce the amount of delinquency among the juveniles concerned'. This reduction is not apparent immediately, but is progressive, and varies according to the age of the estate concerned.

III

It will be clear from the foregoing that our information is sadly restricted and that we have only a few isolated investigations on

[1] Op. cit., p. 70.

which to base our theories and conclusions. Bagot quotes the Chief Education Officer for Birmingham in his 1938 report in support of his general claim that amelioration does appear to take place in rehousing areas over a period of time but no figures are given for the Birmingham area apart from the statement that 'there is some evidence to show that the percentage of delinquencies tends to decline as the influence of the new surroundings makes itself felt'.

A limited amount of evidence from the United States suggests that admission to a new housing project tends to produce a reduction in the measured amount of juvenile delinquency. Chapin,[1] for example, discusses N. Barer's findings for 649 children and their families who had been living in a New Haven Housing Development for between two-and-a-half and four years. By tracing their records back for the years before they had moved and comparing them, after the move had taken place and the family had had a chance to settle in, the results showed that the rates had fallen significantly from 3·18 per cent to 1·64 per cent, in spite of the fact that throughout the area as a whole there had been a substantial rise. This seems to indicate that there is a 'strong presumption that the factor of improved housing played an important role' in the improvement and lends support to 'the hypothesis that good housing may cause a decline in juvenile delinquency rather than merely be associated with a decline'.

Probation officers who have worked over a generation in these new districts support the idea that improvement comes—but painfully slowly. It is however a progressive improvement and the Norris Green ward of Liverpool, which was in its early years a disrupted and delinquent area, is now widely accepted as a normal lower-working class neighbourhood with no unusual social problems.

In the new housing estates which accommodate slum clearance families it seems reasonable then, but by no means certain, to believe that something like a second generation phenomenon occurs. That is to say, those children who are brought up in the better conditions and who attend the new schools in the area are subject to ameliorative influences and become less

[1] F. Stuart Chapin, *Experimental Designs in Sociological Research*, Harper Bros., New York, 1947, pp. 97–9.

delinquent than they would very likely have been in the older blighted neighbourhoods. There is, however, grave danger of complacency if we come to rely too much upon this happening as an inevitable and automatic process. Local authorities may blandly deduce that all they have to do is to provide fresh accommodation and reduce population densities and all will be well. But clearly the successful settlement of a new locality depends also upon whether or not new social institutions are provided to service the incoming tenants. It is almost a truism to say that the shops, schools, churches, parks, playgrounds, public houses, youth organizations and so on should be ready to receive the immigrants and not be left to be provided at some unspecified future date. But in practice, for a variety of reasons, this common-sense policy is infrequently followed and the new-comers find themselves stranded, miles from their former friends and associations, surrounded by seemingly endless open spaces and cut off from all the amusements and facilities upon which they have in the past come to rely for their comfort and support. It is not surprising if, in such circumstances, some people find the life of the wide open spaces of the new housing estate too lonely and uncongenial and if certain behaviour disorders follow, one of which might well be child delinquency.

IV

We have far too little objective information about what really happens on new housing estates and what steps might be taken to ease the transition of families from older urban areas moving into these vast dormitory suburban deserts. There is great scope here for co-operation between local authorities and the universities in carrying out such detailed long-term investigations which would cost little and yet add enormously to our slender fund of knowledge about the relationship between people and their environment. All too often research work of this nature is not carried out because local authority officials are hostile to academic interference and frightened of possible criticism, and equally because the general public, both enlightened and unenlightened, see little need for such enquiries to be made.

As a result of the almost universal apathy we are obliged to jog along in partial ignorance, making use of a few snippets gleaned from a series of *ad hoc* investigations carried out for varying purposes and at widely varying times and which are often conflicting in their findings. Moreover, most of these enquiries have either ignored or only given passing attention to delinquency—apart, of course, from those already referred to by Mannheim, Ferguson and Bagot.

Before we can be certain what effect rehousing and migration have upon crime rates we have got to know where the residents came from and what the delinquency rates were in the older districts compared with the city as a whole. We would also need to compare the rates for the older and younger children and for those born in the estate and those born elsewhere and compare these figures with those for children and, if possible adults, still residing in the older neighbourhoods, as Bagot tried to do in his Liverpool study. This would have to be done systematically over a considerable period of time, say twenty years at the least, and hence would require the co-operation of many local authority departments and research workers in an extensive team effort. A further prerequisite for such an investigation would be that those involved should be concerned to find out the truth and to publicize it rather than, as is too often the case, suppress and deny it. On the whole I am gloomy about the chances of such a vital piece of social investigation ever being launched in a country which, like Britain, flinches from the pain of close self-scrutiny.

So, until these necessary but unlikely surveys are made, we must be content with the very limited knowledge at our disposal. From it, I think, three salient points emerge which require further investigation and validation:

(1) Delinquency is part and parcel of a general pattern of life which is carried over by the immigrants when they move into their new localities, and it tends to remain for a fair period of time at very much its pre-migration level.

(2) After the lapse of time of a generation or more delinquency rates fall and there is a general improvement in behaviour which is usually sustained.

(3) The connection between housing and crime is secondary and probably resides in the association between overcrowding and lack of privacy and amenity, which are themselves aspects of a more general matrix in which social, psychological and economic factors have coalesced to produce what are characteristically criminogenic neighbourhoods.

CHAPTER 12

THE HABITUAL OFFENDER

I

There is, or was, a common stereotype of the habitual criminal as a tough, ruthless, gangsterlike individual, habitually at war with lawful society and a constant menace to decent folk, who must be suppressed at all cost and by every means in society's power. Consequently when there is what the press refer to as a crime wave in the country, that is to say when the criminal statistics reveal an upward trend of rather less than 0·7 per cent, everyone feels increasingly insecure and expects at any moment to be robbed, burglarized, coshed or sexually assaulted. Such a view is utterly unrealistic and false. That such individual criminals do exist I would not wish to deny. That there are many of them in this country is however extremely unlikely. As was pointed out earlier, the ideal picture of the criminal in our society is not a Bill Sykes but a schoolboy. And even when we take that apparently more serious body of offenders, those who are committed to Her Majesty's prisons, it is salutary to remember that 'three out of every four sentences passed by the courts in England and Wales are for six months or less',[1] or in other words for comparatively small offences. Official statistics show that of those people imprisoned for the first time or who, if they have been, are judged not to be bad influences on the others (the so-called Star class prisoners), few return again for later offences. Eighty-seven per cent of men Stars and 89 per cent of women Stars discharged in 1953 and 1954 had not been reconvicted during a three-year follow-up

[1] See C. H. Rolph, *Common Sense About Crime and Punishment*, Gollancz, 1961.

period.[1] Moreover, as Hugh Klare stated in a recent book, 'roughly four out of five first offenders do not offend again, no matter what sentence is imposed.'[2]

The facts then clearly indicate that the majority of offenders are more or less ordinary kinds of folk who suffer from lapses from grace under the stress of peculiar temptations which may never be repeated. Most of the individuals who fill out the vast lists of the Home Secretary's annual statistics are common-or-garden men, women and boys who respond satisfactorily to the usual forms of disciplinary treatment. It is clear, moreover, that many of these people ought not to be sent to gaol at all. Our prisons contain far too many individual offenders who almost certainly would have responded equally, if not more satisfactorily, to less harsh and more constructive forms of treatment. It is also not widely known that a substantial number of people are committed to gaol on remand awaiting trial who are subsequently not given a prison sentence at all. Writing in 1956, Winifred Elkin estimated that between 9,000 and 10,000 persons fell annually into this category of the needlessly incarcerated.[3]

Some 20 to 25 per cent of all offenders may be said to comprise the hard core of persistent criminals. Yet not by the wildest stretch of the imagination could many of them be regarded as desperate characters. The majority are inadequate personalities, eternally down on their luck and promising to go straight again if only they get the chance, or with chips on their shoulders and convinced that the world is especially set against them. They are dull, rather dreary and depressing characters, completely lacking the glamour and panache of the crime film or the detective novel. Much of their lives is spent behind bars where they are usually fairly passive and tractable within limits —a regiment of dull men in dull uniforms going through habitual routines which make little impact on their characters but which society in sheer desperation prescribes to camouflage its own impotence.

[1] *Penal Practice in a Changing Society*, H.M.S.O., 1959, p. 12.
[2] Hugh J. Klare, *Anatomy of Prison*, Hutchinson, 1960, p. 28.
[3] *The English Penal System*, Penguin Books, 1956, 121.

II

The technical name for those men and women who are constantly in and out of prison and who persist in committing the same kind of offence is recidivists. But there are varying kinds of recidivists and regular offenders. Walter Reckless discriminates between the ordinary repeater, the habitual offender and the professional criminal:

'The recidivist, habitual offender, and professional criminal apparently represent gradations on a scale of criminal sophistication, with the habitual criminal occupying the middle position between the untutored second-time offender and the tutored professional. The professional criminal is the most highly processed offender, the one whose career has represented a thorough schooling in criminal techniques, arts, attitudes, and philosophy of life.'[1]

It is probable that all these repeaters are inadequate personalities, although not necessarily of low intelligence. The professional criminal may be more highly skilled—a tradesman in his own right—but he too has a pathetic aspect which belies the popular stereotype of the desperado.

In an interesting article in the *British Journal of Delinquency*, R. S. Taylor in a study of one hundred consecutive admissions to Preventive Detention at Wandsworth, has drawn a vivid picture of this type of offender.[2] Under existing law, preventive detention seeks to protect the public from the constant depredations of habitual offenders, those who are thought unsuitable for corrective training (so called, but more euphemistically than realistically!) whose reformation is regarded as extremely unlikely. P.D. prisons constitute the slums of the prison world, collecting as they do the failures of all other branches. Those undergoing this incarceration must be over thirty years of age, they must, prior to their final indictment, have been committed at least three times from the age of seventeen onwards and have been previously committed to either borstal, prison or corrective detention. Sentences for this category of offenders are severe, ranging from a minimum of five to a maximum of fourteen

[1] W. Reckless, op. cit., pp. 140–1.

[2] 'The Habitual Criminal', *British Journal of Criminology*, Vol. I, No. 1, 1960, pp. 21–36.

years—often in fact the equivalent of a life-sentence or even longer.

Taylor's sample consisted of men almost constantly in trouble with the law who yet, as he points out, on the surface at least, remain great optimists. Their imprisonment is always avowed to be the last time. Another striking feature of 'these men is that crime and prison seem to provide some form of refuge from the world at large, a reaction which seems almost of an hysterical order'.[1]

For the most part they are thieves and housebreakers and very few have committed sex offences or crimes involving violence. The distribution of intelligence amongst the group is normal. Some are emotionally withdrawn while others are buoyantly extraverted. Taylor is convinced that they do not consist of a predominantly psychopathic group, although other assessors might reach the opposite conclusion. Interestingly enough 'only a minority of these recidivists were juvenile offenders', and Taylor suggests that 'it is possible that only a minority of juvenile recidivists become adult recidivists. For a juvenile, a criminal record may have far less serious personal consequences than such a record for an adult whose good character, reputation and career are jeopardized',[2] unlike the juvenile's. The mean average age of the first conviction of the preventive detainee was eighteen, which again seems to differentiate them from the run-of-the-mill offenders.[3] As he points out, after the age of thirteen indictable offences per 100,000 of the population decrease from 1,315 to only 740 for the eighteen-year-old group, which suggests that these men who become habitual offenders in later life are a fairly homogeneous group of inadequate personalities who find that, once they get into trouble, they have neither the ability nor the morale to reform. By no means do all come from homes in the lowest income group and ten of the hundred had enjoyed grammar or public school education. In few cases were there relatives with criminal records to account for their own degeneration. In fact their failure and criminality seemed to be predominantly a personal characteristic, arising from their own inadequacy rather

[1] Ibid. [2] Ibid.
[3] The later the delinquent tendencies show themselves, the more likely it is that they are symptomatic of deep and intractable underlying causes.

than resulting from the delinquent infection of a bad neighbourhood or the corrupting influences of a criminal home background. Many suffered from ill-health, both mental and physical, in the past and in the present, and it is tempting but
speculative to imagine that there is some constitutional factor
at work here which makes such individuals particularly incapable of living socially responsible lives. It must, in fairness, however, be stated that once an adult has a prison or borstal sentence
to his name, it is correspondingly more difficult for him to
reinstate himself in normal society. The odds are heavily against
him, unless he possesses unusual determination or has exceptional luck or help. As has so often been said, the punishment of
a prison sentence begins not on admission but on discharge from
gaol. The problem of the recidivist then is not just the individual
criminal's problem. It is also to a great extent society's problem,
as much the result of social reaction to the stigma of a conviction
and incarceration as of the offender's own psychological condition. Probably the most striking thing about Taylor's group was
their lack of contact with other people, even with other
offenders. Even in their criminal acts they usually were un-
accompanied—a feature which sharply distinguishes them from
the juvenile delinquents I knew in the Liverpool dockland
community and described in *Growing Up In The City*. The
difference seems to be between normality and abnormality:
between offenders (and any of us might conceivably get ourselves into this group) who are actuated by social influences,
gang membership and the like, and those whose lawlessness
springs almost entirely from personal defects.

'It was surprising that eighty-three men committed their last
offence alone, whilst twelve were associated with one other
person, usually someone they met casually . . . equally surprising to find that sixty-five men had committed all their
previous offences alone, whilst eighteen had at some time been
involved with gangs of three or more in the past. As might be
expected, the solitary offenders were usually those who were
first convicted comparatively late in life, whilst those who were
first in trouble as juveniles tended to be gang offenders.'[1]

The picture of habitual offenders that emerges, then, from
Taylor's study, and which is born out by similar enquiries, is

[1] R. S. Taylor, op. cit.

one of personal and social inadequacy, characterized by social isolation and avoidance, by ill-health and retreatism from the pains and frustrations of ordinary life: the dull, grey little men, the dismal failures for whom limited crime and sporadic institutionalization are a lamentable response to their own incompetence; men for whom, in other words, we are bound to feel pity and who remain as a perpetual reminder of the severity of a social system which promotes the strong and depresses the weak still further.

III

So far in this chapter we have concentrated on the habitual offender as a man who on account of serious personal defects has had few, if any, choices open to him in choosing crime as a career. And while this is undoubtedly the case with the majority of the 20 per cent hard core of offenders, we must also face the fact that there is a minority who commit crime as a result of a deliberate and premeditated decision. Amongst the professional criminals, no doubt many are inadequate and even psychopathic personalities, and it would be idle to suppose that neat and clearcut definitions can be made distinguishing the inadequate recidivist from the professional marauder and hoodlum. I think, however, it is worth while saying something about the clever, 'normal' professional thief who might have gone straight had he elected to do so, but who went in for crime as a career much in the same way as a lawyer, doctor, or engineer decides to follow his particular profession.

Such offenders are men who have deliberately crossed the line which divides the true criminal, or enemy of society, from the individual who has merely broken the law but still regards himself as being within the social pale. The true criminals are not likely to experience much remorse or be greatly troubled by guilt feelings. They have developed what may be termed criminal egos which protect them from the pangs of conscience. The world owes them a living and they intend to get it by whatever means seem to offer the quickest and richest rewards.

American criminological literature is our main source of information concerning the activities of big-time crooks, the prototype of whom is the notorious Scarface Al Capone, greatest hoodlum of them all, whose name is still a legend throughout the United States and who brought organized crime and racketeering in the 1920's to the highest pitch of evil perfection. The report of the Kefauver Committee contains what is probably the most detailed exposé of the complex ramifications of what Kefauver himself called 'three fields that have become an unholy trinity in areas of the United States—crime, politics, and business'.[1]

Organized professional crime would not be so successful as a business operation if it were not widely assisted by the institution of graft—if it were not possible to work 'the fix' on the one hand and if, on the other, there were not facilities for disposing of stolen property readily available. Not only are there professional receivers ready to do a deal with the professional thief, but the small-time rogue and even the juvenile finds, as the late Sir Leo Page said, in public houses and markets that there are plenty of '"respectable" persons fully prepared to buy what they know is stolen if only it is a bargain to themselves'.[2]

Thus ordinary members of the community encourage crime by their willing co-operation. Professional criminals, of course, have developed their own social underworld, in direct opposition to the upper world of honest society. Upper- and underworld exist in close relationship to one another. Men in the upper-world make money by legal practices which the rogues dispossess them of by illegal practices. Once they have obtained cash and valuables in this way, the ordinary ethical values are restored amongst the thieves themselves. The swag must be divided fairly amongst the participants that honour among thieves may prevail. If criminals are dishonest with each other beyond a certain degree their social world disintegrates. Underworld values operate, then, very like upper-world values, cementing solidarity and making collaboration possible. This relationship is often strictly business, depending neither upon the charismatic power of any one leader or even upon personal liking or intimate association. 'When a mob sticks together for several years, it is because it has been successful in making money. It is not because of loyalty to a leader or because of personal liking for one another. In some mobs members do not speak to one another socially.'[3]

---

[1] *Crime in America*, p. 225.   [2] *The Young Lag*, Faber and Faber.
[3] *The Professional Thief*, University of Chicago Press, 1937.

The quotation is from the late Edwin Sutherland's fascinating report of his investigations into the lives and attitudes of professional criminals. In that book he tells us what are the run-of-mill rackets of mostly smalltime rogues.

'The principal rackets of professional thieves are the cannon (picking pockets), the heel (sneak-thieving from stores, banks, and offices), the boost (shoplifting), penny-weighting (stealing from jewellery stores by substitution), hotel prowling (stealing from hotel rooms), the con (confidence game), some miscellaneous rackets related in certain respects to confidence games, laying paper (passing illegal checks, money orders, and other papers), and the shake (the shakedown of, or extortion from, persons engaged in or about to engage in illegal acts).'[1]

He has some interesting information about the gentle art of picking pockets. 'A left-breech tool' is an argot term to describe a man who 'can steal from the left-front trouser pocket, which is unusually difficult' for reasons that will be obvious to all male readers. 'The ability to do this', he delightfully informs us, 'is added to any reference to the cannon as is, might I say, Ph.D. to a student. Thus, "Do you know little Butsie, a left-breech tool from Baltimore?" and "He can beat a left-breech", are regarded as very complimentary statements amongst the criminal fraternity.'[2]

While the man who has accepted criminal status for himself is more or less immune from guilt feelings, he does seem to have certain primitive pangs of conscience and to have an immature and incomplete code of ethics. 'Cannons as a rule,' says Sutherland, 'make no distinctions between the rich and the slaves (workers, labourers, factory hands).'[3] But there are some racketeers who 'do not approve or have any part in slave grift, feeling that if the money of a poor man is taken his family will be distressed'. Other nice distinctions may be made concerning potential victims. 'Catholic cannons will rarely beat a catholic priest', and 'There is a generally accepted rule amongst cannons not to beat cripples'. Some of these scruples no doubt have quasi-religious and superstitious genesis in the criminal mind. But more cogent practical reasons lead them to avoid the pockets of policemen! 'Cannons do not generally beat coppers, for it would heat the coppers up against cannons, causing hard-

[1] Ibid., p. 43.   [2] Ibid., p. 48.   [3] Ibid., p. 175 *et seq.*

ship on all cannons.' But the con-man finds 'little difficulty in easing his conscience, for in the con the sucker is always beaten while he is trying to beat someone else . . . the thief gets a feeling of sweet vengeance in beating him.' Cons are contemptuous of suckers, they even regard them with moral indignation some-times. 'They believe that if a person is going to steal, let him steal from the same point of view as the thief does: do not profess honesty and steal at the same time. Thieves are tolerant of almost everything except hypocrisy.' When engaged on the shake, moral contempt for the victim also helps to ease the pangs of remorse. 'The degenerates are beaten, and the repug-nance towards the victim overcomes any thought of his rights.' Shaking homosexuals and other perverts, then, or even jack-rolling (robbing drunks), is thought of as a just retribution.

I have given these extracts from Sutherland's fascinating study at some length because, in their own right, they are bizarrely amusing. Also, because they show that professional thieves are in many ways men very much like ourselves who have, however, set about the business of life from a rather divergent standpoint. Their purpose is to make money and the more easily the better. Many of their values are similar to ours. The main distinction is that they have chosen crime rather than legal business as their career. In place of what is sometimes called business acumen they possess 'larceny sense', its illegiti-mate equivalent. They have consensus together. One hears of them even holding conferences from time to time, just like social workers and other professional people. They have worked out for themselves a group way of life, with their own customs, language and traditions, which, like any other social system, tends to perpetuate itself and become institutionalized over the years. In their book, *The Jack Roller*,[1] Clifford Shaw and Albert Saifir quote from the autobiography of a reformed burglar, one Jack Black, which appeared under the title of 'You Can't Win' in *Harper's Magazine*, February, 1930. In this contribution Mr. Black gave the following description of the code and social castes of the criminal group:

'The upperworld knows nothing about caste compared with the underworld. Crookdom is the most provincial of small villages, the most rigid in its social gradations. Honors and

[1] Chicago University Press, 1930, p. 113.

opportunity are apportioned on the basis of code observance. There is no more caste in the heart of India than in an American penitentiary. A bank burglar assumes an air with a house burglar, a house burglar sneers at a pickpocket, a pickpocket calls a forger a "short story writer", and they all make common cause against the stool-pigeon, whatever caste he comes from. He jeopardizes the life and liberty of his own, which is the great unpardonable crime in the underworld code. He is the rattlesnake of the underworld, and they kill him as swiftly and dispassionately as you would kill a copperhead. . . . The burglar who shoots his partner for holding out a lady's watch goes up in the social scale of the underworld. Like the clubman who perjures himself to save a lady's reputation, he has done the right thing in the sight of his fellows. Each is a better gentleman according to the code.'

While one must always beware of accepting uncritically everything that ex-criminals and convicts have to tell us about their careers and social customs,[1] it seems clear that the underworld has its own class and status stratification, and that at the top of the pyramid are the entrepreneurs of crime who put up the money for the job, organize the operation and, like their counterparts in the normal business world, swallow the largest share of the profits. Such organizers of crime, sometimes called Top Villains or Guv'nors, avoid publicity, keep strictly in the background and dislike violence because of the dangerous limelight it brings to their nefarious trade. There are probably not many such criminals, but proportionately to their numerical strength they cost the community dearly and occupy the full-time attention of some of the finest detective brains in the world—Scotland Yard's famous Flying Squad.[2] There is no doubt that the well-thought-out bank robbery, the carefully planned fraud, the theft of thousands of pounds worth of jewels and above all their rapid disposal are the typical operations of top-line villains. Some of them, no doubt, when they have amassed their pile, retire into relative obscurity, buy houses in

---

[1] Peter Wildeblood, however, in his book *Against the Law*, Penguin Books, 1957, confirms these status gradations amongst criminals.
[2] For very readable accounts of how the police force has geared itself up to crime prevention in the modern world, readers should consult Sir Harold Scott's *Scotland Yard*, Penguin Books, 1957.

the country where they grow prize marrows and tomatoes, become members of the rural district council and even church wardens. Others depart for distant climes when the heat gets too much for them, while some linger too long and are eventually brought to justice and sentenced to imprisonment.

IV

It would be wrong, I think, to give the impression that the criminal underworld is a tightly knit system or thieves' guild, smoothly and efficiently waging war against the law-abiding community like an underground resistance movement in time of alien military occupation. It seems to be rather less stable and united, more divided against itself, and consequently much less efficient than it conceivably could be if overall planning and hegemony could be achieved. It may well be that in certain parts of America, and even in this country too, professional criminals collect money to assist their incarcerated brethren. Sutherland tells us that 'In major cases where a lot of money is needed for a case, subscription papers are taken around to the several hang-outs, and only broke guys do not contribute.'[1] If this touching story is true it proves that there is a strong sentiment of corporate loyalty uniting professionals. But it must also be closely related to the fact that in the U.S.A. it is possible to fix a case, that is to say to bribe the judges and prosecutors, and so secure a felon's release. In this country where such machinations must be either very rare or non-existent such subscriptions could only be raised to help the convict's dependants. There is, however, a shadier obverse side of the medal, which is represented by the widespread phenomenon of informing. The professional informer or 'grass' lives on the fringe of the criminal world by picking up information about crime and giving the police the tip off. The latter have funds available to remunerate informers and, in many cases, information acquired in this way leads to the arrest of wanted criminals and enables the police to prevent robberies occurring.

In the sinister world of crime, therefore, we do not find two cohorts relentlessly opposed to one another. Criminals, informers and police exist in a quasi-symbiotic relationship and

[1] Op cit., p. 7.

occasionally work together as well as in opposition, while, in and around the stage on which the drama of organized crime and crime-prevention continually takes place, gather an unknown number of queers, perverts, drug-addicts, dead-beats, inadequates and psychopaths who are attracted to its strange and powerful lure and who from time to time participate in the crowd scenes, sometimes as victims and at other times as offenders. It is not a clear-cut picture that emerges. Any criminal may turn informer, either to vent his spite against a fellow villain or to satisfy a vain desire to feel superior or even to save his own skin. While there may be some sort of honour amongst thieves, it is also true to say that sometimes dog eats dog. If it were not so, the threat of organized crime to respec - able society would be much graver than it is, even in a coun ry which, like the United States, is so exposed to graft and political corruption.

V

We might venture a very tentative analysis of the social stratification of the criminal world in some such way as this:

Class 1. The Top Villains, professional criminals concerned with the planning and organization of the more serious and remunerative types of crime.

Class 2. Professional crooks possessing specific skills, operating either alone or in groups, e.g., burglars, counterfeiters, etc.

Class 3. Lower grade professional thieves, often of limited mentality and probably suffering from some psychiatric disability resulting from earlier deprivations, e.g., cannons and sneak thieves.

Class 4. A miscellaneous, heterogeneous rabble of hangers-on who commit petty and often persistent offences and who are almost certainly inadequate and psychopathic personalities.

Classes 2, 3, and 4 are to varying degrees manipulated by the class 1 criminal, but in class 2 are a number of sturdy individualists—type of the master craftsmen of old—who follow their own line and are self-employed. Classes 3 and 4 are almost certainly the most numerous and constitute the kind of habitual offenders already discussed in R. S. Taylor's paper, pathetic and isolated men who are more of a nuisance than a menace to society.

It will be obvious that both from the viewpoint of crime prevention and of penological treatment these four general classes present us with widely different problems. One group has chosen crime as a business career; the other and much larger group have fallen into the ways of crime because of personal inadequacy or because our individualistic and highly competitive society has failed to provide them with the support, training and discipline that their crippled personalities require. In the light of this analysis we may have renewed sympathy with prison officers and officials who are obliged to cater, often with totally inadequate means, for so diverse and debased a section of the population.

CHAPTER 13

A NOTE ON SEX OFFENDERS

I

Probably no aspect of our social experience is so bedevilled by prejudice and dishonest humbug as the topic of sex. Naturally sexual offences and sexual offenders create a stir out of all proportion to their extent and seriousness. Demands for more repressive measures and severer punishment (usually with thinly veiled sexual overtones themselves) follow quickly upon reports in the press of assaults on children, outbreaks of exhibitionism and either attempted or successful rape. Some of the more widely read Sunday papers indeed thrive upon the juicy sex cases dug up from every major and minor court in the country. At noon on most Sundays throughout the year, members of the male proletariat, young and more elderly, are to be seen propped upon half-cleared breakfast tables, puffing their third and fourth cigarettes of the day and deeply engrossed in such stories as that of the medical practitioner who administered sleeping draughts to female patients before sexually assaulting them, or of the self-styled advertising expert who appears to have had little difficulty in inducing respectable housewives to pose naked to be photographed beside their washing machines in the belief that by so doing a famous manufacturing firm would financially reward them.

Bearing in mind the warnings given in an earlier chapter about trying to build elaborate theories from all too fallible criminal statistics, it is quite impossible to estimate with any accuracy the amount of sexual crime in present-day society. By its very nature and the privacy with which at times it is necessarily accompanied, sex offences are not open to accurate recording. Moreover, no form of illegal activity is more exposed to swings of public opinion so that an increase in the number of prosecutions can never be taken as a true index of what some hoary moralists like to call 'the state of the nation's morals'.

But there can be no doubt that the amount of *known* sex crime has gone up greatly in recent years. More people are brought before the courts on sexual charges than ever before. Prosecutions for indecent assaults on females, defilement of girls under the age of sixteen and indecency with males have risen very substantially during the past fifty years. There can be no doubt about this, although there is considerable disagreement about its significance. Some people claim that we are more frank and open than we used to be, that we suppress such activities less than we used to do. Others maintain that there has indeed been a sharp decline in standards of moral behaviour throughout all classes.

II

I do not wish to enter very deeply here into an examination of the nature, extent and motivation of sexual crimes but to offer a number of observations from the sociological viewpoint which may be helpful. In a treatise of this kind, in which I have striven to show that criminal behaviour is nearly always socially conditioned and in a great many cases perfectly normal, I feel that I cannot entirely burk the issue raised by sexual offences and misdemeanours. For surely, if anywhere, it is in the understanding and explanation of these offences that the psychologist and psychiatrist come into their own. Are not sex activities, be they proper or perverted, acceptable or illegal, the full responsibility of the individual and are they not explicable purely in terms of the individual offender's personal psychology?

While I hope I have not given the impression that I am trying to grind the sociological axe at the expense of psychological analyses and insights (but rather to bring them both together into a truer focus), I must point out that even here, in the one field which, at first sight, might appear to be the peculiar province of psychologists, it is misleading entirely to ignore the social factors and influences which are also constantly at work. In order to demonstrate my thesis, I will take but two examples of sexual problems—namely homosexuality and prostitution—

as they have been very much to the fore in public discussions over the past few years following the publication of the report of the Wolfenden Committee.[1]

Let us take homosexuality first. This term of course includes female sexual inversion, often known as lesbianism. Neither of these conditions is in itself illegal or prohibited: only certain active manifestations in the male sex but, somewhat paradoxically, not amongst females, are forbidden and punishable by law. As the authors of the Wolfenden Report say homosexuality 'as a propensity is not an "all or none" condition' but may exist in all gradations and in most individuals at some stage of their development. Some psychoanalysts would indeed maintain that every individual must pass through the homosexual before attaining the fully adult heterosexual state. It is a topic that invariably generates intense emotion, and all I want to do here is to point out that the moral fervour aroused does nothing to help but greatly aggravates a rational social approach to the alleged problem. Unfortunately the minds of many professing Christians, both past and present, often seem to be obsessed with sexual activity to the point of neuroticism. Sex and sin are frequently used as synonyms. The abhorrence of sexual activities, either permitted or prohibited, is a curious cultural phenomenon that we cannot go into here, but Augustine's famous saying *inter faeces et urinam nascimur* illustrates how far the attitude of repugnance to generation can go. One is permitted, I think, even as an agnostic to ask whether this viewpoint is helpful to humanity, or even theologically sound.

The student of social institutions cannot fail to be perplexed by a society like ours which legally proscribes homosexual relations yet, at the same time, organizes certain aspects of its life in a manner to encourage their development. We know well enough that what happens in childhood and youth largely determines our adult attitudes and behaviour. Yet we persist in throwing members of the same sex together at vital stages of their physical, psychological and social development so that latent and potential homosexual tendencies are richly encouraged. Sexual segregation as practised and stoutly defended in most of our schools is a glaring illustration of this paradoxical

[1] *Report of the Committee on Homosexual Offences and Prostitution*, H.M.S.O., 1957 (Cmnd. 247).

principle. In boarding schools, where, for two-thirds of the year, boys are kept in close contact with other boys and with men, and girls are similarly confined to their own sex for emotional relationships, this tendency is seen at its extreme. Yet in the day schools, both private and statutory, the same inveterate tendency towards segregation operates.[1] I remember in my own schooldays that it was forbidden for a boy to talk to or be seen in the company of a pupil from the neighbouring girls' grammar school. I recall being rebuked for walking to school one day with a girl I happened to know who was the younger sister of my elder brother's friend and with whom, in leisure hours, we all played cricket and 'shoot'. It seemed to me then and seems to me much more so now an absurdity. And what seems even more absurd is that these prohibitions are still in force in some schools. I know of one boarding school, for example, where the pupils are beaten if found talking to any member of the opposite sex under the age of forty! I doubt very much whether all the ladies of the surrounding locality carry their birth certificates in their purses but if they do not the poor boys must have a difficult time. Some, I know, take the risk and endure the thrashing when detected.

The object of regulations such as these is to promote avoidance, to drive a wedge between boys and girls and make the whole concept of a sexual relationship seem, if not positively dirty, at least undesirable. The reasons given to defend the practice of segregation deserve a study to themselves—a treatise in sexual psychopathology. It would not, perhaps, matter very much if the instances I have cited were isolated and unusual. But they are widespread and generally approved by adults and parents—the very people who, in their capacities as responsible mediators of public opinion, express repugnance and horror against the sexually inverted. It seems that, on balance, we are prepared to risk homosexual tendencies (which we all have in varying measures) developing rather than take the other risk of extramarital sex relationships taking place during adolescence. We prefer the encouragement of latent homosexuality to the occasional unmarried mother and illegitimate child.

[1] Youth organizations also, in the main, reflect the same bias and operate on uni-sexual lines, although in more recent years the growth of 'mixed' clubs has been strikingly successful.

A NOTE ON SEX OFFENDERS

Two things, therefore, seem to my mind worth saying before we leave this topic. If by law and moral precept we wish to promote heterosexuality, our social institutions charged with the training of the youthful should facilitate and not impede such a development. Moreover, the practice of sentencing convicted sodomites to segregated prisons and the equally iniquitous isolation of adolescents and teenagers in borstals and approved schools can only encourage the growth of practices which ostensibly we wish to extirpate.[1]

Secondly, and here I quote from the Wolfenden Report, we must honestly face the fact that homosexual tendencies are not merely evil or unnatural, but may, and indeed often do, have valuable social resultants: 'amongst those who work with notable success in occupations which call for service to others, there are some in whom latent homosexuality provides the motivation for activities of the greatest value to society. Examples of this are to be found among teachers, clergy, nurses and those who are interested in youth movements and the care of the aged.'[2]

That quotation ought to be read and pondered on at some length. If it is true, if it contains indeed a substantial portion of veracity, then certain things must necessarily follow. If it is false, it must be shown to be so and rigorously exposed to condemnation. For my part I consider it to be true. Hence, I believe certain things must follow. The first is that we should acknowledge that human sexuality is more complex and many-sided than some have supposed, that manifestations can occur in more ways and at different times which appear to be, but are not necessarily, contradictory. And the law must take account of these differences and complexities and, when legislating, one manifestation should not be treated as less human or more degenerate than another. That homosexual relations of any active kind should be permitted in private between consenting adults in this country was the recommendation of the Home Office Committee. It was a majority, not an unanimous, view with certain members writing in their individual reservation. It seems to me a policy which would, in the main, help to

---

[1] There have been many instances of young men being sexually assaulted in prison itself, due partly to the seriously overcrowded conditions in the cells.

[2] Op. cit., p. 13.

create a wiser, more humane, less guilt-laden, and even richer, social order than we have yet attained.[1] To allow consenting adults their sexual freedom does not mean that we intend to permit a man to entice a boy to commit indecency or go free of the consequences. He would no more be free to seduce a juvenile than the heterosexual male adult would be to seduce a young girl. Indeed, the offence would be treated similarly and, I should hope, with similar gravity. Both are risks that, in the present state of our knowledge, are unavoidable in any kind of society. But to regard one as a legitimate risk to take and the other as an illegitimate one seems to me illogical and perverse. We do not want either offence to occur and must do our level best to prevent them both!

III

The question of what is indecent conduct in the broad sense is not so easily determined in spite of the lack of doubt in so many self-assured minds. We would probably all agree in the main that the public must be safeguarded against certain dubious acts and influences. But where to draw the line between the permissible and the prohibited is often a matter of opinion and taste as much as a clear moral issue. From time to time the police raid certain night clubs where, it is alleged, indecencies are taking place. The actors appear naked or take part in a dance highly suggestive of sexual intercourse or something of that kind. But can it be shown that such expensive cabarets exert any undesirable influence on the common citizen, or that any but the lewdly inclined will patronize such shows? How difficult it is, too, to distinguish between art and pornography. The recent court case over Lawrence's novel, *Lady Chatterley's Lover*, brought this issue dramatically to the fore and was ultimately resolved on the basis of expert literary taste. A youth whose sexual development is undergoing stress and difficulty might find the novel a temporary source of erotic excitement but should the book be banned for this reason? Even the Bible contains erotic passages which such a person could conceivably

---

[1] It would also substantially reduce the number of blackmail cases. Homosexuals are, for obvious reasons, particularly exposed to this pernicious exploitation.

use as a source of stimulation and pseudo-gratification, but ought they on that account be deleted?

It so happened that roughly about the time that Janacek's opera, *Cunning Little Vixen*, was being performed by Sadler's Wells the proprietor of a Soho revuebar was prosecuted for putting on an indecent floor show in which there was a scene in which a girl dancer playing the part of a stowaway was whipped on deck as the old custom was. In Janacek's opera the Cunning Little Vixen is also portrayed by a female and seen writhing on the ground and trying to avoid the switches of the boys.

In what way can we distinguish between the two mimed flagellations? In the last analysis, we can only do so on the basis of motivation and the relationship of the act to a central unfolding theme. In one case, the whipping is organically related to a serious artistic purpose and is functional to the plot, as in *Nicholas Nickleby*, while, in the other case, it is enacted to titillate the jaded sexual appetite. Nobody could maintain that the sight or description of flagellation does not stimulate the type of person who is erotically excited in this way, and, if we are honest most normal people are capable of being roused by what may be called sexual violence. But within the whole context of play, opera or novel such scenes and moments are both organic and subsidiary. They occur, as they do in real life, occasionally but are not indulged in orgiastically. And the dividing line between an undesirable orgy and true artistic purpose has to be drawn by experts, and what the experts say in 1960 and what they said in 1900 and what they are likely to say in the year 2000 is dependent upon changes in the general climate of public opinion. It is therefore subject to social definitions, and we can never completely reconcile the moral with the merely social and legal point of view. In spite of the fact that a certain novel or play has legally been declared fit for publication or public performance, a moralist may still maintain that it is objectionable. Similar considerations hold good of sex offences. Sex relations with a girl under sixteen are illegal and punishable at the moment. But in a few years' time, taking into account the possibly earlier physical maturity of young people to-day, the age of consent may be lowered to fifteen. What is now an offence will then become acceptable practice.

These movements in the climate of public opinion are constantly taking place and affect our ideas of what is pathological in human behaviour. In this way we see how psychological and social evaluations constantly interweave and modify one another and how the law is influenced by both.

IV

The topic of prostitution which the Wolfenden Committee also discussed is another illustration of how our values change, and of how the psychological interpretation is affected by and, at the same time, deeply influences purely social considerations. Prostitution of course is not an offence. The offence committed by prostitutes is that of soliciting in public, which is held to be a nuisance. This is a curious legal position which epitomizes our basic conflict over sexual activities. We find it difficult to forbid extramarital sex relationships, however much we may deplore them. Adultery is not a criminal offence in law in spite of the hardships and pain that such conduct may entail for many innocent relatives and dependants.

It has often been maintained that prostitution of females is the price we have to pay for monogamous marriage, which is, of course, a social institution of a particular kind not found in all societies. This view stems from the belief that men are naturally more promiscuous than women and that their sexual urges are less easily controlled and sublimated. It is wryly amusing that our Victorian forebears held this view with some force. In Victorian England, which is sometimes held up to us as a model of moral purity and religious rectitude, there operated what has come to be called 'the double standard of morality': one for the men and another more lofty ideal to which the women were obliged to conform. The men were permitted a degree of promiscuity and extramarital sex relationship while their spouses were expected to maintain the strictest standard of propriety and never to cast amatory glances at another male. This hypocritical attitude was bound up with the nauseating idea that women were inferior beings. They were part of their husbands' property and possessed few legal rights. As McGregor says in his fine study of divorce, 'Outside the family married women had the same legal status as children and lunatics; within it they were their husbands' inferiors.'[1] No wonder, then, that the divorce rates in those golden years of the past were low. And no wonder that prostitution flourished in British society to an extent our own more relaxed and venial age cannot equal. It is probably not generally known that in the heyday of Victorian England prostitution was legally recognized. In 1864 Parliament passed a Contagious Diseases Bill compelling the registration and medical treatment of prostitutes in certain naval and garrison towns. This was extended two years later to include the cathedral strongholds of Canterbury and Winchester and some other towns. A register was kept and prostitutes were forced to submit to periodic medical examinations in order to safeguard the health of Her Majesty's fighting men. It was this cynical bureaucratization of the double standard of morality on the part of frock-coated, top-hatted, bewhiskered Christian gentlemen that incited Josephine Butler and her supporters to launch their bitter and ultimately successful campaign for moral welfare.

The influence of the double standard mentality has also no doubt been responsible for the fact that it is the women who solicit and not the men who consort with them who fall foul of the law. But, as psychiatrists point out, prostitution involves a dual relationship. Not only ought both parties to come within the censure of the law, if justice is to be done, but both must contain within themselves the seeds of psychopathological disorder. In a stimulating paper given some years ago, Dr. Edward Glover[2] advanced the thesis that, contrary to popular views, many prostitutes exhibit acute sexual frigidity. They derive little or no pleasure from the sexual act but unconsciously are antagonistic towards the male partner. Glover maintains that in these cases the women, as a consequence of a disturbed childhood, have unconscious homosexual desires which produce much overt or latent hostility towards the male sex. For this reason they often steal from their clients, adding a further insult, as it were, to the basic financial exploitation whenever possible. Such women of the streets are often unusually drab and unprepossessing in their appearance, careless of toilet and appearance, and contrast with the merely unstable adolescent

[1] O. R. McGregor, *Divorce in England*, Heinemann, 1957, p. 67.
[2] *The Psycho-Pathology of Prostitution*, I.S.T.D., 1945.

girl, often in rebellion against her home and defying repressive discipline, who may indulge in the practice not so much for money as for companionship and the rewards of a free and easy life.

Clearly prostitutes shade off into irresponsible, misguided adolescents who in turn merge into the 'gold digger' type who may or may not give value for money. Some are professionals, others amateurs, some merely kept women serving a lodging house of foreign sailors for instance. But there are also, I believe, a number of women who, like the professional criminals, accept prostitution as a business career, believing that this offers the only prospect for them to make a good living. Such women may even have children and combine maternity with a career, being good mothers in the home by day but going forth at night to earn the bread and butter. Others almost certainly drift into prostitution quite casually and accidentally as a result of opportunities happening to be available or not at a particular time.

Prostitutes, like other sex delinquents, do not form a neat homogeneous group. But the majority have probably suffered in their early formative years from emotional difficulties arising from an unsatisfactory home life.[1] Their prostitution is not so much the way out of their difficulties as the logical outcome in given social and economic conditions. According to the McCords crimes against the person, which include sex offences, seem 'to be a reaction against either maternal domination or paternal rejection. Retaliation against the cruelty or neglect of their fathers and the over-protectiveness of their mothers seems to be the primary motivation.' 'Sexual crimes', they add, 'apparently stem from thwarted desires for maternal affection. Most of the sexual criminals had been raised by either passive or neglecting mothers. They also had neglecting or rejecting fathers.[2]

[1] Dr. Glover has put forward the interesting thesis that in the relationship between regular prostitute and a man who is a habitual customer, they are both giving expression to 'bad' images repressed in childhood. For the woman, the client represents 'the deteriorated image of the father' while man, still fixated to 'his old infantile profane love' is seeking the 'bad' image of his mother. If this view is correct it means that both are the victims of earlier normal sexual impulses which at a later stage they have failed to outgrow. For a fuller discussion see *The Psycho-Pathology of Prostitution*.

[2] William and Joan McCord, *Origins of Crime*, Columbia University Press, 1959, pp. 149 *et seq.*

A NOTE ON SEX OFFENDERS

Unfortunately for theories such as these, we have no satisfactory method of proving that there is a causal relationship between the rejecting or passive parent and the children's subsequent criminality. For one thing, we do not know, nor are we ever likely to know, the incidence of parents exhibiting such psychological defects in the population at large and whose offspring nevertheless turn out to be law-abiding conventional citizens. What evidence we have is mainly clinical and statistical, consisting of retrospective enquiries into the past histories of ascertained offenders. But, in the absence of other more satisfactory explanations, I think that we can accept these *post facto* psychological theories as useful hypotheses with which to work. If we refrain from accepting them uncritically and temper our speculations and researches with necessary scepticism, they should prove useful stepping stones towards further and fuller understanding of problems which are, by their nature, immensely complex.

As Dr. Glover has indicated, normal sexual adaptation, which would to a considerable extent apparently exclude the likelihood of many kinds of sex offences occurring, would 'involve a radical change in our present system of sexual upbringing' which needs to be much more liberal and loving and honest. Even where there are genuine subjective factors at work, Glover believes that 'it is still possible that improvement in conditions of upbringing will make all the difference between reasonably normal and definitely abnormal behaviour'.[1] That this may be so is to some extent illustrated by changes in the social status of women which have taken place over the past forty years. From a position of comparative inferiority they have achieved, if not parity with men, then a considerable loosening of economic and social restrictions and, as a result of the spread of knowledge of contraception, much more sexual autonomy and freedom both inside and outside marriage. At the same time 'there is some reason to believe that this in turn has led to a reduction in the number of confirmed professional prostitutes'.[2]

V

There is thus seen to be a constant interplay between social influences and personality factors in the production of many

[1] Glover, op. cit., p. 15.   [2] Ibid., p. 14.

kinds of sex offenders, and even in a field where psychological and psychiatric interpretations are probably pre-eminent, the sociological component cannot be ignored. As in our discussion of the more common types of offences committed against property, a consideration of sexual offenders has ultimately led us to the point of suggesting possible ways to mitigate the severity and incidence of such offences which involve the manipulation of the environment. Once again adequate home life, the blend of love and discipline, is seen to be important if not indeed crucial. There are also some purely medical measures which offer hopeful prospects for treatment in the future. In cases where glandular disturbance or other physiological conditions are suspected as being the source of aberrant and forbidden sexual behaviour certain drugs seem to be helpful. Stilboestrol, a chemical medicament similar to the female hormone oestrin, has been given to male perverts apparently with temporary improvement of their condition. It may well be that the future treatment of the grosser kinds of sexual abnormality will yield to bio-chemical measures. If so, the public alarm over the more unusual and dramatic kind of sex offence may diminish. There is no doubt that it is the sadistic sex murders and assaults rather than the activities of voyeurs and exhibitionists which create the greatest anxiety in most people's minds.

The case of Neville Heath is typical of such sadistic sexual homicides.[1] Heath murdered two girls and savagely assaulted them in the process. One victim he flogged and both were found to be covered by terrible bruises, cuts and wounds in the sacral regions. After death, he bit off the tips of their nipples. The details of the case, like many others committed by abnormal sex-maniacs, sound terrifyingly like the activities of the perverted characters portrayed in the American horror comics. The bald recital of such events makes us wonder whether such beings as participate in them can be called human. Our next line of defence is to describe them as maniacs, and write them off as mad. But the jury who listened to the prosecution of Heath thought differently and he was subsequently executed.

The case of Heath and of Clarke, who found sexual relief only in putting his hand on women's throats or in being caned

[1] For the full account see W. Lindesay Neustatter, *The Mind of the Murderer*, Christopher Johnson, 1957.

by prostitutes, raises once more the question of responsibility discussed in an earlier chapter. Neither Heath nor Clarke was admitted to be insane in the legal sense under the McNaughton rules. Yet both were adjudged insane in the medical sense by some psychiatrists. But whether legally or medically insane, most people would agree that their behaviour was of such a character that they ought to be permanently lodged in a place of secure restraint. We might make yet another category and call them socially insane. Yet when a Scots youth aged sixteen was found guilty of strangling a seven-year-old girl, after indecently assaulting her, in August 1961, he was merely sentenced to ten years' detention. Thus by the time he is twenty-five he will in all probability be permitted to live in ordinary society once again, and one cannot help wondering what will happen.

Medical insanity, or rather psychosis, seems, in cases where such individuals commit serious crimes, a strangely confused concept. At what moment do we judge that the insanity is operative? Shall we wait until the little girl has been raped and strangled before taking action? Shall we even accept that once a man has committed such an offence he must therefore be insane? There must be a division between eccentricity, abnormality and madness. But where does it lie?

These profound questions have no easy answers. They lie deep at the roots of human criminality. I raise them here, not to offer any trite conclusions, but to indicate the importance of being able to distinguish between normal and abnormal human behaviour if we are to understand and treat criminals correctly. It seems to me that we ought to be intensifying research into these tremendous problems, rather than concentrating, as we often tend to do, on devising and assessing new ways of dealing with the less serious kinds of criminals and delinquents, who commit their offences mainly against property.

Chapter 14

CRIME AND PROSPERITY

I

It is commonly and, I believe, erroneously supposed that while crime in the past is understandable if not excusable, in modern times it ought not to exist. Social critics frequently point out that at a time of increasing material progress, when the provisions of the social services have never been so inclusive and extensive, the official criminal figures show a substantial upward trend. In the past, it is assumed, poverty, bad housing, the lack of many supposedly necessary social and physical amenities, together accounted for the existence of an embittered, hostile and criminal minority who developed feelings of antagonism, despair and frustration to such a degree that they fought against the existing regime in order to wrest for themselves and their families the means of existence. The drunkenness, despair and depravity of slum-dwellers in the midst of prosperous Victorian society led social reformers to the naive hope that, if only the adverse physical and material conditions could be eliminated, criminality would also be checked and contained. Such hopes have been cruelly disappointed. For crime and higher living standards have advanced hand in hand, and, as we saw in a previous section, the amount of known crime has actually about doubled over the past twenty years.

General dismay has resulted from awareness of these facts. Typical of many such headings is one that appeared in *The Observer* not long ago. *Affluence and crime advance together.*[1] It went on to report a speech by Mr. R. Brooman-White, joint Scottish Under-Secretary, to a conference on penology held in Dunblane.

[1] *The Observer*, 5th, March 1961.

'Of all the field of psychology', I quote from the report of his address, 'knowledge about human delinquency had perhaps advanced the least. They had very little real knowledge of why offenders offended and what punishment or treatment would stop them doing it.'

A recent Home Office Report, *Penal Practice in a Changing Society*,[1] commences on a similar note of puzzled dismay:

'It is a disquieting feature of our society that in the years since the war, rising standards in material prosperity, education and social welfare have brought no decrease in the high rate of crime reached during the war: on the contrary, crime has increased and is still increasing.'

This is an understandable complaint and one frequently heard from enlightened people who care about the quality of life in our society and who are saddened by the implications of increasing lawlessness, even, and perhaps especially, among children and young people. When one addresses conferences of teachers, magistrates or social workers, the same question inevitably emerges. How can you reconcile the existence of full employment, the Welfare State and increased criminal activity?

II

I think one must begin to answer this question by clearing the ground of some conventional but probably misconceived ideas. It may well be that an increase in crime is connected with greater material prosperity but the relationship is not nearly as simple as it seems. The idea that less poverty and more prosperity would of itself automatically reduce crime was a naive one. It assumed that crime sprang from one simple root cause. This is clearly not the case. Crime as we have shown is not a simple phenomenon. It is a term we use as a carpet-bag into which we throw a whole series of diverse and utterly different forms of behaviour. And, just because we have thrown them all in the same bag, we deduce that they must be similar. But we forget that it was we ourselves who put them into that bag. What we should have done, of course, was to provide ourselves with a whole number of bags into which we could have put roughly similar types of offences. In other words, we

[1] Cmnd. 645.

were treating heterogeneous phenomena as though they were homogeneous. And then complaining that it didn't make sense!

Our whole concept of crime was astray. We thought of it merely as wrongdoing or immorality. But it is in fact a socio-legal concept of immense complexity. It is graphically to be represented by a Hydra. It is many-headed. Its causes are multiple. Even from the purely sociological viewpoint it can be said to arise from a number of different sources: from status and financial frustration, from inadequate socialization in the home, from a conflict of cultural values, from the rebelliousness of youth and from residence in an under-privileged neighbour-hood, to name the most important ones only. There is indeed no such thing as Crime except as a very abstract philosophical notion. Pragmatically there are only crimes and criminals. Progress in criminological science can only be achieved if, as in other sciences, we begin by classification of the phenomena under study. We must begin by grouping things roughly similar and sharply distinguishing them from things quite dissimilar. At a later stage we will no doubt have to divide and sub-divide the things which at first we thought were the same. Definition and observation will lead to more accurate classification, and accurate classification will alone enable us to discern and describe causes. But there is not a cause of crime as such, only different causes of different crimes committed by disparate criminals. The hope is that in time we will be skilled enough to begin to see a causal pattern underlying the origins of certain types of offences and offenders. Just as medical science learned in time to distinguish between, say, measles and chicken-pox, but could make no progress at all by searching for the cause of disease. Each disease is different in origin and nature, though some diseases are sufficiently alike for them to be usefully grouped together. Obviously virus infections cannot be treated or regarded as being similar to functional disorders arising from states of mental hysteria.

It is therefore to my mind misleading to say, as the McCords did in a book which I have already for other reasons highly commended, that 'Property crimes seem to be motivated pri-marily by a desire for attention' and only 'to some extent for material welfare'.[1] Such a partial explanation leads ultimately

[1] *Origins of Crime*, p. 151.

to unscientific confusion. It is the original sin of over-simplifica-
tion and unwise generalization in the search for causes. It may
well be that with a certain type of offender theft arises from a
quest for affection or attention or both. But it is utterly misleading to even hint that such motivation is primary in most cases
and that the acquisitive purpose is usually secondary or even
non-existent. This is the weakness and danger of attempting to
explain all human behaviour in terms of the psychology of the
individual—a tendency that all too many writers and investigators nowadays evidence.

III

It will by now be abundantly clear that the viewpoint I myself
favour involves a combination of psychological and sociological
analysis. In preceding chapters I have stressed the significance
of the social structure in promoting and encouraging certain
kinds of behaviour. Moreover, I believe that the purely sociological explanations of criminal and delinquent activity have
to a great extent been lost sight of because of the undue attention that has increasingly been given to psychological and
psychiatric theories. As a result, the work of criminologists has
been seriously impaired and much confusion has resulted.
Psychiatrists have gone on concentrating attention on the reactions of the individual and the operations of the private mind
and have taken society itself for granted. Meanwhile, incidentally, nobody has given much attention to an evaluation of
psychiatric treatment or carried out an objective follow-up
study of delinquents who have been through medical hands to
see whether this approach to the crime problem was itself fruitful. Indeed, short-term clinical methods have become an end
in themselves, and reliance upon 'psychiatric treatment' and
the work of the child guidance clinics is widely accepted on
faith rather than demonstrable truth.[1]

To return to our original starting point, while the welfare
services have been expanding and full employment has been

[1] 'Psychiatrists and psychologists have played a large part in suggesting
the lines of attack which are most widely used today *though their efficiency has
yet to be proved*', Dr. T. C. N. Gibbens, *Trends in Juvenile Delinquency*, W.H.O.,
1961, p. 40. My italics.

achieved in most parts of the country and, we might also add, psychological interpretations of criminal behaviour have also been greatly in vogue and more psychiatric treatment has been made available, the numbers of offenders seem to have gone up and up. In other words, the Welfare State, economic prosperity, more humane methods of treatment, increasing psychological and medical services appear to have had very little effect on the crime rates. Rather these things have all marched side by side, if not hand in hand.

Two popular explanations for this state of affairs have been put forward. In the first place, it is argued, moral standards have deteriorated and there has been a flight from organized religion. The churches are more than half-empty, their message ignored and even held in disrepute. The present is an irreligious, godless, materialistic, hedonistic generation, given over to violence, sexual indulgence and the pursuit of transient pleasures. Secondly, there has been a loosening of the bonds of family life, the sacrament of marriage is denigrated, divorce is rife, and the home life of the nation in a state of corruption and disintegration.

These two explanations are intimately bound up with one another. They boil down to the same thing: spiritual decay. If they are true, the condition of contemporary British society is indeed lamentable. Small wonder, then, that crime is everywhere on the increase and likely to become more widespread.

I have not the space here to deal with these doctrines of despair in detail or to refute each single accusation of national degeneracy. I would, however, point out that the evidence for such a wholesale condemnation of modern society is very dubious indeed. It may be true that fewer people go to church, but those who do, attend for reasons of greater sincerity than ever in the past. It may be that fewer people find pietism a rewarding way of life but notions of social justice, equality of opportunity and individual dignity are more universally honoured in all forms of social organization than ever before. It may be that the divorce rate has risen steeply, but that is as much a proof of the high value attached to marriage and family life as a denial of their meaning.

In other words, the past half century has witnessed many social changes. But these changes are not all unmitigated disasters. Some are undeniable advances. There is probably more tenderness for other people and a greater respect for their individual aspirations and basic rights than our much-lauded Victorian ancestors dreamed either possible or desirable. More honesty, too, in personal relations; a greater willingness to face realities, however painful, and to admit fallibility if not sin. Such attitudes do not to my mind stem from spiritual degeneracy. I even find them consonant with the great ethical pronouncements embodied in the Sermon on the Mount. And this suggests to me that while churchianity is certainly dying, Christianity may yet be a powerful leaven working its silent transformation of the great social lump.

IV

It is only, I believe, by taking into account the sociological as well as the moral and psychological views that we can possibly hope to understand the changes that are everywhere going on around us in contemporary society. Above all, as we have argued in preceding chapters, it is only an examination of the nature of society itself that will give us the clue to explain why crime and delinquency rates have gone up *pari passu* with improved social conditions.

Society exists *sui generis*. It is a thing, a noun. It is impersonal, objective and relatively stable and enduring. It is built up of a number of parts which together interweave to create solid social structures. These structures, which are variously institutions, processes and organizations, exist in relation to the individuals who make up the population rather as the bony skeletal frame of the body does in relation to flesh and blood. Without structure, society could not exist. It would disintegrate into 'a dust of individuals'. Without the skeleton the body would be nothing but a jelly.

In the general social structure certain ideas and notions have become institutionalized and made semi-permanent. The class system, for example, which is related to the need for some individuals to exercise power and authority, is not just a result of individual selfishness. It does not arise merely because certain psychopathological men wanted to impose their wills on their fellows as a compensation, say, for being unloved by their mothers or savagely weaned by their nurses. In fact, such mentally perverted individuals do seek power and ruthlessly strive to exploit their brethren. In fascist and totalitarian states we can see this urge to dominate explicitly at work. Democracy exists as a very real obstacle to the concentration of absolute dictatorial power in the hands of any one individual or small group. The social and political structure of a democratic state may be said to limit personal power and prevent dictatorship from arising. In such states it can only come into being by force, through a military coup, which destroys the old structure and replaces it with a new politico-social system.

It will be clear, then, that democratic principles are not merely ideas and philosophies. To be effective they have to be made into social reality by organization. If the structure of society is dictatorial, aristocratic or oligarchical, democratic principles are socially frustrated and may find few adherents. The ideas, values and attitudes that individual citizens have are to a considerable extent influenced by the social forms in which they are educated. This does not mean that there can never be any change, or that the individual mind and conscience is utterly at the mercy of the social framework. The relation between the individual and society and the way in which social changes occur are of tremendous importance in sociology, but we cannot pursue them further here. The point must, however, be borne in mind that social structure not only influences behaviour and attitudes, *it also embodies principles and ideas in the first place.* One of the things we have to take responsibility for as individual citizens is to make sure that our social institutions embody and promote the social philosophies that we *on other grounds believe* to be right.

We must now relate this analysis (over-simplified as it undoubtedly is!) to the phenomenon of crime.

V

Crime like other human behaviour is learned. In a minority of cases it may arise more or less spontaneously as a result of individual illness or mental unbalance. But, in the main, as I have argued earlier, it is essentially normal behaviour. Normal in two ways. First, it is normal psychologically, in that it has by and large the same motivation and goals that ordinary 'law-abiding' people's behaviour has. And normal, secondly, in that it arises in response to pressures generated by the social structure, by society itself, which as a system has institutionalized these goals, attitudes and motivations. It is not so much that the social structure, as such, forces people to become delinquents as that it makes it much more likely in cases where individuals fail, for a whole variety of reasons, to make a success of their lives as success is defined by generally accepted values. Crime is to such people an alternative road to achievement. In this view it is possible to claim that a society has the criminals it deserves or helps to create, or, to use a metaphor from chemistry, it precipitates its own delinquency.

Terence Morris puts it this way:

'The competitive society has something of the character of the compulsory game. We are all forced to play and penalized if we do not achieve at least some measure of success. The delinquent is the person who, unable to win, has either sneaked round the back to get at the prizes or who has turned aggressively against the other competitors in the bleakness of despair.'[1]

While Robert K. Merton, approaching the topic from a rather different angle, has pointed out the basic similarity and near-identity of the economic roles of both legitimate and illegitimate business men:

'Both are in some degree concerned with the provision of goods and services for which there is an economic demand. Morals aside, they are both business, industrial and professional enterprises, dispensing goods and services which some people want, for which there is a market—and in a prevalently market society, we would expect appropriate enterprises to arise whenever there is a market demand for certain goods and services.'[2]

VI

We have already drawn attention to two remarkable facts which emerge from a study of criminal statistics. Crime is predominantly a male activity in our society, and it is characteristically

---

[1] 'The Carrot Out of Reach', *The Listener*, 4th, June 1959.

[2] *Social Theory and Social Structure*, The Free Press, Revised and Enlarged Edition, 1957, p. 79.

committed against property. The institution of private property in our kind of society is intimately bound up with the type of offence that is most common. Both the male role as bread-winner and the careful husbandry of personal possessions are part and parcel of the social structure. Other forms of social organization are possible, but these are ones which have been chosen and which have also developed in the course of history in western culture.

As Malinowski has shown, in primitive and small societies, although much property may be personal and may even be handed on from father to son, the sort of crime that afflicts our highly complex, comparatively huge industrial society has little place. In a south-sea island village community, theft of a permanent kind is almost impossible. If you take another man's canoe, you have to bring it back to the harbour and everyone in the locality knows who it belongs to. There is no hiding place for stolen goods, unless you opt out of that community altogether and take your stolen canoe with you hoping to join up with some other small settlement. But in the world of the Trobriand islanders you cannot steal, you merely borrow. That is to say, you commit a breach of custom rather than commit a crime.[1]

In the infinitely complicated mass societies which characterize western industrial civilization, crime unfortunately does pay. Or, people consider the risk worth running. You have something like a fifty-fifty chance of success. Moreover, strong social pressures are continually exerted on all of us to acquire more and more goods, more and more personal possessions. In fact, our economic buoyancy has been said to depend very largely upon convincing more and more customers to buy more and more goods so that production may increase. Waste rather than conservation is the key to prosperity—the reverse of wartime conditions when as individuals we furiously conserve in order to indulge in communal waste.

Consumer demands and expectations are constantly rising in the more prosperous and successful societies, be they capitalistic or communistic in political organization apparently.[2] The

---

[1] See B. Malinowski, *Crime and Custom in Savage Society*, Kegan Paul, 1936, passim.

[2] N.B. We are not saying here that Communism is any better or more desirable!

difference between the two seems to be largely a matter of control.

In Britain, America, Sweden and the other capitalist democracies, which we know a fair amount about, we might indeed go so far as to say that, in existing conditions, a high crime rate may be taken as an index of economic success.

In these countries, to which we might also add Federal Germany, Norway and Italy, the increase in property offences has been paralleled by improved living standards and conditions. There has in most countries, also, been an increase in offences against the person and sex offences. These three things are undoubtedly inter-connected, and arise in the main from changes in social structure rather than from widespread lapse from grace on the part of the populations.

If we take the U.S.A. as an extreme example of a country which has achieved a high standard of living for its citizens together with an exceptionally high crime rate, we obtain clues which enable us to understand what is happening on a somewhat more lowly degree in our own society. When Donald Taft accused American culture of being criminogenic he was saying in effect that a socio-economic system based on free enterprise capitalistic principles is positively criminalistic both in the way it is organized and in the attitudes of mind it characteristically produces. Taft goes on in the same context:

'American culture is, even if decreasingly, the embodiment of materialism. The dollar is dominant if not almighty. The symbol of success is still what Veblen called conspicuous consumption. Honest dollars may be preferred to dishonest dollars, but not a few unearned dollars *have* brought prestige.'

Thus it is the successful, rather than the honest or public-spirited, businessman who is afforded status, and both his success and his prestige are largely estimated by financial gain.

'Whatever the economists may say, speculative gains look more like luck than hard work, and more nearly approximate the something-for-nothing philosophy of the pickpocket.'[1]

Marshall Clinard in his study of black market activities previously referred to has said substantially the same thing about American business methods and attitudes. He maintains that

[1] Donald Taft, *Criminology*, New York, Macmillan, 3rd edition, 1956, p. 39 *et seq.*

there is as yet no consensus of opinion in the United States which is prepared to consider 'business violations as crimes . . . even though they were, on the whole, wilful and evasive transgressions of the law'.[1] Indeed, he goes so far as to say that, during the periods of national emergency, many people believed that even then the government had no right to interfere in business in any way! There should be no bar against individual money-making enterprise, and the desire to make profits, while others were dying to defend their country, should be allowed to continue uncurbed! For men who hold such extreme views, business and free enterprise and the prospect of unlimited financial gain are a positive way of life. They are in fact a religion.

Sutherland, Shaw and McKay and many other criminologists and sociologists have indicted American society on similar grounds. Their verdict is that the social structure is itself powerfully criminogenic. Such critics, be it noted, are patriotic Americans, not cynical Europeans making easy gibes from outside. And the findings of the Kefauver Committee overwhelmingly endorse this severe censure. The weird tale of the activities of the Mafia, a shadowy international organization controlling much of America's vice, the career of Greasy Thumb Guzik who walks in the footsteps of the notorious Al Capone, the impunity with which the Capone Syndicate has operated since the demise of its master, the devious ways whereby the racketeers infiltrate into legitimate business and still, where necessary, use murder to obtain their evil ends as well as the normal fixing and corruption, are all to be found in Kefauver's own account of the Senate enquiry of which he was so able a chairman. At the end of his book he was moved to passionate outcry:

'Why, I ask, in the name of everything sacred to our democratic civilization, should these killers and extortionists—the master racketeers and the erstwhile bosses of Murder Inc.—be permitted to get away with it? Even assuming that the gangsters have forsaken crime as they claim—and of course they lie in their teeth when they say it, for all of them are still up to their armpits in crime—why should they have been permitted to slide into legitimate fields and escape unpunished?'[2]

They escape unpunished, of course, because they *have* infil-

[1] Clinard, op. cit., pp. 341–2.   [2] *Crime in America*, p. 235.

trated ordinary business, because their deeds are not very dis-consonant with the *mores* of the businessmen's world, as Clinard and others have indicated. It is certainly not because Americans are more wicked than other nations (they are a deal more honest than most!), but because their society is so organized that it is hard for public-spirited men, whose integrity is above reproach, to collect the evidence necessary to bring them to justice. Interestingly enough, the gangster and racketeer is said to be much more in fear of the income tax officials than of the law enforcement machine![1]

The freedom enjoyed by the crooks is the inevitable con-comitant of the freedom enjoyed and desired by honest men. It represents the dark reverse side of a precious medal. In a country where the individual is supreme, individualism can be abused. If too many curbs and controls are placed on personal freedom in order to prevent villainy, some of the highest values incorporated in this sort of democracy may be sacrificed. And the price may be too high a one to pay.

Similarly the Freudians have argued with some justification that aesthetic creativity and altruistic dedication are the out-come of individual frustrations, which may or may not be purely sexual. If we could eliminate the source of the frustrations it would almost certainly mean the end of much artistic and ethical inspiration, and the world would accordingly be a much less interesting place to live in. If we had a choice, which luckily we usually have not, which would we choose? Many of us would, I think, prefer to have the immortal works of a Leonardo, a Beethoven or a Shakespeare to three well-adjusted uncreative pedestrian lives which, in any case, would be fleeting and soon forgotten.

VII

Now, while it cannot be argued that here in Britain we have anything like the freedom, the wealth or the crime that America enjoys, a similar analysis can be applied. But we must realize that British society is in some important respects very unlike American. For one thing we have accepted the idea of con-trols in public life. Our freedom as individuals is much more

---

[1] Al Capone himself was finally brought to trial on a charge of falsifying his tax returns and not for his gangster activities as such.

circumscribed than our transatlantic cousins. We have also a much more comprehensive system of social welfare. The Welfare State, which in theory, if not always adequately in practice, protects us from the cradle to the grave, creates, and, in its turn, arises from, a rather less extreme attitude of mind than American people understand. Many Americans are suspicious of too much welfare because it is alleged to weaken 'moral fibre' and curtail freedom. We might say in this country that we operate a system of compromise capitalistic democracy in which some forms of individual freedom have been surrendered in return for certain individual securities.

Another characteristic of British society is its class structure. We are, by comparison with many other countries, extremely class conscious. Social mobility as an ideal is not so widely accepted here as it is in the United States. There is no British dream exactly corresponding to the American dream. Our ambitions are much more lowly, and we are in the main satisfied with second-best for ourselves. Our vitals are not so constantly gnawed by aspiration and the advice of the admassmen to get on and get up and get rich leaves us rather cooler. Being an older society we are perhaps more sceptical. Pioneering is a thing of the past. Moreover, we are all a little cynical about flamboyant success. If anyone we know makes a lot of money, we are inclined to ask 'What dirty tricks did he get up to?' rather than applaud or envy his rise. There is a strong tradition in the middle classes for what may be termed public service—an old, imperial *noblesse oblige* approach to life which does not necessarily equate personal or social value with money or possessions. Many of the men who went out to the colonies and dependencies as officials—not as commercial exploiters who were also there!—did so as a form of service. Rightly or wrongly they believed they had something to give as well as to get and were content with comparatively modest financial returns for their life's work. The same tradition inspires the best in British social work today and is the heart and soul of our prolific voluntary organizations.

All these things—the Welfare State, the traditional class structure, the upper class tradition at its best, coupled with an almost inborn anglo-saxon scepticism and love of compromise—have made British society much less dynamic and much more stable than American. For these reasons I believe, crime and delinquency are for us much less severe problems.[1] Being more content with our lot, we are less open to economic and social frustration. But in so far as our society is geared up to naked success, to moneymaking and the profit motive we must also suffer from many of the unavoidable handicaps. Britain is no better than America, but it is different—a minor variation on a common theme.

Thus, if my thesis be correct, the structure of British society, while in some of its aspects it is plainly criminogenic, in other aspects possesses built-in safeguards against their excess. The divorce between the law-makers and the law-enforcement officers, between the executive and judiciary, is also a powerful bulwark in Britain against the corruption which threatens to poison the good blood of American democracy.

It is true that crime in this country is about double what it was before the Second World War. It is true that many people still pursue purely materialistic ends. Paul Ferris has told the story of how the market reacted to the Conservative Party victory in the elections of 1959, of how, when the 'threat' of nationalization was lifted from the steel industry, the shares added £60,000,000 to their value in the space of a single hour. 'It was pandemonium,' he wrote, 'and if you had your fingers in the honey, it was lovely.'[2]

While it is still possible to dabble in the honey and the lolly so greedily, crime, as an alternative route to the same success, is not likely to diminish. Poorer people and those who feel themselves cut off from the riotous indulgence in the so-called good things of life will still be open to severe temptations to break the law or violate the social norms. It is something that all classes are exposed to, not merely the lower socio-economic groups. We have little concrete evidence to show that crime and illegal practices are widespread throughout the whole of our society, and one of the fields of criminological research which is in need of development is that which relates type and frequency of

---

[1] In New York, it has been shown, there is on the average day, one homicide, 27 felonious assaults, 3 rapes, 140 burglaries, 69 grand larcenies, and a whole variety of miscellaneous offences that make Great Britain, even London, seem like a kindergarten by comparison.

[2] *The City*, p. 29.

offence to social class. But what evidence we have is highly suggestive. Says Sutherland, contrasting the somewhat crude and physical type of crime associated with slum-dwellers with the highly sophisticated subtleties of upper income people groups, 'The people of the business world are probably more criminalistic . . . than are the people of the slums . . . the crimes of the business world . . . are indirect, devious, anonymous and impersonal. . . . The Perpetrators . . . do not feel the resentment of their victims and the criminal practices continue and spread.[1]

VIII

Prosperity, therefore, far from allaying the necessity for crime, tends to exacerbate it further in a society which has institutionalized the goals of financial reward and free enterprise. That this increase in crime in Britain is still retained within reasonable bounds is the result of the built-in safeguards already mentioned. But, if economic prosperity increases over the next quarter of a century, we can look forward to rising crime rates as the probable concomitant, unless we decide to undertake a substantial revision of society as a whole. Skilled social work techniques may help to contain, but they will never reduce, the problem, for the simple reason that they do not touch the heart of the matter. Crime is intimately bound up with the social structure. If we seriously want to eliminate or greatly reduce its incidence, then we must alter the social system. We must create a new society. But the price we will have to pay to achieve so vast and comprehensive a change may be too high for many of us to contemplate. Revolution is not an easy or comfortable experience. So much good may be lost in order to avoid some of the evils of crime that we may well decide, on balance, that it must be to some degree accepted. Like the sufferer from high blood pressure we may elect to live with our disability and come to terms with our complaint. The cure for hypertension may be having to live a life of such insufferable boredom that we would rather be dead.

I would myself advocate the reconstitution of society. I would like to see our social institutions overhauled and renovated to bring them into line with agreed moral purposes. But I must

[1] Op. cit., pp. 46–7.

confess that I see no prospect of this happening. Even if we would collectively arrive at an accepted moral code, I doubt if we would ever agree on the way in which it could be achieved and incorporated in social organization. It seems that the most we can reasonably hope for is that we should try to work out together some *modus vivendi* which will produce the minimum discomfort and crime with the least social dislocation for us all. How we may, as a nation, come to terms with crime and perhaps contain it within manageable proportions is the theme of the final section of this book.

CHAPTER 15

CONCLUSIONS AND PRESCRIPTIONS

I

The main argument of this book has been intended to show that society itself is in some respects criminogenic and to a considerable extent precipitates its own delinquency. My plea has been that we should concentrate more on the concept of crime as essentially normal and not abnormal behaviour.

I have argued that delinquency is found in every stratum of society, that it links hands with business and commerce and is not solely associated with slum neighbourhoods, as many often suppose, but extends throughout the length and breadth of the land. In a phrase, crime is endemic, not epidemic, in our society.

Some kinds of crime are normal because they are associated with motivations which maintain the dynamic life and expanding prosperity of our society. They are normal also because they result from common psychological impulses within individuals. A truly free society must contain within itself the potentiality of deviance. Freedom to choose must mean both the possibility of making wrong choices, i.e. crime, and of making unpopular choices.

We ought not, therefore, to expect the complete elimination of crime and delinquency, for the more perfectly our society attains certain of its objectives, the more the social structure promotes some of the values and attains the ends that are implicit and explicit in some forms of social and economic organization, the more delinquency is likely to be stimulated.

Moreover, from the mental health viewpoint, also, it may not be desirable to eliminate all traces of delinquent behaviour.

CONCLUSIONS AND PRESCRIPTIONS

'There is much to indicate that delinquency is a disorder with a comparatively good prognosis and may represent a valuable safety valve,' says Dr. Gibbens. He goes on to quote from Penrose, who, in 1939, showed that in many countries there is an inverse relationship between the numbers of people in prison and those in mental hospitals. 'Where the mental hospital population is large, the prison population is small and *vice versa.*'[1]

II

To many, this view is merely a doctrine of despair. It implies that crime will always be with us: that, whatever we do, it is ineradicable. What is the use then of trying to rid ourselves of it? Are not all our efforts foredoomed to failure? Should not all magistrates, probation officers and other social workers concerned with the prevention and treatment of delinquency abandon their present jobs and go off into the country to keep chickens?

I think we must answer those who get depressed by the seeming failure of all our efforts to reduce the volume of crime by pointing out that, although their work may seem to be futile, it is in fact more successful and necessary than they suppose. If some crime is like physical pain it may well be both necessary and useful, nevertheless we want to prevent its increase. We do not acquiesce in its continuing. As soon as it registers its message, its work is done. We can only tolerate so much. Beyond a certain point, pain destroys the organism and makes life utterly intolerable.

So, too, crime and delinquency cannot be tolerated beyond a certain level. What that level may be is probably impossible to determine but a good working philosophy is that we should *aim to eliminate although only expect to restrain* it. Otherwise there is a danger of creating a criminal society and not merely a society in which crime is normal. In a healthy society crime plays a part, but only a small part, in the total social process. In a truly criminal society something akin to jungle law obtains. That is to say it is not a society in our sense of the word at all

---

[1] T. C. N. Gibbens, op. cit., p. 21. This statement implies that in some countries the anti-social are sent to prison, while in other countries they are placed in hospitals.

but merely a network of predatory relationships within a specific geographical area.

It is the function, then, of the social services, and particularly of those services which are linked with courts and the treatment of offenders, to contain criminal activity within as narrow limits as is compatible with social health. They provide the safety valves, as it were, to relieve internal pressures when they become dangerously high.

III

In the above paragraphs I have been speaking mainly about normal, not abnormal, crime. The distinction is immensely important, because abnormal crime is malignant and must be extirpated. Its origin is always psychopathological. It is altogether of a different order and kind from what we may call benign delinquency. Its presence both in the individual and in the society is definitely disastrous. Fortunately, it is not very common and is certainly never widespread, but its impact can be truly terrifying. In the attack on abnormal, malignant criminality we can all unite forces with a good conscience and strive unceasingly to achieve its destruction.

I want now, by way of summary of the foregoing chapters, to say something about the treatment and prevention of crime under the two main rubrics of 'benign' and 'malignant' offences.

In so far as the future existence of our country depends on originality, initiative, daring and controlled aggressiveness, we must agree that such potentially valuable tendencies in young people should be fostered rather than suppressed. If we are to do this then we must give young people a fair amount of latitude. This in turn means that we must be prepared to tolerate some forms of misbehaviour, even of violence and predation, without reacting with excessive repression. Demands for the reintroduction of the cat and the birch, even encouragement of wider use of corporal punishment in schools, longer prison and borstal sentences may be described as socially over-reactive behaviour. They seek to put the clock back and dam up energies which could be utilized to the general benefit. They are as archaic and inept deterrents as were the treadmill, the pillory, the hanging-drawing-and-quartering which I doubt if even the most back-ward of backwoodsmen in the penological field would nowadays dare to advocate.

The reasons behind this over-reaction to crime are fairly clear. As my senior colleague, Professor T. S. Simey, often says, we all have to restrain anti-social tendencies in ourselves. It is, as he puts it, a matter of brakes. None of us has a set of entirely effective brakes and we often show signs of slipping and this experience makes us afraid. So we develop an interest (often a morbid interest) in the business of the inefficiency of other people's brakes, especially if we believe our own to be broken or bad. Moreover, bad braking by others is a threat to our own security. The criminal alarms us deeply and so we fear and hate him. Thus we read a newspaper account of criminal acts with avidity and develop both individually and as a society an interest in crime and punishment, which is well-nigh patho-logical and almost totally unrelated to the number of criminals in our midst.

Benign delinquency, as I see it, springs from two main sources: on the one hand, it is bound up with the values and goals of normal society, and, on the other, it is intimately associated with group sentiments and the natural desire of people to belong to social groups in which they feel secure and valued members. The juvenile gang is not an evil phenomenon. If it indulges in excessively dangerous criminal acts it becomes undesirable. It must, therefore, be transformed. The good qualities must be retained, the undesirable results eliminated. Mere suppression will not achieve this end. We have to find outlets for these groups which are socially acceptable substitutes for the be-haviour which in another context we deprecate. It is therefore an educational rather than a penal problem. We are to concentrate on habit formation. To do this we need to control the environ-ment.

IV

When Barbara Wootton headed an article on the report of the Ingleby Committee *What Shall we do with Naughty Children?*[1] some readers may have felt impatient with the innocuous im-plications. But most offenders are 'naughty children', not

[1] *The Spectator*, 2nd December 1960.

desperate outlaws. What they need is education or, rather, re-education, not punishment.

As far as our treatment of this sort of benign offender is concerned (and there are thousands of them constantly coming before the juvenile courts every year) we make the mistake of separating social training into two distinct categories; the scholastic and the penal. As Lady Wootton has argued, a child's upbringing is concentrated in two centres, the school and the home, and these two institutions should mutually support each other. The school supplies what the home lacks, but the school cannot do its work effectively without parental backing. With the vast majority of middle- and upper-class children nothing more is required to effect their social training. They enjoy, however, as a result of the differential class structure of our society, an education that goes on throughout childhood and adolescence. The children of lower- and working-class families leave school at fifteen, and for them the facilities of Further Education on a part-time basis are in theory, but not always in practice, supplied. Under the heading of Further Education we include the work of County Colleges (when they come into being), Day Continuation Classes and the Youth Service. Clearly the existing educational and recreational services available for seventy per cent of the young people of the country are inadequate and are failing, for a whole variety of reasons, to do their job properly.

We must therefore begin the containment of benign delinquency, not by building more approved schools or new detention centres, but by bringing our existing educational service up to scratch and by expanding and developing whatever new facilities are necessary under the umbrella of Education.

I will not deal here with the deficiencies of the ordinary day schools, for that is a vast topic worthy of sustained and serious consideration. I will only say that much of the primary and secondary modern education now being given in the tough neighbourhoods of the big cities is failing from lack of adequate support, and this failure is the responsibility of both parents and education authorities.[1] The successful prevention of much delin-

[1] I would refer interested readers to two books by myself which deal specifically with this important problem. *On the Threshold of Delinquency* and *Education and the Urban Child*. Both are published by the Liverpool University Press.

quency depends to an enormous extent upon schools doing a much better job than they are at the moment enabled to do.

I want, rather, to reiterate Lady Wootton's plea for an integration of all existing methods for educating children, be they delinquents or not, under the one broad administrative framework. As she points out, 'a formidable apparatus already exists' to deal with naughty children, but it is unfortunately not all incorporated within the same system.

'Already our educational provision includes (on paper) schools for every variety of handicapped or difficult child, including schools for the maladjusted. If the Approved Schools now under the control of the Home Office and even the Attendance Centres now run by the police were integrated into the same system by transfer to the Ministry of Education, surely the educational world would be fully equipped to provide the education *"and discipline"* required by any normal child *and to do this within the framework of its ordinary schooling*. Only in the event of a proposal to send a child away to a residential institution against both his own and his parents' wishes should it be necessary to invoke judicial process—and with patient co-operation between the education authorities and the parent such cases can be rare.'[1]

The immense advantage of such a programme would be that delinquents would no longer be exposed to further undesirable stimulation or enjoy the halo effect of being court cases. They would not easily be able to assume anti-social status, nor would they be stigmatized for life by the possession of a criminal record. The details of such a gigantic reformation of our existing methods for dealing with juvenile delinquents would, of course, need to be worked out with considerable care. For one thing, the juvenile courts as we know them, which endeavour to carry out the often conflicting functions of welfare committees combined with legal obligations and penal powers, would have to be drastically altered. Moreover, the age of criminal responsibility would have to be raised, as the Ingleby Committee report suggested, at least to twelve, or, better, to fifteen. It might even be necessary, when the school leaving age goes up to sixteen, to make it impossible for any young person under that age to be the subject of a criminal charge, save, perhaps, that of homicide.

[1] Ibid. The italics are Lady Wootton's.

Tremendous new responsibilities would thereafter be placed on the shoulders of educationists. The numbers of teachers would have to be increased and recruitment encouraged by enhanced status and higher pay. Specialization would also become necessary during and after the completion of a basic training course; specialization not only into arts and sciences but into residential and non-residential, therapeutic and instructional. Such categories would not have to be narrowly divided; every teacher ought to be able to understand the basis of delinquent and non-delinquent behaviour where they differ, as well as the techniques for imparting knowledge of a particular subject.

I am inclined to believe that the teaching profession as a body would respond to the challenges involved in such a radical reorientation of their work. Many would welcome greater emphasis on the mainly social and welfare side of their job and there might well be a closer tie up between pedagogy and social work. At the moment the two are sharply differentiated, some teachers stoutly denying that they should do more than instruct their pupils in the subjects of the curriculum and many social workers, deluded by the notion that their role is more allied to that of the doctor and the psychiatrist than that of the educator, claiming that the task of prevention and treatment is theirs alone.

V

While we are on the topic of Further Education and the deployment of the social services as part of the general programme to maintain stability and so help to reduce the incidence of crime and unrest, I feel that I must make a brief but nonetheless urgent mention of the work of the Youth Service in this connection. As one who spent the more active years of early manhood as a boys' club leader and later as a Settlement warden, I can speak with some experience and feeling on this subject. The contribution that a well-staffed, adequately maintained Youth Service could make to the easement, if not to the solution, of many of the problems that beset the lives of young people is incalculably great, but seldom appreciated by the general public, who have all too hazy and limited a view of what youth clubs can achieve and mean in the lives of many youngsters. I can perhaps epitomize this latter point best by quoting the comment made to me by a Liverpool dockland youth after he had ceased to be a member of the club for which I was responsible. He was a tough young man, a keen boxer, not intellectually very bright and with a streak of recklessness in him that had made his schooldays and early adolescence a period of considerable risk. When we were talking about the club one day he said suddenly and with a spontaneity and warmth that surprised me: 'You know, Warden, if it hadn't been for York House, I'd be in Borstal now.' He then went on to tell me things about his past life that confirmed that statement up to the hilt. I was thrilled and rather humbled by this confession, for, at that time, he was a lad I had rather disliked and a little feared. I had thought him a bad influence on the other boys and so, when he passed his eighteenth birthday and became no longer eligible for membership, I heaved a little sigh of relief. But how wrong I was! Not only had the club made all the difference to the course of his life but as an 'old boy' he gave years of invaluable voluntary service, helping the younger ones to develop healthy bodies and keep clear of the trouble of which he had too keen a memory.

There must be hundreds of stories from all over the country that parallel mine and testify to the creative influence of club work on the characters of adolescents. One does not want to be pompous or sentimental about this or to claim more than can be justified for the Youth Service. But I know, beyond any shadow of doubt, that the best work I have ever done in my life was the work I did as an underpaid youth leader for something like twelve consecutive years on Merseyside. If only we could develop this service more adequately and realize its enormous potentiality for good in underprivileged and difficult neighbourhoods, we would find, I am sure, a safeguard against a great deal of the juvenile and youthful misbehaviour of which we hear so much these days.

As far as the normal juvenile offenders are concerned we want to keep them out of a court of law for as long as possible and to link them up more firmly with everyday life and society. Their homes need help, too, and their parents require in some cases further support, both financial and emotional. What many need is not so much 'deep casework', in the current sense of that term, as guidance, friendship and, in some instances, direction. If the children need discipline, so do many adults. School and home ought to be brought together into a firm working relationship by the development of the Parent-Teacher movement, but more insistently by teachers with special training for the purpose going out into difficult neighbourhoods to meet, counsel and befriend their parents. In the operation of a children's Adventure Playground in Liverpool I was immensely impressed by one aspect of the work of the play-leader we appointed to this exacting post.[1] She was a girl who had a fund of sympathy and good sense at her command and we found, as the weeks went by, that the work she was doing was as much connected with parents and home life as with the organization of their children's play.

I am convinced that social workers based on a neighbourhood have a lot to contribute to the solution of many social problems arising from ignorance, fear, apathy and other non-criminal attitudes. We certainly found that our play-leader's friendship was greatly appreciated by young and old alike. Moreover, the need for such help and encouragement was a revelation to me. It is a mistake to assume that one needs four years' intensive training and weekly contact with a psychiatrist to undertake this common-sense, common humanity kind of social work. Social casework, I am afraid, has suffered immense harm from its attempt to swallow whole and uncritically a good deal of dubious and tendentious psycho-analytical theory in recent years.

VI

An interesting and highly controversial scheme which has been in operation in Liverpool for the past ten years or so is the police Juvenile Liaison Officer service. The basis of this scheme is that special plain clothes officers, appointed to each police division of the city, are responsible for dealing with first offenders or other children brought to their notice who are giving evidence of delinquent tendencies. Not all first offenders are dealt with in this way but only such cases as the police themselves consider

[1] J. B. Mays, *Adventure in Play*, Liverpool Council of Social Service, 1957.

likely to benefit from this service or those whose delinquency does not seem to be very far advanced or serious in character.[1]

The scheme was intended to be a contribution to the problem of recidivism as well as an attempt to reduce the overall numbers of children coming before the courts by tackling the incipient and first offender without prosecution and at a stage when simple remedial measures and serious warning might still be effective. A juvenile dealt with in this way is cautioned officially, in the company of his parents. Thereafter, for an indefinite period, the liaison officers work in co-operation with the home and with such social welfare agencies as may exist in the locality, supervising the child's leisure time activities and associations. Schools have been particularly co-operative in this work as have some youth organizations and ministers of religion.

The supervision given by the liaison officer is no doubt somewhat authoritarian in character. A good deal of advice is offered, to both child and parents, and it is hard to believe that the officers operating the scheme spend very much time on the niceties of the caseworker-client relationship. It is doubtful if their clients would in fact appreciate such subtleties. But many school teachers and shopkeepers undoubtedly appreciate this kind of approach to the problems presented by small-scale larceny, especially when they have cases of neglected children doing petty pilfering which they do not want blowing up into official court proceedings. To call in the juvenile liaison officer and be sure that henceforth some supervision and help will be offered to such children and their families is a happy solution to their dilemma and one which offers better prospects of prevention than more formal procedures. It is analagous to the many other time-honoured practices we have established in schools and business organizations for dealing with our internal delinquencies informally and by mutual agreement. And there is no doubt that it is a sensible and practical approach to the problem of the small 'naughty' boy in need of a little discipline and supervision to keep him out of further mischief. It is not, of course, intended to be a method of treating the disturbed child or the neurotic whose difficulties are likely to prove more

[1] For a full official account of this work see *The Police and Children*, published by the Liverpool City of Police, 1956.

intransigent. It is perhaps best thought of as the modern equivalent of the policeman's traditional slap, which for a variety of very good reasons, cannot be transplanted from the village to the urban community.

But the scheme has encountered much opposition. The main objections are that: (a) it apes probation; (b) its officers are not trained to carry out this sort of work; (c) it infringes the duties of the juvenile courts by preventing the child coming before them; (d) it postpones the moment when the child can obtain the professional help he requires; and (e) it is a job outside the scope of police work.[1]

Objection (b) seems to me the only one which carries any great weight and this is something which could easily be overcome by setting up special training and selection methods for potential liaison officers. Objection (e) is purely legalistic. According to this view the police should now take it upon themselves to apprehend, deal with and treat an offender. This sort of thing is after all the very basis of the much hated police state. Of course, we must be vigilant in keeping a close eye on all police activities, but, in my view, there are many other police practices, such as searching individuals' property without a warrant or the dubious way in which some fingerprints are obtained from suspects, to which we could more profitably direct our attention. I can see no grounds for such legalistic anxieties. I am quite satisfied that the families who have participated in the operation of the scheme do not feel that their rights have in any way been abrogated. On the contrary, very many people must be grateful for the second chance their children have been offered by the service.

Official figures for the whole ten year period are not to my knowledge available, but those given for the first five years of the scheme's operation showed that of the 3,955 cases dealt with in this way no less than 3,622 children were not prosecuted subsequently. It is a condition of operating the service that any child who is a known offender or who has been brought to the notice of the police previously must be dealt with in the normal

---

[1] Interestingly enough nobody has objected to the police running Attendance Centres on this score, nor did they object to the police carrying out judicial whipping. Could it be because these jobs are distasteful to social workers?

process of prosecution and appearance before the juvenile court. This is a most important safeguard which means that it cannot be used as a device for manipulating the delinquency rates. In fact it has dealt with a great many children who otherwise would never have come to the notice of the officials at all. Undoubtedly the scheme has been effective in Liverpool. Few other cities have adopted it nor, in view of the cold douche administered by the Ingleby Committee's Report, are they likely to do so in the future. The latter's comment is typical of the tepid and sterile approach adopted by that most abortive of enquiries: 'While, therefore, we have nothing but commendation for the aims and achievements of those who have instituted and worked police juvenile liaison schemes, we are unable to recommend that the Government should encourage their general adoption.[1]

VII

Whatever we do, of course, in the nature of pepping up the environment by providing new and extended social services and by making our educational system more truly egalitarian and effective, we will still have our quota of delinquents. Many families will still present tough problems; some parents will resist all efforts to help or advise them, and some children will, apparently unaccountably, go wrong.

Dr. Stafford Clark in Lord Pakenham's enquiry put forward four vital elements in a good home.[2] They are as follows:

a. The emotional atmosphere, which ideally should embrace love, security, and the complete acceptance of each other as individuals of infinite worth by every member of the family.

b. The example, set primarily by the parents, of mutual respect, love, loyalty and trust.

c. The precepts set out by the parents, including religious and philosophical beliefs.

d. The relationship between the home as a unit and society

---

[1] *Report of the Committee on Children and Young Persons*, H.M.S.O., 1960, par. 147.

[2] Lord Pakenham, *Causes of Crime*, Weidenfeld and Nicolson, 1958, p. 55.

as a whole, the internal security of the home being re-
flected in an external security within the framework of
society and law.

As Lord Pakenham commented, 'A penetrating analysis,
surely. How far is it ancient wisdom wrapped up in modern
dress?' And how far can we hope to achieve such a high ideal
of family and home life? We must be content very often with
only second or third best and be satisfied with solid pedestrian
prose rather than yearn for poetic flights. There will always be,
even when social conditions and welfare services have been
drastically altered, some incorrigibles for whom a form of
institutionalization is necessary.

We must have a second, even a third line of defence. This will
in part be provided by the boarding schools and will, I hope,
follow more closely the lines of such schools for educationally
subnormal and emotionally maladjusted children than of
approved schools. I am myself immensely impressed by the
pioneer work which such men as George Lyward and David
Wills have done for children with problems. I want to see their
method more commonly practised. Their approach which may,
in a quick phrase, be characterized as 'love in action', is often
lacking from even the most scrupulously administered hostels
and approved schools. While the latter tend to insist on discipline and order (sometimes it seems even for their own sakes),
the emphasis with Wills or Lyward is on self-determination and
affection. One employs authority as its main technique, the
other love. One offers an institution (no doubt a good one in
many cases), the other offers a home.[1]

VIII

As an example of the sort of thing we ought to avoid but often,
in the present state of affairs, do not, I want to refer to a case
which came up in 1959 before a Lambeth magistrate's court. A
woman of nearly forty, the mother of four children, all of school
age, and of whom three were said to be suffering from tuber-

---

[1] See for a full account of this work, W. David Wills, *Throw Away Thy
Rod*, Gollancz 1961 and Michael Burn, *Mr. Lyward's Answer*, Hamish
Hamilton, 1956.

culosis, was sentenced to two months' imprisonment for failing to declare her earnings to the National Assistance Board. Her husband, who also suffered from T.B., had died six years previously. While in receipt of an allowance from the N.A.B. she earned between £2 and £3 a week by taking in sewing. It was claimed that she had consequently been overpaid by £226, for which she was prosecuted and sent to prison. In the press report, the sentencing magistrate declared it to be a 'lamentable case' but said he could not do otherwise than order a short term in prison. It was also added that the children were being temporarily looked after by neighbours. This is a story which could be used to harrow the emotions unbearably. One could make much of the tuberculotic history, the need for additional comfort; one could describe the physical and nervous strain of that extra sewing done by artificial light in a cramped room after the long day's toil in the kitchen. One could go on to point out the dilemma of the J.P., of how he was constrained by the law to do something he did not wish to do. One could make, too, if one had the pen of a Charles Dickens, a few scathing comments on the allegedly Christian society which permitted such a state of affairs to arise. The point I would like to stress, however, is that the neighbours looked after the children—a simple act of human kindness set against the legal and administrative framework of a society so obsessed with money and material things that even its charity is hedged about by restrictions and an almost pathological fear of being defrauded.

One thinks of the fifty odd million pounds expended upon Blue Streak and wonders if that odd two-hundred-and-twenty-six was not doing a better job than all the expensive pyrotechnics—even though it was doing it illegally. One asks was the law made for man or man for the law?

IX

While, as I have suggested, we must do what we can, humanely and sympathetically and constructively, to contain the problem of benign and more normal delinquency, we must exert every effort to extirpate more severe and malign crime. Malignant crime falls into two main sub-categories: one in which the root cause seems to be associated with a definite psychological disturbance or illness; the second where the individual has deliberately adopted crime and fraud as a way of life.

Much of what we have already said in this chapter would, if implemented, help considerably to assist us to deal with the psychiatric offender. If one thinks of the dramatic and terrible offences committed by men like Straffen, Heath, and Hume, the question one invariably asks is why steps were not taken earlier to treat them. This is a topic where one must tread warily for the infringement of the rights and liberty of the subject and reliance upon purely medical diagnosis is wide open to abuse and contains many serious dangers. The enquiries which led up to the passing of the Mental Health Act, 1959, revealed these risks most clearly. At the same time, one has a right to ask that the psychological medical services should be made more widely available for both ascertainment and treatment of potentially criminal individuals than they are at the moment. I have neither the space here nor the expert knowledge to say precisely how this might be achieved. But there is no doubt that a programme which included such things as closer contact between social workers, teachers and families, an extension of facilities for obtaining psychiatric treatment and advice, marriage guidance counselling, a more flexible educational system permitting needy children to be brought up in boarding schools, rather than waiting for them to break the law, would all help considerably to ease the gravity of this problem. Whatever is done to improve family life and to bring love into the lives of those who have never experienced its healing and creative influence will help to diminish the incidence of psychological disturbances and hence the risk of psychiatrically motivated crime.

The expansion and development of mental health services within the general framework of the health service is long overdue. For I am sure that the methods of psychiatry have a major contribution to make in dealing with the less usual type of delinquent. Unfortunately so much nonsense has been talked about psychiatry and so many absurdly exaggerated claims have been made (not usually by psychiatrists themselves!) that a good deal of hostility and prejudice has been created in the minds of responsible people who have no wish to abandon the quest for scientific understanding to the new 'white magic', and who are determined not to give up their personal responsibility to a branch of modern witchcraft. My own contact with psychiatrists has been reassuring. I have usually found them thoroughly common-sensical in their approach, not easily bluffed, undogmatic and deeply sympathetic. But there are villains in every profession, and the mental health service has its quota of obscurantists, quacks and pseudo-scientists.

In his book, *Psychological Disorder and Crime*, Dr. Lindesay Neustatter has some frank things to say about his brand of medicine. He estimates that, judging from the published results of psychiatric treatment of psycho-neurotics, 'about one-third improve greatly, one-third moderately so, and one-third not at all'. These findings, he says, 'remain so curiously constant, irrespective of the methods by which the patients have been treated, that one is sometimes tempted to wonder a little cynically if the true formula for success is not another instance of "did nothing in particular, but did it very well?"'[1]

It is clear that a psychiatrist cannot diagnose or treat a patient with the certainty of an ordinary medical practitioner, dealing with a case of, say, pneumonia; there are few clear-cut symptoms invariably associated with any psychiatric disorder, nor are there any stock medicaments with a long history of clinical success behind them. I suspect that it does not very much matter what analytical school the psychiatrist favours or what precise concepts he employs, but that it is his own sympathy of approach, even empathy for the patient, together with his willingness to listen and to reassure by every available means in his power that provides the therapy. In the last analysis it is the psychiatrist's own personality and human sensitivity that produce such successful results as there are. His healing art is more akin to poetry than to mechanics. To say this is not to denigrate his skill but to indicate its rarity.

Clearly we need more such people working in the delinquency field than the orthodox medical schools can ever hope to provide. Moreover, although there are advantages in having a medical degree before passing on to study psychological analysis and treatment, I think that there may well be room in the future for this work to be shared with psychologists and even social science graduates, so that the supply of skilled workers

[1] Christopher Johnson, 1953, p. 229.

may be more commensurate with the great demand. Such a view may well appear heresy to some psychiatrists. Nevertheless, I put it forward hopefully, in the belief that the promising work accomplished by psychiatrists may grow and prosper. Perhaps psychiatric social workers could be called upon to do more actual remedial work than they have been accustomed to doing in the past. But, wherever we get the skilled social workers from, of the great need for them there can be no doubt. I am convinced that many people, young and old, who are displaying delinquent tendencies, could be greatly helped by the sort of approach that psychiatrists can give. I am not certain that only fully qualified medical practitioners can do this work. There is a dangerous mystique associated with 'the man in the white coat'. As Dr. Neustatter himself has said, in the work already quoted, success depends more on individual qualities than upon book learning:

'Here I would like to add my own strong view that successful management of delinquents is far more dependent on natural insight and imagination, than on any amount of theoretical knowledge, book work or academic qualification—which holds for psychiatrists as well as ancillary workers. For, unless there is a natural flair for understanding problem cases, the study of psychopathology and mental mechanisms only results in highly imaginative findings. Worse still, these flights of fantasy are usually committed to paper when, richly embellished with jargon, they are incorporated into interminable reports which are submitted to magistrates noted for their dislike of psychiatrists. Thus one more nail enters the psychiatric coffin.'[1]

Sometimes, we must admit, abnormal mental fixations occur which are not amenable to educational influences or even to environmental treatment. In such cases, it seems to me, we have, as a community, no other recourse than to provide for such unhappy individuals some place of restraint where they will be prevented from causing untold harm to other people. But this restraint must be as humane and decent as we can contrive. None of us, I am sure, likes the idea of locking a man up for the rest of his life or even for long indefinite periods. The one ray of hope in severe cases of psychic disorder which is opening up is that we may at some future date be able to dis-

[1] Op. cit., p. 232.

cover physiological conditions which are the root causes of such psychiatric crime and then, by dint of medical research, we may learn how to treat and overcome them. It is a remote prospect but all we have to cling to in such cases.

X

The attack on organized crime—crime as a business—indulged in by professionals is more properly a police concern than a topic for a sociologist to discuss. As we said earlier, there is a logical connection between so-called legitimate business and crime, and, as with the former, the less it can be made a paying proposition the more infrequently is it likely to be adopted as a career. But while we are all, in our different ways, bent on achieving the same economic goals for ourselves the likelihood of ever being able to rid society of the depredations of professional thieves is very faint indeed. Some would say it is the quintessence of utopianism. Meanwhile the war, for that is the only word for it, between the crook and the racketeer and the law-enforcement officers must go on relentlessly. One hardly likes to point out the obvious connection between the prestige of the police service and their remuneration and their effectiveness in detecting crime and hounding down the criminals. But obviously improved status and pay would go a long way towards attracting even more able men to the police service and in making good the actual numerical deficiency that now exists in many parts of the country. Here again the development of scientific techniques and measures to detect and prevent crime pays enormous dividends, and the need for research in this field in order to keep abreast of the constantly changing and improved techniques of the criminals is an urgent priority. But if less time and energy had to be expended on dealing with the petty offenders and the juvenile delinquents, this economy in manpower might go some way towards making the detection rate higher. At the present moment crime does appear to pay some people. There is little certainty of detection or arrest to deter the calculating marauder. Until there is, we are almost certain to have him in our midst at an immense cost to the national exchequer and as an undesirable model for disaffected youth to emulate. To a considerable extent we have already within our grasp the means to reduce the amount of crime and prevent its incidence increasing amongst juveniles more especially. We have the means. We seem to desire the end. Yet, as a society, we do not will it. The necessary legislative and administrative action is not being taken. There is uncertainty where there should be decisiveness, ambivalence where singleness of mind and purpose should prevail. We worry about delinquency rather in the same sort of way that we fret ourselves over inflation in the economic field. And, like inflation, delinquency seems to be closely bound up with the way in which we allow our communal affairs to be managed. It parallels what Galbraith condemned as 'private opulence' in the midst of 'public squalor'. 'The greater the wealth the thicker will be the dirt', he wrote describing the fundamental tendency of our time. 'As more goods are produced and owned, the greater are the opportunities for fraud and the more property that must be protected.' 'If the provision of public law enforcement services does not keep pace, the counterpart of increased well-being will', he warned, 'we may be certain, be increased crime.'[1] There is no mystery about this explanation. The only mystery is why we go on being puzzled about the phenomenon of crime in our midst; why we do not take a more vigorous control over shady financial transactions and dubious take-over bids; why, above all, we do not drastically overhaul our entire educational and recreative provisions for children and young people. To quote Galbraith again: 'Presumably a community can be as well rewarded by buying better schools or better parks as by buying bigger cars. By concentrating on the latter rather than the former it is failing to maximize its satisfactions.'[2] It is merely a matter of public choice. Goering offered the German nation at one time the alternative of 'Guns or butter?' Galbraith puts it rather differently as a choice between 'Television and the violent mores of Hollywood and Madison Avenue' and 'the intellectual discipline of the school'. The essential moral challenge presented by the existence of increasing delinquency in our society does not result in the waywardness of individual offenders but in our corporate inability to do anything positive and constructive

[1] J. K. Galbraith, *The Affluent Society*, Penguin Books edition, 1962, pp. 211–12.
[2] Ibid., p. 212.

CONCLUSIONS AND PRESCRIPTIONS

about it. A society which still pretends to draw its inspiration from the Christian religion cannot fail to stand self-condemned by the facts. More people than ever before lie in our national gaols or are committed to approved schools and borstals. Their presence in such institutions is the measure of our collective sin.

CODA

I am aware that some readers may be of the opinion that I am anxious both to eat my cake and still have it! They may consider that there is an unresolved paradox in my claim that crime is both inevitable and yet must be fought and restrained.

This discrepancy, if such it be, arises from the fact that one has to work simultaneously on two different levels. As a social scientist one has to face the hard facts of life as it is lived within the framework of a particular kind of social system. One asserts that crime is closely associated with our present manner of living even as its existence is always a potentiality in human nature itself. One knows that as a society becomes more complex, as individual desires and greeds and egotism are excited, as material prosperity increases, stress, strain and temptation will still lead many to fall foul of the law. Not until our society has achieved the stability of perfection will these tensions relax: not until love is the experience of every living being will we reach a time when police officers and social workers are as dead as the dodo or as redundant as mastodons crashing about in the primordial swamps.

On the other hand as a citizen and a parent, as a humanitarian and teacher, one cannot for a moment acquiesce in any individual being exposed to the social stigma and ultimate isolation which are the ultimate logic of the criminal process. In this personal context one is bound conscientiously to work to prevent children from becoming delinquents because the status of the criminal in our society is not a happy one. As no less a person than Winston Churchill said half a century ago in his capacity as Home Secretary, the attitude of the public to criminals is a sure test of the level of its civilization. He urged 'tireless efforts towards the discovery of curative and regenerative processes; unfailing faith that there is a treasure, if you can only find it, in the heart of every man; these are the symbols which, in the treatment of crime and criminal, mark and measure the stored-up strength of a nation, and are sign and proof of the living virtue in it.'[1]

Those are splendid and stirring Churchillian words that have the authentic tang and freshness of truth on them, now as on the day they were uttered. Not only must we be vigilant in promoting penal reform and in creating a sense of responsibility in the mind of every citizen for the criminal and delinquent. Not only must we believe and act as though the offender has the right to treatment and rehabilitation, but we must constantly scrutinize the ideas and attitudes deeply embedded within the social structure which promote crime and militate against humane reformation.

As one studies the problem of crime in society one is struck by the strange inconsistencies of policy everywhere apparent. An ill-tempered father in an uncontrolled moment strikes his nine-month-old son so violently that his brain is injured and he is blinded for the rest of his life. We deal with such a case by committing the man to six months' imprisonment. Another man, in a mood of acute sexual jealousy, believing his wife to have a relationship with another man in the locality, strangles her after they had both attended a dance. We sentence him to a year in gaol, and the judge summing up on our behalf says, 'No one can have heard this case without feeling profoundly sympathetic, but wives who are suspected of infidelity must not be strangled, and that is what you did.'

One goes into a juvenile court and hears how a thirteen-year-old boy with two previous convictions against his name has stolen fifteen shillings' worth of goods from a shop and is committed to an approved school for three years, while another small child, said by his parents to be beyond control (often an excuse for getting rid of him!) is similarly dealt with. It is still possible for a juvenile in this country to lose his liberty solely because he plays truant from school.

A man who strangles his wife gets a year, a man who blinds his baby half a year, yet we acquiesce in the loss of freedom for much longer periods for children who have shoplifted or 'sagged' school. We are told that going to prison and being committed

[1] Quoted in C. H. Rolph, *Common Sense About Crime and Punishment*, Gollancz, 1961, p. 175.

for training in an approved school are two entirely different things. But both are punitive in effect, both involve loss of liberty, both mean restraint and close supervision, and both leave a social stigma in their wake.

I can only conclude this analysis of the meaning, nature and extent of crime and delinquency in contemporary society by urging, not only the necessity for more scientific research, but also for more honest self-scrutiny of our own behaviour and a more realistic appraisal of what actually goes on in the day by day processes of our economic, commercial and public life. The seeds of crime are blown on every wind, and richly receptive cultures wait everywhere to foster and nourish them.

It is a splendid and encouraging fact that within this criminogenic community there are also forces making for humanity, social equality and for that righteousness based, not on the letter of inflexible law, but upon affection and self-giving. Whatever the intellectual content of this book may imply, I hope that its emotional message will be clear enough. It is that while serious crime remains a blot and a disgrace to our national life, we have good reason to be proud of those cleansing and recuperative agents which are also at work—the devoted magistrates, the probation officers, the teachers and youth leaders, the after-care workers in every field, and, above all, those vigilant advocates of penal and social reform who constitute so mighty a minority. They are the living embodiment of the social conscience, and the outlook for our society would be bleak indeed without them.

APPENDIX I

CASE HISTORIES

In a book of this size there is little space for detailed case studies. But I would like to give one or two pictures of the boys I used to know in order to illustrate some of the points I have been making above.

．　　　　．　　　　．

Tony was a lively, friendly youngster who, at the time of my enquiry, had just left school and was working as a clerk. His father was dead and he lived with his mother and married sister in a new flat. He was very much the family 'baby' in relation to his older brothers and sisters who were all married. He complained that, as a consequence, he was 'always being growled at by somebody'. His mother used to go every night to the pub, where she took part in a regular sweep. She entered his name in it to make up the number. None of the family attended church at that time. Tony had not been since he was seven. Up to that age his sister took him with her to a local mission. He was always fond of practical jokes and at one time he used to throw lighted fireworks on to passing buses. In his younger days he was regarded as 'a bit of a bully in the Dwellings'. One horrifying activity was to catch cats and drop them over the balconies. He and his friends killed and injured several in this way.

He had been an active member of a fairly well-knit gang which was entirely composed of boys living in the same block of flats. Most of their activities were quite harmless. They took over an empty storeroom as their headquarters and ran their own football team which played regular matches with street sides and teams from other blocks. Sometimes these games were played in the park but more often they made use of the square in the centre block. After the older members were called up for the Army the gang's activities came to an end. Tony spoke nostalgically about the 'old days'.

His pocket money as a young wage earner was seven shillings and sixpence a week, and this had to cover fags, pictures, bets, and club dues but he managed to save half-a-crown towards his summer holiday at Butlin's. He spent about sixpence a week on horses, and the same on pools and the sweep. He also used to make a number of *ad hoc* bets with other boys and at weekends he nearly always played cards for money.

He was convinced that his club membership had greatly assisted him and had prevented him from becoming involved with the law-breaking gangs in which the area abounded. He said his mother had to stop going out at night because of the danger of having the electric meter robbed and that his Gran, who ran a tontine, had additional locks put on her doors and cupboards. Tony knew who was responsible for such raids in the neighbourhood. It was a boy who lived in the same block and who would almost certainly 'end up in Borstal'. He had produced a very suspicious number of shillings when playing cards. While Tony did not avoid this boy when knocking about in the Dwellings, coming to the club was, amongst other things, a most useful alibi, as it was very dangerous to be seen in the vicinity of a flat which had been raided. When you were vouched for at the club nobody could 'pin things on you'.

Tony had never appeared in the juvenile court, although he might well have done so if luck had not gone in his favour. He told me how when he was about nine he and his mates used to play in a burned-out warehouse. They liked 'nosing around' and climbing. One day they found money bags containing copper and silver which was divided among the gang members. Young children, he said, like to explore and 'you can't stop them'.

One of his elder brothers was a regular thief and went down town shoplifting almost every day. He had three or four court appearances. Tony himself had a spell of lorry-skipping. They stole sugar, nuts, fruit etc. along the dock roads. At the age of eight or perhaps nine he stole from city shops in the company of other lads. Saturday mornings were the favourite times for shoplifting.

Tony told me that a lot of theft took place at school holiday camps. Country shopkeepers are so unsuspecting! One boy at his school was notorious. He used to load up his mackintosh pockets with loot, and in the dormitory at night he auctioned it. He would make in this way as much as £6 a week and would return home rolling in cash. Tony bought two expensive compacts from him to take home as presents for his sisters. He bought several things he knew had been stolen, but the bargains were so good that nobody could resist the temptation. He admitted that he had no qualms in the matter. It was to your advantage, so you just did it!

He gave up shoplifting when he was about thirteen, as he became aware of the dangers. He said he knew that he had been open to many bad influences, but had no father and apparently his mother was not very particular. Not only did she allow him to smoke but she actually encouraged him to gamble. There was also the influence of the elder brother, who was a regular thief. The family was, however, an affectionate one and this may have been Tony's salvation. He was very lucky indeed to survive to early manhood without a conviction being brought against him. It would seem that he never received any direct ethical training yet, being an intelligent boy, he emerged more or less unscathed from his delinquent phase and succeeded in throwing off the more deleterious effects of his environment. His story is, I think, in many ways typical of the better adjusted and more stable boy, coming from a united if not very well-organized home, who is, however, constantly a delinquency risk in a slum district. Not all such boys are as fortunate as Tony. They may be unwisely handled or merely less lucky and find themselves round about the time of the onset of puberty in fairly serious trouble with the law.

·   ·   ·

Edward lived near Tony and went to the same school but his story was very different. He was an official delinquent, had appeared in court more than once and had been on the brink of being sent to an approved school. He was a powerfully-made boy, not more than average in intelligence, and somewhat restive by temperament. Games rather than lessons appealed to him, and when it came to a choice of employment he naturally enough gravitated to manual work.

His family was small and very 'respectable'. His only brother, three years his junior, was almost scholarly—a rather solitary unathletic boy who loved music and the arts—in many ways a complete contrast to Edward. Yet they were good friends and often went off on all-day cycle rides together.

Edward's employment history was very chequered, he changed his job no less than five times in two and a half years. But he could not for this reason be called an unstable or unreliable youth.

As a club member, he was intermittent, until the age of sixteen. About this time he seemed to settle down and take a more responsible attitude to life. He was a good athlete, a fine swimmer, and the club gave him every opportunity to develop these interests. His probation officer seemed to be giving him the right kind of support during this period and Edward always praised his and the club's efforts on his behalf. Without their help, he said, he would very likely have developed into 'a complete rogue'.

He had a bad record, in many ways typical of the district. But it is hard to see why he became a delinquent while his brother did not. It may be that he felt a little inferior intellectually. It may also be that his restless energetic personality found little during his early years to engage his interest and loyalty. The fact that he was somewhat adrift and exposed to the temptation of a criminogenic environment may have made all the difference in his case. Had he been more of a scholar and more inward-turning like his brother, he might have kept on the right side of the law. As it was he made his first appearance in court for larceny at the age of thirteen. His father paid the fine. A year later he was charged with the same offence and placed on probation. At sixteen, while still on probation, he committed a further offence. But this time the court appearance seems to have shocked him into a realization of the ultimate consequences of that kind of behaviour. Thereafter he was exceptionally cautious. If out after dark without a light he would walk his cycle home rather than risk any further todo with the police. He threw himself into club activities and made close friends with reliable boys and had no further charges brought against him. He did, however, do some shoplifting while away on holiday. Twice he stole presents to take home. He said that boys think it is easier to steal in strange localities and that it is natural for them to take presents which they cannot really afford to buy.

Looking back on his boyhood, Edward said that what he and his pals between eleven and thirteen wanted was adventure. He remembered when they were in school how they waited for the four o'clock bell as a signal for adventure. They would get a skip on a wagon as far as the Pier Head, stealing sugar, fruit and nuts on the way, and enjoying the thrill and fun of it. The risk of capture and sheer physical danger seemed to supply the stimulus they needed to feel really alive.

Edward neither drank, smoked nor gambled. Yet he nearly embarked on a criminal career. He is probably a good example of the easy-going, good-natured boy who takes a very long time learning to adjust himself to the demands of increasing maturity. In an environment which lacked delinquent suggestions and illicit rewards, he might have been a somewhat different kind of boy. As it was he was a serious risk. Yet I could never quite see why. He had many admirable qualities and I would have been happy if he had been my own son. There was nothing furtive or dangerous about Edward. But he did break the law quite frequently. His story epitomizes the problem presented by many young delinquents who live in similar kinds of deteriorated neighbourhoods in our big cities.

I think I should end by saying that Tony and Edward are both now married men doing well in life. They are both fathers. Both have settled down in a newer neighbourhood. But one realizes, with something very much like a stab of mental pain, how very fine indeed is the line which at times divides the social failure from the social success.

APPENDIX II

A NOTE ON CRIME PREDICTION

Of recent years some criminologists, tired of the unsuccessful pursuit of the alleged root causes of crime, have sought to by-pass the problem by developing statistical instruments of prediction for which straightforward notions of cause and effect are not necessary. They have contented themselves by isolating a number of factors which are much more often than not found to be associated with either criminal or non-criminal behaviour. These factors are not to be taken as causes. They may in fact be nothing more than indications of more deep-seated conditions which are at present beyond the reach of our diagnostic skills. But for practical purposes, since they are known to be frequently associated with the condition we are studying, we can make use of them for prediction. That is to say, we can treat them as though they were causal, while, at the same time, preserving our intellectual freedom and scepticism about their real nature. This is indeed a satisfactory solution to a problem which at one time looked like holding up the progress of criminological science indefinitely. While we blundered deeper and deeper through the forest of proliferating data in pursuit of a probably chimerical quarry called a Cause, we had no time to follow up more concrete lines of enquiry which might be expected to give us some control of crime together with a more objective evaluation of its treatment. We were often bogged down in philosophical swamps when we needed to be plodding the hard road of practicality.

Ernest Burgess and the Gluecks in America had already begun to construct this utilitarian thoroughfare many years before; in this country, Hermann Mannheim and Leslie Wilkins undertook their epoch-making enquiry into the effectiveness of Borstal training in which they made use of similar ideas and methods.[1]

Wilkins indeed went so far as to reject the concept of cause altogether as having little scientific usefulness. In its place he put the concept of probability or of likelihood and uncertainty. This depends, as has already been indicated, upon certain factors having a close statistical association with the condition we are interested in: on the basis of whether or not these associated factors are present or absent in a particular case we can essay a reasonable prognostication of what is likely to happen. Insurance companies make use of similar criteria in evaluating the risk involved in taking on new clients. Past experience has shown them that there are certain broad classes of 'good' or 'bad' risks for life policies. For instance a man's age is an obvious factor to be taken into account in deciding what premium he should be asked to pay. Another is his occupation. Anglican parsons for example, have been shown to live longer than coal miners, and, as clients, they are therefore less likely to die before they have paid a fair number of premiums into the company's coffers. Of course, even an Anglican rural vicar might drop dead twenty-four hours after being medically examined. But the chances are that he will not, and, on the basis of these generalizations from experience, the company officials can make a handsome profit for their shareholders.

Mannheim and Wilkins here and the Gluecks and others in the United States have been trying to make use of such actuarial sagacity in the field of criminology. While they not unnaturally regard their efforts as something of a major 'break-through', they have not lacked critics, and the whole topic is still in what we might call its 'debating stage'. It is the subject of academic seminar discussion but, as far as I know, has not yet given rise to any change of policy or procedure in dealing with offenders.

So far I have been talking about prediction when in actual fact I should have coined a different term, such as retrospective prediction. For the researches that have so far been carried out in this field have always worked upon past history. The investigators have been obliged to confine their enquiries to cases of

[1] *Prediction Methods in Relation to Borstal Training*, H.M.S.O., 1955.

known criminals and ascertained delinquents. This is a serious methodological weakness but one that is more or less inevitable at this early stage of such investigations. Until more people have more confidence in statistical methods and overcome their repugnance for their 'cold-blooded' objectivity, research workers will have to go on using existing case records of known offenders only. But what they have already done with them suggests that the so-called 'predictive approach' to crime looks like being a most fruitful idea and one which, if handled with due safeguards, may give considerable help in the future to magistrates, judges and penologists, as well as assisting social workers to concentrate their energies upon certain specific and crucial aspects of social life.

The Mannheim and Wilkins Study showed, for instance, that *without using any more material than was available to the court at the time the case was heard,* and without ever having personal contact with the boys in question, they were able to 'predict' the outcome of 338 Borstal detainees with much greater precision than the governors and housemasters who had handled the boys prior to release. Of the 338 cases they predicted correctly in 212 instances—roughly four times as accurately as the so-called experts with all their intuition and skill based upon long years' experience in the penal service! All that Mannheim and Wilkins had to go on were the case records of these boys as supplied to them by the official sources. To this body of raw material they applied a predictive instrument which they had previously worked out in an earlier study of 385 Borstal boys whose post-release histories they knew. They were thus able to isolate a number of factors associated with success and with failure after Borstal training. Over sixty such concomitant factors were studied and their mathematical relationship to failure and success in Borstal were worked out. They finally constructed their prediction table on the basis of a selected number of these factors which appeared from the evidence at their disposal to have a very close association indeed with what actually happened to the individual boys. Each factor, called a predictor in this case, was given a due numerical weight in accordance with its observed importance and a hierarchical place in the table.

This table, which is printed below, may be applied quite

automatically by anybody. Unlike most of the psychological projective tests it does not need a highly trained initiate to interpret it. Provided all the relevant data can be assembled the instrument should work satisfactorily.

Factor

	ADD
If evidence of drunkenness	24
If any prior offence(s) resulted in fine	9
committal to prison or approved school	8
a term on probation	4
If not living with parent(s)	7·5
If home is in an industrial area[1]	8
If longest period in any job was:	
less than 1 month	11·7
over 4 weeks up to 6 weeks	10·4
,, 6 ,, ,, ,, 8 ,,	9·1
,, 2 months ,, ,, 3 months	7·8
,, 3 ,, ,, ,, 4 ,,	6·5
,, 4 ,, ,, ,, 6 ,,	5·2
,, 6 ,, ,, ,, 9 ,,	3·9
,, 9 ,, ,, ,,12 ,,	2·6
,, 1 year ,, ,,18 ,,	1·3
,,18 months	0
Total	

If one obtains a total score of 15 points this would indicate a 65 per cent prospect of success. A score of 35 gives only about a 30 per cent chance. Those that score 40 and over showed a 1 in 8 chance of success, while those who scored 9 and under showed a 7 in 8 chance of doing well after Borstal training.

It is important to realize that by applying such a table to an individual case you obtain only a probabilty statement, not a certain prognosis. This is of course a weakness of such procedures but when one realizes that they have only to compete with old-fashioned hit or miss methods, this weakness will not seem unduly depressing. The strength of the predictive table is that it is much more reliable than the judgements of experienced individuals. Its utilization might be expected to result in a

[1] Any town where the ratio of the rateable value of industrial to total hereditaments exceeds 0·009.

sounder overall sentencing policy, but it would not, of course, ensure success with specific individuals. This is something we have not yet succeeded in doing, nor is it something we can reasonably expect in the future. There always will be some element of doubt in treating offenders in any way and by whatever method of selection we use.

The work done using the Gluecks' prediction methods should be briefly mentioned, as they corroborate the findings of the Mannheim-Wilkins Study.[1] The Gluecks evolved three separate tables based on different factors; one of these, which they called their Social Prediction Table, is of special interest to sociologists. It is based on five factors and was initially presented in their book, *Unraveling Juvenile Delinquency*. I list them below, together with the Gluecks' own findings regarding their applicability.

1. *Discipline of the boy by his father* (72·5 per cent of the boys whose discipline was classifiable as overstrict or erratic turned out to be delinquents compared with only 9·3 per cent of the cases where discipline was firm but kindly).

2. *Supervision of the boy by his mother* (83·2 per cent of the cases in which maternal oversight had been unsuitable proved to be delinquents compared with 9·9 per cent of cases where it was judged to be suitable).

3. *Affection of father for boy* (the incidence of delinquency where the father's attitude was hostile or indifferent was 75·9 per cent as contrasted with only 33·8 per cent where it was warm and affectionate).

4. *Affection of mother for boy* (a similar contrast obtained here between 86·2 per cent and 43·1 per cent of the cases).

5. *Cohesiveness of the family* (96·9 per cent of boys from unintegrated families were delinquent as compared with only 20·6 per cent of those brought up in cohesive families).

Richard Thompson carried out some valuable work making use of the Gluecks' social prediction scale, first with a hundred cases selected from the files left over from the Cambridge-Somerville Youth Study and secondly with cases handled by a Boston clinic. Thompson showed that not only were the Gluecks'

[1] See Sheldon and Eleanor Glueck, *Predicting Delinquency and Crime*, Harvard, 1959, pp. 16–17.

scales validated but that they were much more reliable in fact than the prophecies of experienced clinicians and psychologists who had examined the children at the beginning of the Cambridge-Somerville Study.

Evidence is therefore slowly accumulating to the effect that statistical devices can indeed cut down the element of uncertainty in attempts to predict children's future histories, on the one hand, and the outcome of specific treatment on the other. If they could be utilized more widely, it is to be presumed that, not only would individual offenders stand a better chance of receiving the appropriate form of treatment, but, what is equally important but apt to be overlooked, Borstals, approved schools and the like would also stand a better chance of succeeding with the individuals committed to their care. Some useful sorting out of sheep and goats could be essayed which would be to the advantage of all concerned. While nothing so infallible as a litmus paper test could be expected, certain gross errors might well be eliminated from the penological field. More square and fewer round pegs would be put into square holes, and the grave problem of recidivism might possibly be alleviated.

Exaggerated claims however should not be made for any future application of predictive techniques to treatment. Much work remains to be done in validating their effectiveness and in developing similar devices for the other forms of rehabilitative and remedial care at our disposal.

In an interesting article R. L. Morrison, discussing the findings of the Mannheim-Wilkins Study, has shown that when the distinction between 'open' and 'closed' Borstals is taken into consideration there is an overall difference in the success rates of the two types of institution of 8 per cent.[1] He points out that if a lad in the good prospect group is sent to a closed and not to an open Borstal his chance of success is accordingly reduced. This shows how immensely complicated are all endeavours to systematize the findings of criminological research; for not only, in the matter of Borstal training, have we to face the difference between the two basic types, but we have also to take into account somehow the fact that no two Borstals *of any kind* are identical. Furthermore, an individual institution changes as its

[1] *British Journal of Delinquency*, Vol. 6, 1955–6, p. 100.

staff and detainees change, and it is clear that throughout the entire gamut of treatment there is a continuous process of mutation at work.

Immense problems await solution before prediction can hope to replace the esoteric randomness of established procedures. Objections must be honestly faced, particularly in relation to the rights of the individual and the notion of justice itself. Dr. Grunhut in a paper delivered to the Royal Statistical Society said:

'It is still an open question whether we are justified to decide on a man's destiny by assuming that because he exhibits symptoms similar to those of a group out of which 80 per cent are persisting in crime, he himself has a chance of 4 to 5 to belong to the 80 per cent persistent criminals and not to the 20 per cent who become straight.'[1]

In other words, while predictive devices might show us that a man is a good risk ought we to refuse a man who is adjudged a bad risk his slender chance of making good by the particular form of treatment? It is indeed a grave question but one, so it seems to me, which in time we will learn to grapple with successfully, when further research has been done. If there is an offender who is adjudged a serious risk for prison but a much less serious risk say for psychiatric treatment ought we not, in an enlightened country, to order the latter rather than the former? The offence may unfortunately be one that by existing law is punishable only be imprisonment, in which case no dilemma need arise. In our allegedly enlightened society, however, it would seem to be necessary to legislate in such a way that courts have a degree of flexibility in sentencing which would permit adequate choice. In which case, as and when we reach such a pitch of humane sophistication, the court may seek to match the punishment or treatment to the offender rather than to the offence with a greater expectation of success than they can in the present state of affairs. It is a juridical cliché that justice must not only be done but must also clearly be seen to have been done. This means, if I understand it aright, that a fair balance must be attained between deterrence and rehabilitation. It is a matter of public opinion what that balance is;

[1] 'Statistics in Criminology', *J.Roy.Stat.Soc.* Series A. (General), 114 Part II, 1951.

whether we ought to give greater weight to reform than to mere punishment. This depends in turn upon the moral conscience of the entire nation. Not until the general will is in tune with the view expressed by William Thomas and Florian Znaniecki that the difference between socially normal and anti-social actions is quantitative rather than qualitative, are we likely to place rehabilitation of the offender above the vindication of the outraged law. But from the viewpoint of these authors 'the question of the anti-social individual assumes no longer the form of the right of society to protection, but that of the right of the anti-social individual to be made useful'.[1] When more of us are of that opinion, we may expect that predictive techniques will be brought into legal practice and that the pioneer work we have been discussing will be made use of in the service of the common man and to the benefit of the common weal.

[1] *The Polish Peasant, in Europe and America*, New York, Knopf, 1927, p. 80.

APPENDIX III

Class	1938 thousands	1948	'51	'59	'60	'61	1961 thousands
				1938=100			
Violence against the person	2·7	190	239	510	579	652	17·6
Sexual offences	5·0	218	292	399	397	408	20·4
Breaking and Entering	49·2	229	195	272	308	335	165·0
Larceny	200·0	175	178	223	245	266	531·4
Receiving, Frauds and False pretences	19·5	118	190	227	244	274	53·4
Others	6·8	170	218	258	288	281	19·1
All	283·2	185	185	239	263	285	806·9

II. Persons found Guilty of Indictable Offences

Class	1938 thousands	1948	'51	'59	'60	'61	1961 thousands
				1938=100			
a Violence against the person	1·6	201	248	578	648	719	11·5
b Sexual offences	2·3	164	209	265	257	270	6·2
d Breaking and Entering	10·9	217	199	277	293	332	36·2
e Larceny	56·1	149	155	161	172	191	107·2
c Receiving, Frauds and False pretences	5·3	179	185	205	217	257	13·6
Others	2·3	253	238	294	322	326	7·5
All	78·5	165	169	195	208	232	182·2

Source: Criminal Statistics, 1959, 60 and 61 Chapter III para. 8
and   Criminal Statistics, 1959, 60 and 61 Appendix I
        Criminal Statistics, 1956 Appendix I

APPENDIX III

III. Persons found Guilty of Indictable Offences —by Class of Offence and Age of Offender

Class[1] Age	(a) Violence against the person			(b) Sexual Offences		
	8–	17–	21–	8–	17–	21–
1938	116	163	1304	475	354	1492
			1938=100			
1948	199	248	195	156	123	177
1951	301	302	237	200	160	224
1957	655	1003	359	249	191	253
1958	896	1279	366	235	225	235
1959	1061	1452	426	267	255	268
1960	1362	1694	454	256	288	249
1961	1480	1844	521	248	308	260

Class[1] Age	(c) Receiving and Frauds etc			(d) Breaking and Entering		
	8–	17–	21–	8–	17–	21–
1938	602	437	4294	6793	1395	2665
			1938=100			
1948	177	144	183	186	257	275
1951	243	155	179	179	218	238
1957	284	175	152	177	282	276
1958	362	222	167	210	395	339
1959	400	257	172	226	392	344
1960	424	293	181	247	421	344
1961	533	343	207	279	482	397

Class[1] Age	(e) Larceny			All		
	8–	17–	21 and over	8–	17–	21 and over
1938	19750	8847	27495	28116	11451	38896
			1938=100			
1948	140	106	169	158	132	180
1951	154	101	174	169	124	183
1957	142	126	150	160	166	172
1958	159	151	157	184	208	183
1959	158	153	165	189	215	194
1960	168	175	173	204	243	201
1961	189	193	192	229	269	224

[1] See Table II.

245

IV. Persons found guilty of indictable Offences Rates per 100,000 popn.—in Age/Sex Groups

Age	8–	14–	17–	21–	30–	All
			Males			
1938	798	1131	767	487	173	393
1948	1433	1902	1084	871	281	612
1951	1503	2044	1192	930	303	645
—	—	—	—	—	—	—
1957	1091	2058	1555	969	264	612
1958	1176	2274	1974	1070	269	680
1959	1168	2313	2033	1170	281	710
1960	1254	2436	2189	1243	279	747
1961	1425	2535	2275	1377	300	818

Age	8–	14–	17–	21–	30–	All
			Females			
1938	46	90	102	68	39	51
1948	123	212	191	118	59	87
1951	119	195	160	104	55	79
—	—	—	—	—	—	—
1957	75	198	182	97	51	73
1958	96	227	221	116	56	84
1959	93	240	201	114	57	84
1960	110	275	236	128	61	93
1961	142	310	265	152	72	111

Source—Criminal Statistics, Appendix, II

APPENDIX III

V. Persons found Guilty of Indictable Offences per 100,000 popn. in Age/Sex Groups

Sex	Males				Females			
Age	8–	17–	21 and over	All	8–	17–	21 and over	All
Class a Violence against the person								
1938	4	11	8	8	0	1	1	1
1948	4	32	15	16	0	2	2	2
1957	24	146	30	36	0	4	2	2
1959	37	211	35	46	1	4	2	2
1960	48	237	37	51	1	4	2	2
1961	52	242	43	57	1	5	2	2
Class b Sexual Offences								
1938	16	27	11	13	0	0	1	0
1948	29	35	17	20	0	2	1	1
1957	38	62	25	30	0	0	0	0
1959	39	82	27	32	0	0	0	0
1960	38	89	25	31	0	0	0	0
1961	37	89	26	31	0	1	1	0
Class c Receiving, Frauds, etc.								
1938	19	28	27	26	2	6	4	4
1948	38	45	45	44	4	8	8	7
1957	51	60	38	42	4	10	5	6
1959	69	88	43	50	7	14	6	7
1960	73	97	46	53	7	15	6	7
1961	91	104	52	62	10	19	6	8
Class d Breaking and Entering								
1938	232	104	20	61	4	1	0	1
1948	477	295	50	125	17	8	1	3

Table V—(*contd.*)

Sex	Males				Females			
Age	*8–*	*17–*	*21 and over*	*All*	*8–*	*17–*	*21 and over*	*All*
1957	379	354	49	120	11	6	1	3
1959	463	490	61	153	16	8	1	4
1960	505	501	61	161	16	12	1	4
1961	570	540	69	182	21	14	1	4
Class e	*Larceny*							
1938	633	582	166	275	55	89	36	42
1948	957	637	258	380	126	161	55	70
1957	816	866	228	361	93	149	46	59
1959	866	1069	248	399	113	159	53	67
1960	905	1166	254	417	134	189	58	76
1961	1005	1198	274	453	165	212	70	92
All Indictable Offences								
1938	918	767	242	393	62	102	45	51
1948	1587	1084	402	612	152	191	70	87
1957	1352	1555	387	612	110	182	58	73
1959	1524	2033	435	710	139	200	66	84
1960	1627	2189	446	747	162	236	71	93
1961	1810	2275	487	818	200	265	84	111

APPENDIX III

VI. NON-INDICTABLE OFFENCES

Persons found Guilty (thousands)

Type of Offence	1938	1958	1959	1960	1961
Traffic Offences	475·1	596·1	635·1	622·6	712·6
Drunkenness	52·7	62·4	62·5	65·2	71·6
Breach of Local and Other Regs. (Inc. Disorderly Behaviour)	35·3	25·2	26·7	23·3	24·8
Revenue Offences	33·5	24·1	26·4	30·7	29·3
Railway Offences	8·6	20·0	21·2	20·1	20·8
Betting and Gaming	18·5	15·5	13·0	10·6	4·9
Assaults	10·7	11·0	11·6	12·0	11·9
Offences by Prostitutes	3·2	19·5	12·3	2·7	2·3
Malicious Damage	9·6	13·1	12·9	14·5	15·1
Others	61·8	59·1	65·5	70·0	76·9
All Non-Indictable Offences	709·0	846·5	887·5	871·7	970·2
Indictable Offences	78·5	146·7	153·2	163·5	182·2
All Offences[1]	787·5	993·2	1040·7	1035·2	1152·4

[1] Excluding a small class of offences against Defence Regulations.

APPENDIX IV

A SELECTED BOOK LIST

Andry, R. G. *Delinquency and Parental Pathology*, Methuen, 1960.

Bagot, J. H. *Juvenile Delinquency*, Cape, 1941.

Bowlby, J. *44 Juvenile Thieves*, Bailliere, Tindall & Cox, 1944.

Bovet, L. *Psychiatric Aspects of Juvenile Delinquency*, W.H.O., 1951.

Burt, Sir Cyril. *The Young Delinquent*, University of London Press, 1st ed., 1925.

— *The Causes and Treatment of Backwardness*, University of London Press, 1952.

Clinard, Marshall B. *The Black Market, A Study in White Collar Crime*, Rinehart, New York, 1952.

Cloward, R. and Ohlin, L. *Delinquency and Opportunity*, Routledge & Kegan Paul, 1961.

Cohen, Albert. *Delinquent Boys, The Culture of the Gang*, Routledge & Kegan Paul, 1956.

Coser, Lewis. *The Functions of Social Conflict*, Routledge & Kegan Paul, 1956.

Durkheim, Emile. *The Rules of Sociological Method*, 8th ed., Free Press, 1938.

— *Suicide*, ed. by George Simpson, Routledge & Kegan Paul, 1952.

East, Sir Norwood. *Society and the Criminal*, H.M.S.O., 1949.

Edelston, H. *The Earliest Stages of Delinquency*, Livingstone, 1952.

Elkin, W. *The English Penal System*, Penguin Books, 1956.

Ferguson, T. *The Young Delinquent in his Social Setting*, Oxford, 1954.

Ferris, Paul. *The City*, Gollancz, 1960.

Fyvel, T. R. *The Insecure Offenders*, Chatto & Windus, 1961.

Gibbens, T. C. N. *Trends in Juvenile Delinquency*, W.H.O., 1961.

Glover, E. *The Psychopathology of Prostitution*, I.S.T.D., 1945.

Grygier, T. *Oppression*, Routledge & Kegan Paul, 1954.

Glueck, Sheldon and Eleanor. *Unraveling Juvenile Delinquency*, The Commonwealth Fund, New York, 1950.

— *Predicting Delinquency and Crime*, Harvard, 1959.

— *Family Environment and Delinquency*, Routledge & Kegan Paul, 1962.

Healy, W. and Bronner, A. *New Light on Delinquency and its Treatment*, Yale University Press, 1936.

Klare, H. J. *Anatomy of Prison*, Hutchinson, 1960.

Kefauver, Estes. *Crime in America*, Gollancz, 1952.

McCord, W. and J. *Origins of Crime*, Columbia University Press, 1959.

Malinowski, B. *Crime and Custom in Savage Society*, Kegan Paul, 1936.

Mannheim, H. *Juvenile Delinquency in an English Middletown*, Routledge & Kegan Paul, 1948.

— *Group Problems in Crime and Punishment*, Routledge & Kegan Paul, 1955.

— and Wilkins, L. T. *Prediction Methods in Relation to Borstal Training*, H.M.S.O., 1955.

Marsh, D. C. *The Changing Social Structure of England and Wales, 1871–1951*, Routledge & Kegan Paul, 1958.

Mays, J. B. *Growing Up in the City*, Liverpool University Press, 1954.

— *On the Threshold of Delinquency*, Liverpool University Press, 1959.

Merton, R. K. *Social Theory and Social Structure*, Revised ed., Free Press, 1957.

— and Nisbet, R. *Contemporary Social Problems*, Harcourt, Brace & World, New York, 1961.

Morris, T. P. *The Criminal Area*, Routledge & Kegan Paul, 1957.

Neustatter, W. L. *Psychological Disorder and Crime*, Christopher Johnson, 1953.

— *The Mind of the Murderer*, Christopher Johnson, 1957.

Pakenham, Lord. *The Causes of Crime*, Wiedenfeld & Nicolson, 1958.

Pearce, J. D. W. *Juvenile Delinquency*, Cassell, 1952.

Reckless, W. *Criminal Behaviour*, 6th impression, McGraw Hill, 1940.

Rolph, C. H. *Common Sense About Crime and Punishment*, Gollancz, 1961.

Salisbury, Harrison, *The Shook-Up Generation*, Michael Joseph, 1959.

Silcock, H. *The Increase in Crimes of Theft 1938–47*, Liverpool University Press, 1949.

Shaw, Clifford and McKay, H. *Juvenile Delinquency and Urban Areas*, University of Chicago Press, 1942.

Sheldon, W. H. *Varieties of Delinquent Youth*, Harper Bros., New York, 1949.

Sutherland, Edwin. *The Professional Thief*, University of Chicago Press, 1937.

— and Cressey, D. *Principles of Criminology*, 5th ed., Lippincott, New York, 1955.

Taft, Donald. *Criminology*, 3rd. ed., Macmillan, New York, 1956.

Thrasher, F. *The Gang*, 2nd revised ed., University of Chicago Press, 1936.

Trenaman, J. *Out of Step*, Methuen, 1952.

Wertham, F. *The Seduction of the Innocent*, Museum Press, London, 1955.

Whyte, W. F. *Street Corner Society*, University of Chicago Press, 1943.

Wilkins, L. T. *Delinquent Generations*, H.M.S.O., 1961.

Wills, David. *The Barns Experiment*, Allen and Unwin, 1945.

— *Throw Away Thy Rod*, Gollancz, 1960.

Wolfgang, M., Savitz, L., Johnston, N. *The Sociology of Crime and Delinquency*, John Wiley, 1962.

Woodward, M. *Low Intelligence and Delinquency*, I.S.T.D., 1955.

Wootton, Barbara. *Social Science and Social Pathology*, Allen & Unwin, 1959.

— *Contemporary Trends in Crime and its Treatment*, nineteenth Clarke Hall Lecture, 1959.

Government Publications:

Report of the Committee on Homosexual Offences and Prostitution, H.M.S.O., 1957.

Penal Practice in a Changing Society, H.M.S.O., 1959.

15–18, Report of the Central Advisory Council for Education—England, H.M.S.O., 1959.

INDEX

INDEX

INDEX

Jazz, 93
Jews, 148, 152
Journal of Royal Statistical Society, 241 n.
Journal of Social Issues, 90 n.
Juvenile Court(s), 33, 58, 127, 213, 215, 218, 219, 228, 232

Kefauver Committee, 43, 49, 149, 172, 202
Kefauver, Estes, 49 n.
Klare, Hugh, 167 n.
Kretchmer, 99

Lady Chatterley's Lover, 184
Lancet, 110 n., 116 n.
Lander, Bernard, 150–1
Lange, Professor, 100
Law and Social Class, 36, 40, 41
Lewis, Hilda, 109
Libido, 108
Listener, 100 n., 102 n.
Liverpool, 49, 50, 85, 133, 134, 135, 155, 161, 162, 163, 165, 216, 217 n., 219
    Dockland, 84, 94, 170, 215
    Irish, 148
    see also Merseyside
Liverpool Daily Post, 50 n., 62 n.
Lombroso, 98
Lyward, George, 220

Mafia, 202
Malinowski, B., 87, 200
Mannheim, Hermann, 10, 151, 157, 160, 165, 236
Marcus, B., 125–6
Marsh, David, 10, 34
Maternal Deprivation, 107, 125, 128; *see also* Bowlby
Mays, J. B., 65 n., 126 n., 216 n.
McCarthy, Joe, 161
McCord, William and Joan, 124–7, 188, 194
McGregor, O. R., 186–7
McNaughton Rules, 115, 191
Menday, R. P., and Wiles, J., 121, 131
Mental Deficiency in relation to crime, 114
Mental Health Act (1959), 116, 222
Merseyside, 12, 76, 148, 215; *see also* Liverpool
Merton, Robert K., 90, 92, 93, 95, 199
Middlesbrough, 144 n.

Miller, Emanuel, 110
Morris, T., 95, 96, 199
Morrison, R. L., 240
Mothers at work, in relation to juvenile crime, 79
Mother's role, in relation to juvenile crime, *see* Parental Role
Motoring Offences, 21, 27, 28, 42, 132

National Assistance Board, 221
Negroes, 143, 144, 147–53, 155
New Haven Housing Development, 157, 163
Neurosis, 103, 104, 112
Neustatter, W. L., 190, 223–4
New Housing Estates, in relation to crime, 160–5
New Statesman, 24 n.
New Testament, 39, 40, 197
New York, 61, 91, 92, 205 n.
Notting Hill, 144

Observer, 192 n.
Oedipus Complex, 108, 128
Offences:
    indictable, 27, 29–31, 35–6, 169, 243–248
    non-indictable, 27, 28, 249
    peak age of, 32, 33, 34, 37

Page, Leo, 172
Pakenham, Lord, 219, 220
Parental Role(s) in relation to juvenile delinquency, 119–29, 187, 188, 239
Parsons, Talcott, 77
Pearce, J. D. W., 106, 145
Peer Group, *see* Gangs
Penology, 19; *see also* Punishment
Penrose, L. S., 209
Persistent Offenders, *see* Recidivists
Physiological Maturity, 33, 185
Pick-pocketing, 23, 173
Pinkerton, P., 10
Police:
    attitude towards offenders, 21, 22, 23, 40, 41, 91, 92, 150, 173, 176, 177, 218
    detection rate, 28–9
    Juvenile Liaison Officer Scheme, 22, 216–19
    procedure, 22, 23, 24, 29
    role in organized crime, 44–6, 48–9, 225, 226

255

Date Due